INVESTIGATING VICTORIAN JOURNALISM

Investigating Victorian Journalism

Edited by

Laurel Brake

Lecturer in Literature
Birkbeck College, London

Aled Jones

Lecturer in History
University College of Wales, Aberystwyth

and

Lionel Madden

Keeper of Printed Books
National Library of Wales, Aberystwyth

MACMILLAN

First published 1990

Published by
THE MACMILLAN PRESS LTD
Houndmills, Basingstoke, Hampshire RG21 2XS
and London
Companies and representatives
throughout the world

Filmset by Wearside Tradespools,
Fulwell, Sunderland

Printed in Hong Kong

British Library Cataloguing in Publication Data
Investigating Victorian Journalism
1. Great Britain. Journalism, history
I. Brake, Laurel   II. Jones, Aled
III. Madden, Lionel
072

ISBN 0–333–49761–9

Contents

List of Abbreviations

The following abbreviations are used in the references.

DWB	*The Dictionary of Welsh Biography down to 1940.* (London, 1959; supplement 1970)
JNPH	*Journal of Newspaper and Periodical History*
Reynolds's	*Reynolds's Weekly Newspaper*
VPN	*Victorian Periodicals Newsletter*
VPR	*Victorian Periodicals Review*
WR	*Westminster Review*

Notes on the Contributors

Margaret Beetham is Senior Lecturer in the Department of English and History at Manchester Polytechnic. She has published articles on the Manchester periodical press, and on feminist theory and practice in teaching. Her research interests are nineteenth-century periodicals and feminist theory and she is currently co-writing a book on women's magazines.

Scott Bennett is Director of the Milton S. Eisenhower Library, Johns Hopkins University. He was previously Assistant University Librarian for Collection Management at Northwestern University. He has written widely on library matters, textual editing, bibliography and Victorian periodicals. The early nineteenth-century publisher Charles Knight is the focus of his recent work.

Lucy Brown was Senior Lecturer in History at the London School of Economics from 1966 to 1982 and is now retired. She published *Victorian News and Newspapers* in 1985.

Dennis Griffiths has worked in the regional and national press of Great Britain for 40 years and was Production Director of Express Newspapers, London. There he was also archivist of the *Standard*. He is a member of the Advisory Group of the British Library Newspaper Library.

Michael Harris is Lecturer in History at Birkbeck College, University of London. He has written extensively on the history of the newspaper press and on the history of the English book trades. His recent publications include *London Newspapers in the Age of Walpole*, *The Press in English Society* (joint editor with Alan Lee, 1987), and *The Economics of the British Booktrade 1605–1939* (joint editor with Robin Myers, 1985). He is General Editor of the *Journal of Newspaper and Periodical History*.

Deian Hopkin is Senior Lecturer in History in the University College of Wales, Aberystwyth. He was founding editor of *Llafur*, the journal of the Welsh Labour History Society, and has written extensively on British labour history and the early socialist press. In 1986 he was a founding member of the Association for History and Computing and edited (with Peter Denley) *History and Computing* (1987). He is currently working on a history of the Labour Party in Wales.

Anne Humpherys is Professor of English and Dean of Arts and Humanities at Lehman College, City University of New York. She has written two books on the work of Henry Mayhew, and published articles on Dickens, Reynolds, and the history of the press. She is currently working on a book on the relationship between the press, the stage and the early Victorian novel.

Philip Henry Jones is Senior Lecturer in the Department of Information and Library Studies, University College of Wales, Aberystwyth. He has undertaken research into the nineteenth-century Welsh publisher Thomas Gee, and is currently investigating the Welsh-language press of the 1840s and 1850s as a preliminary to a detailed study of Gee's newspaper, *Baner ac Amserau Cymru*. In addition to articles in Welsh on the Welsh periodical press he was responsible for compiling the recently-published third edition of the standard *Bibliography of the History of Wales*.

B.E. Maidment. After holding teaching posts in Leicester and Aberystwyth he has worked at Manchester Polytechnic since 1973. He currently teaches Art History and English. He has written and lectured widely on Victorian literature, popular culture, and publishing history. His critical anthology of writing by and about Victorian artisan authors, *The Poorhouse Fugitives*, was published in 1987. His current research is centred on popular wood-block illustration.

Lyn Pykett teaches in the English Department of the University College of Wales, Aberystwyth. She is the author of a number of articles on Victorian fiction and on the periodical press, and has just completed a book on Emily Brontë.

Brynley F. Roberts has been Librarian of the National Library of Wales since 1985. He was previously Professor of Welsh Language and Literature at University College of Swansea. His main research interests are in medieval literature and seventeenth-century *virtuosi*. He has worked on Welsh library history, printers and binders, and on the history of Welsh scholarship in the nineteenth century. He recently completed a short study of Prince Louis-Lucien Bonaparte.

Edward Royle is Senior Lecturer in History and Head of the Department of History at the University of York to which he first came in 1972. He was previously Lecturer in History at Selwyn College, Cambridge. His publications include two studies of radical freethought – *Victorian Infidels* (1974) and *Radicals, Secularists and Republicans* (1980); two short seminar studies – *Radical Politics, 1790–1900* (1971) and *Chartism* (1980); and two text books – *English Radicals and Reformers, 1760–1848* (with James Walvin, 1982) and *Modern Britain: A Social History, 1750–1985* (1987).

Joel H. Wiener is Professor of History at City University of New York. His books include *The War of the Unstamped* (1969), *A Descriptive Finding-List of Unstamped Periodicals, 1830–1836* (1970), *Radicalism and Freethought in Nineteenth-Century Britain: The Life of Richard Carlile* (1983) and *William Lovett* (1989). He has edited *Innovators and Preachers: The Role of the Editor in Victorian England* (1985) and *Papers for the Millions: The New Journalism in Britain, 1850s to 1914* (1988).

Introduction: Defining the Field

This new work on print journalism contributes to three broad areas of scholarship, namely the teaching of communications, the study of discourse, and press history. It is aimed principally at readers of journalism, and teachers and students in history, media, cultural studies, English literature and librarianship. Each discipline offers particular insights into different aspects of the press, but combined they have the potential to transform our understanding of British journalism. These essays, then, are investigative in two senses: they interrogate the practices and study of journalism, and they explore the possibilities of interdisciplinary work.

The political and social uses to which British journalism has been put have long been matters of public concern. One former editor of *The Times* argued in the late 1930s that 'a free Press, conducted in a spirit of responsible citizenship, may be at once the central problem and the main safeguard of modern democracy'.[1] The ambivalent role performed by journalism in society is a subject of this book, and a number of the essays set out to analyse the central, if complex, relationships established between the newspaper and periodical press and areas of British political and cultural life. However, understanding the functions of journalism depends on the ability to construct and utilise adequate critical methods of research. The book attempts to develop such methods and, in the process of initiating a discourse which theorises journalism, it also presents a critique of current practice and proposes new directions for the study of media.

With the aim of fostering discussion of method, the editors organised a conference of the Research Society for Victorian Periodicals on press production, bibliography and theory. Although some of the material here had its origin in that occasion, we have attempted to focus this collection more precisely. Bibliography generally is absent, while theoretical questions – such as definition of the genre, and the common valuation of categories such as the local, metropolitan and provincial press – are to the fore. Two key issues were discussed at length and form the basis of the present volume. It seemed necessary to shift attention from journalism as a source for other studies and to treat it as a subject in its own right, and to develop a particular blend of analytical skills in order to effect the shift. Investigating journalism required an unambiguous commitment to interdisciplinarity.

This particular form of cultural production, then, can be best understood if the disciplinary boundaries between bibliography, English literature, history and economics are dismantled. Although scholarly interest in journalism has increased in recent years, study of the press still tends to fracture under the pressures of institutional subject classificiation into component single disciplines. The implications of these diverse, if parallel, methods and writings, and considerations of ways in which they may be combined have given rise to this book. In short, our organising principle is that the study of journalism, past and present, demands the recognition of a discrete, interdisciplinary field.

Anyone who turns to the newspapers and periodicals of the eighteenth and nineteenth centuries will find in them numerous reflexive articles on the press, its ethics, its social and political functions and its history. It is only as academic specialisation developed that journalism was defined principally as a practice, the study of which fell outside history, economics and literature. If it was studied at all in higher education, it was by bibliographers (themselves at the margins of diverse disciplines), or by vocational students of librarianship or journalism. In consequence, the most prolific literary form of the nineteenth century, and the precursor of modern journalism, has largely been ignored by scholars and students in higher education. The recent popularity of media studies in schools and colleges is an encouraging development, but the tendency to focus on twentieth-century forms of communication is artificially constrained. Work on nineteenth-century journalism provides a valuable counterbalance to the overemphasis on contemporary institutions in such courses.

The essays are divided into three parts. Part I explores broad theoretical questions pertaining to journalism. Looking at the field as constituted by some recent theoretical models, Lyn Pykett considers the kinds of evidence which periodicals produce, what is context and what text in a variety of theoretical frameworks, and defines the text as 'the object of a freshly constituted interdisciplinarity'. Tensions within a hypothetically identifiable genre occupy Margaret Beetham. Rhythms of continuity of the run and closure of the single issue, and the combination of single and collective voices in a single periodical are gauged and related to readership. Anne Humpherys looks at the implication of one discourse with others, the ways news stories rely on popular structures of melodrama and romance to produce meaning. Edward Royle, like Lyn Pykett, addresses modern research; he examines its appropriation of historical 'information' from the press, and argues that journalism as an historical source should be approached with caution and sensitivity. Together these writers dislodge premises, such as transparency of narrative and models of reflection or influence, which commonly underlie raids on the press by colonisers from other disciplines, and suggest methods which a new, discrete field might adopt.

Part II draws attention to the rich diversity of Victorian journalism. The nineteenth-century press enjoyed a relationship with society and politics quite different from that of its more centralised modern equivalent. Aled Jones argues that the history of journalism should begin at the local level, by investigating links between titles and their producers, correspondents and readers in and outside London. Four local case studies from the contrasting areas of Wales and London illustrate these connections. Brynley F. Roberts surveys the growth of the Welsh periodical press, while Philip Henry Jones studies the first nine years of *Yr Amserau* ('The Times'), the first commercially successful Welsh-language newspaper. Similarly, Michael Harris surveys the London locals, analysing the structure of their development, and Dennis Griffiths traces the early management of the *Standard* between 1827 and 1900. Finally, Lucy Brown outlines the growth of the national press which had grown to dominate British journalism by the 1890s.

Part III looks to some future directions in journalism studies. B.E. Maidment takes on the limited accommodation of the Victorian press by twentieth-century academic journals, and argues for attention to Victorian journalism as such, while Joel H. Wiener suggests materials for undertaking this in a piece on sources for the study of newspapers. Scott Bennett raises the urgent matter of the physical preservation of Victorian periodicals, and Deian Hopkin considers the extent to which electronic journalism is likely to replace print journalism in future.

These investigative essays are designed to open new avenues of research, and to stimulate further work on ways in which nineteenth-century journalism may be read, and its histories written.

LAUREL BRAKE
ALED JONES
LIONEL MADDEN

Note

1.   Henry Wickham Steed, *The Press* (Harmondsworth, 1938) p. 3.

Part I
Theorising Journalism

1

Reading the Periodical Press: Text and Context

LYN PYKETT

I

It is indeed a subject of wonder, that periodical publications should have existed so long ... without having become subject to a regular and systematic course of criticism.[1]

These words are, of course, not my own preface to an heroic attempt to subject the periodical press to a regular and systematic course of study, but the words of James Mill writing anonymously in the *Westminster Review* in 1824. Over 150 years later the project announced by Mill did not seem a great deal further advanced when Joanne Shattock and Michael Wolff echoed Mill's words in their introduction to *The Victorian Periodical Press: Samplings and Soundings*.

> The systematic and general study of [the Victorian periodical] press has hardly begun ... for the press as a whole, we appear to have little choice except to be satisfied with a casual or glancing knowledge, believing that anything broader or deeper or more systematic is beyond the bounds of reasonable humanistic ambition. ... The sheer bulk and range of the Victorian press seems to make it so unwieldy as to defy systematic and general study. ... And yet, despite what prudence and common sense would tell us, a case can be made that the very impenetrability of the Victorian press requires of us that we attempt a systematic and general study.[2]

From Mill's early attempts to provide a coherent description and analysis of selected contemporary periodicals, to the latest efforts of Shattock, Wolff, and their contributors, students of the Victorian

3

periodical press have persistently confronted the double problem of defining the object of study, and devising an appropriate methodological framework within which to conduct that study. This particular problem raises a number of theoretical questions, which derive both from the nature of the material itself, and from the nature of the institutionalised fields of knowledge within which periodicals have traditionally been studied. My interest in this essay is in the theoretical questions which arise from the intersection of the methodologies of historical and literary studies.

The study of the periodical press is inevitably interdisciplinary. It not only challenges the boundaries between hitherto separately constituted fields of knowledge, but also challenges the internal hierarchies and sub-divisions within discrete academic disciplines. The ideal student of the Victorian periodical press would employ the methodologies of these disciplines and sub-disciplines in a new combination. I am aware that I am here in danger of making an appeal for the super-scholar who makes a ritual appearance in most of the attempts to define the project of periodicals study in the last fifteen to twenty years. Michael Wolff, for example, outlining the project in influential pieces in *Victorian Periodicals Newsletter* (*VPN*) in the early 1970s, requires scholars of such awesome erudition that one fears that they would sink under the burden they carry in their pursuit of the periodicals equivalent of the 'key to all mythologies'. Wolff considers what would constitute an adequate description for the new era in British journalism announced by Joel Wiener's paper on 'The Press and the Working Class 1815–40':

> We would need to know the range and type of newspaper and magazine publication in both 1815 and 1840; we would need to know a lot about circulation and content, and about the writers, editors, and proprietors, and their attitudes towards the hoped-for readership ... whether the object of each periodical was to make money or to influence people or, if both, in what proportion – and these factors would have to be seen not just at a given moment but dynamically through the runs of the serials. We would need to know something ... about the readership ... who bought what, what was distributed free to whom, what clubs or places of entertainment made what available, and what sort of reading aloud or word-of-mouth extension of news and opinion

took place, and, finally and most difficult of all to recapture, how seriously particular publications were read or listened to and how their actual influence might be measured.[3]

The desire for plenitude which pervades this passage, its language of totality, mastery and control seem to be typical of the discourse of periodicals study. Many students of the periodical press, apparently, aspire to the total knowledge of a past culture, and seek a degree of conceptual possession of a 'documentary' culture which must elude them even in relation to a living culture.[4] However, ultimately, as Wolff recognised, it is not simply a question of *what* we need to know (and there is no escaping that we need to know a lot), but it is also a question of *how* we need to know it, of what *kinds* of knowledge we need, what *models* we use, and what *patterns* we construct.

With these questions in mind, I shall examine the theoretical premises of the phase of periodicals study which launched *Victorian Periodicals Newsletter* before going on to look briefly at the different models offered to the student of periodicals by the interdisciplinary fields of cultural and media studies. Finally, I will consider James Mill as an early theoretician of periodicals study, and suggest some theoretical approaches which seem to be useful pointers for his successors.

Michael Wolff was surely right in his pioneering essay, 'Charting the Golden Stream',[5] to identify newspapers and periodicals as 'primary research materials' for the relatively new project (at the time of the essay) of the investigation of Victorian culture as a whole. But, while he dismisses the practice of using the periodicals to provide 'secondary confirming evidence', important questions remain: what kind of primary research material are they, and how are we to use them? These are theoretical questions, or at least raise theoretical questions. While no theory or methodology can eliminate the need for exhaustive (and exhausting) empirical work, the theoretical framework adopted will to a great extent determine the object. In this particular case the theoretical framework adopted will determine our perspectives on the periodical press, what we are looking at, the kinds of structure in which we locate it and how we read it.

The implicit theoretical framework for the early answers to the questions posed by Wolff was a mixed reflective/constructive model. For Wolff himself the periodicals, on the one hand, 'reflect' Victorian culture: 'The years that we call Victorian are best mirrored in the serial publications – literature, argument, the tastes and preoccupations of just about every level and sort of society, all display themselves in the newspapers and journals'.[6] On the other hand, periodicals are a means of constructing opinion and identity: 'One might almost claim that an attitude, an opinion, an idea, did not exist until it had registered itself in the press, and that an interest group, a sect, a profession, came of age when it inaugurated its journal'.[7]

Walter Houghton also adopted the reflection model in his introduction to *The Wellesley Index*, which presents the periodicals as 'a remarkable record of contemporary thought' which 'reflect the current situation'.[8] Similarly, John North, in an essay which seeks to persuade mainstream historians and literary historians of the importance of periodicals to their specialist fields, describes the periodical press as a 'sensitive . . . record of a civilization'.[9] North's is also a foreground/background model; although the periodicals take us, on the one hand, to the very heart of Victorian culture, on the other hand, they provide the background against which, and in the context of which, we read the foreground of the eminent and the important writers. In other words he proposes using the periodicals as a context for what Raymond Williams calls the selective tradition.[10]

Clearly one of the most obvious objections to the reflection model of the media, as Tony Bennett has argued, is that it 'implies that the media are secondary and derivative, somehow less real than the "real" they reflect, existing above society and passively mirroring it rather than forming an active and integral part of it'.[11] And, to be fair, both Wolff and North while broadly relying on the reflection model also point beyond it. North, for example, directs attention to the 'multifarious' nature of the Victorian periodical press and suggests (at least implicitly) that it is the specific structure, organisation and function of that press which makes it a uniquely sensitive instrument for registering the course of a civilisation. Wolff (as I have already noted) also calls attention to multifariousness, and directs his readers beyond the exhaustive mining of the elite journals towards the recognition of the periodicals and the totality of the press as primary evidence: 'attention to context puts the history of journalism squarely into the history of the period as a whole'.[12]

Subsequent redefinitions of the project of periodicals study have further challenged the reflection/record, background/foreground models of the role of the periodical press in Victorian culture, and in our present historical knowledge of that culture. Structuralist, poststructuralist, and a variety of Marxist theoretical initiatives within historiography, literary studies and, perhaps most important, within cultural and media studies, have variously helped to displace the reflection model. Periodicals can no longer be regarded in any simply reflective way as 'evidence' (either primary or secondary), as transparent records which give access to, and provide the means of recovering, the culture which they 'mirror'. Far from being a mirror of Victorian culture, the periodicals have come to be seen as a central component of that culture – an 'active and integral part', and they can only be read and understood as part of that culture and society, and in the context of other knowledges about them.

Reading the Victorian periodical press backwards through the twentieth-century mass media, Shattock and Wolff redefine that press, and implicitly redefine the project of periodicals study.

> The mass media, however carefully some Victorians tried to insulate themselves, are the inescapable ideological and subliminal environment of the modern world. The press, in all its manifestations, became during the Victorian period the context within which people lived and worked and thought, and from which they derived their . . . sense of the outside world.[13]

The periodical press is now defined not as a mirror reflecting Victorian culture, nor as a means of *expressing* Victorian culture, but as an 'inescapable ideological and subliminal environment', a (or perhaps *the*) constitutive medium of a Victorian culture which is now seen as interactive.[14]

This shift of theoretical perspective has both proceeded from and necessitated an ever-increasing emphasis on interdisciplinarity. Interdisciplinarity was, of course, central to Wolff's early attempts to define the project in 'Charting the Golden Stream', where he relates the importance of periodicals to 'a new phase in the historiography of [Victorian England]' which for the literary historian,

> means an increasing awareness of the context within which

authors worked and of the definite but extremely complicated ways in which . . . this context impinged on the literature. These developments have inevitably blurred the lines between disciplines; they have forced scholars to begin asking questions about the internal quality of historical events.[15]

One might also add that these developments have forced scholars to ask questions about the historical determinations of language and of literary forms and genres.

Twenty years on interdisciplinarity is even more important and has radically changed our notions of the ways in which 'contexts' 'impinge' on 'the literature', and about the nature and structure of historical events. Under the gaze of semiology, structuralism, a variety of Marxist poststructuralisms, Post-Foucauldian historiography and the formalist historiography of, for example, Hayden White, ideas of history and of literature have changed. Literature and context can no longer be seen as separate or separable entities. They are more likely to be viewed as indivisible elements of a signifying system, or ideological or discursive formation. In short the lines between disciplines have not simply become blurred, they have been dissolved to constitute multidisciplinary disciplines such as cultural studies with its 'capacity . . . to "think" the connections between culture and society non-reductively'.[16]

None of these theoretical developments obviates the need for extensive empirical knowledge of the field. However, they both provide various ways of constituting the field, and of undertaking a systematic analysis of it. In Britain our view of the nature and function of the periodical press has been radically altered by developments within cultural studies from the late 1950s onwards. Raymond Williams has been a key figure in this process, from his early insistence that culture is everywhere, 'Culture is ordinary',[17] to his later work in cultural materialism, which he describes as 'the analysis of all forms of signification, including quite centrally writing, within the actual means and conditions of their production'.[18] The analysis of culture thus defined must inevitably be interdisciplinary, since it will involve the analysis of 'the organisation of production, the structure of the family, the structure of institutions which express or govern social relationships, the characteristic forms through which members of the society communicate'.[19]

When Williams tested his early theoretical model in an actual analysis of the culture of the 1840s in England, his first move was to recover the field of journalism from the operations of the selective tradition and to locate the nineteenth-century newspaper press within the history of writing, and within specific social, political and cultural formations. The press, he argued, must be seen as part of the wider structure of social (or, as some would say, signifying) practices, and could not be isolated from 'the cognate forms of other writing, publishing and reading ... other kinds of political and cultural formation and organisation – from political movements, new industrial organisations, educational developments, changes in the theatre. . .'[20]

The changing emphasis in Raymond Williams's approach in fact parallels broader developments within the field, particularly within Marxist approaches to cultural studies. Since the 1960s European Marxisms have increasingly moved away from a reductionist base/superstructure model of the relationships between culture, ideology and the economy, and have instead turned their attention to theorising and investigating the question of the relative autonomy of the cultural sphere. Williams's work also provides an interesting example of the operations of the two major traditions of cultural studies. Although identified predominantly with the culturalist approach, which emphasises the role of human agency in the making of culture, Williams also increasingly emphasises the concept of structure, which informs the second major tradition within cultural studies. 'If we study real relations, in any actual analysis, we reach the point where we see that we are studying a general organisation in a particular example, and in this general organisation there is no element that we can abstract and separate from the rest.'[21]

Where the culturalist approach views all cultural forms as objectifications or expressions of what Williams calls 'structures of feeling,'[22] a variety of structuralist approaches start from the basic position that experience is not 'the ground of culture but ... its effect, the product of the ways in which individuals are transformed into thinking, feeling and perceiving subjects of different kinds in the context of differently structured relations of symbolic exchange'.[23] The genetic structuralism of Lucien Goldmann, the structuralist semiotics of Roland Barthes, the poststructuralist discourse theory of Michel Foucault, Lacanian theories of the subject, Louis Althusser's concept of ideology and Antonio Gramsci's theory of hegemony have all provided important theoretical and methodological models for the analysis of cultural structures. All these approaches provide a variety of models within which we might read the ideological, semiotic, cultural, social, political and psychological functions and determinants of the Victorian periodical press. They also provide a variety of methods for analysing its place in what we might call the chain of significations and determinations, and its nature and function as a signifying practice and a reproducer of ideologies.

The changes which I have described in the way in which the Victorian periodical press is perceived, and in particular the abandonment of the reflection/background model which dominated the earlier phase of periodicals study, may be directly attributed to these developments within cultural studies. Similar theoretical developments have also been extremely important in the relatively new interdisciplinary field of media studies. Here, as in cultural studies there has been a movement away from a crudely reductionist model, in this case that of the positivistic American social science of the 1950s, towards a multiplicity of Marxist, structuralist or poststructuralist theoretical initiatives. A supposedly empiricist media studies which viewed the media as sustaining or reflecting a consensual reality already in existence, has been overtaken by a succession of theories which view the media as (in various ways) producing or manufacturing that consensus. This theoretical shift has been accompanied by changes in methodology. Descriptive and quantitative content analysis has been replaced by a new focus on 'the media message, as a symbolic sign-vehicle or a structured discourse, with its own internal structuration and complexity',[24] and a variety of techniques and theories from linguistics, semiology and psychoanalysis have been employed in the analysis of the structure and effects of media messages.

Of course, one has to retain a degree of scepticism about the usefulness of simply transferring theories and methodologies developed in relation to the study of modern mass media, to a study of the nineteenth-century newspaper and periodical press. Raymond Williams, for example, quite properly points out the dangers of simply reading backwards through our knowledge of what the nineteenth-century media turned into,[25] and I would certainly want to emphasise the importance of focusing on the historical specificities of nineteenth-century culture and society, and of the conditions of their production. Nevertheless, the theories and methodologies of modern media studies would seem to be indispensable to our study of the nineteenth-century press. The work within media studies on theories of ideology and hegemony, and also the development of various theoretical approaches to the analysis of media messages, and the study of media institutions and media power, offer some particularly useful models to the student of nineteenth-century periodicals.[26]

II

My suggestion that we locate the periodical press within the multidisciplinary terrains of cultural and media studies would seem to take us a long way from Michael Wolff's original 'back of the mind' conviction that 'the basic unit for the study of Victorian cultural history is the individual issue of a Victorian periodical'.[27] The cultural/media studies model would not automatically rule out this approach, but it would radically alter the project. It would determine the kinds of question one asked about that single issue, would raise questions about the methodologies we should use, and about how, and within what structures and frameworks, we should attempt to contextuate it.

However, consideration of the single issue does narrow the field considerably. In a single move we shift from the vast domain of a cultural system or network of media institutions, to something that might look like a single text. But to describe it thus would be to beg several questions. What is a text in the field of periodicals study? Is it the individual essay? The issue? The volume? A run defined in some other way – say by the period of a particular editorship?

The idea of the text that I want to consider is not the text that is used as evidence by the historian, nor the text as annotated by the literary scholar or sensitively responded to by the practical critic, but rather the text as the object of a freshly constituted interdisciplinarity. Roland Barthes has suggested that the change that has taken place in our conception of language and the literary work

is clearly connected with the current development of (amongst other disciplines) linguistics, anthropology, Marxism and psychoanalysis . . . What is new and which affects the idea of the work comes not necessarily from the internal recasting of each of these disciplines, but rather from their encounter in relation to an object which traditionally is the province of none of them. It is indeed as though the *interdisciplinarity* which is today held up as a prime value in research cannot be accomplished by the simple confrontation of specialist branches of knowledge. Interdisciplinarity is not the calm of an easy security; it begins *effectively* . . . when the solidarity of the old disciplines breaks down . . . in the interests of a new object and a new language, neither of which has a place in the field of the sciences that were to be brought peacefully together . . . there is now the requirement of a new object, obtained by the sliding or overturning of former categories. That object is the *Text* . . . the Text is a methodological field.[28]

I would like to take Barthes's concept of the text as a methodological field and site of interdisciplinarity as a reference point for an examination of a particular periodical essay, which undertakes an analysis of periodical literature in the guise of a review of the *Edinburgh Review*. The essay in question is James Mill's contribution to a *Westminster Review* series which attempted to submit the contemporary periodical press to a 'regular and systematic course of criticism'.

In his essay James Mill, adopting a Barthesian strategy, proposed to unmask and demystify periodical literature. He begins with the *Edinburgh* and the *Quarterly*, publications which he sees as being engaged in a form of covert activity: 'under the guise of reviewing books [they] . . . have introduced the practice of publishing dissertations'.[29] More significantly, he considers the periodical press as a specific cultural formation. He explores it as a mass medium, and analyses the specific nature of periodical publication and its ideological implications. Mill distinguishes periodical from book publication, arguing that, by its very nature, periodical literature must make an immediate appeal, 'must have immediate success, to secure so much as existence', 'must catch at immediate applause'. A press so characterised cannot be oppositional or critical, since 'To please the great body of men, which is the object of the periodical writer, he must flatter their prejudices'. Mill thus develops a theory of hegemony.

Periodical literature depends upon *immediate* success. It must, therefore, patronise the opinions which are now in vogue, the opinions of those who are now in power. It will obtain applause, and will receive reward, in proportion as it is successful in finding plausible reasons for the maintenance of the favourite opinions of the powerful classes and plausible reasons for the discountenance and rejection of the opinions which tend to rescue the interests of the greater number from the subjection under which they must lie to the interests of the smaller number.[30]

If we translate Mill's discourse into Althusserian terms we might argue that he sees the periodical press, or the particular section under scrutiny, as an ideological state apparatus which reproduces and reinforces ruling class hegemony. His exploration of the paradoxical process by which the (powerful) smaller number finds plausible reasons for maintaining the subjection of the (less powerful or powerless) greater number also anticipates Althusser, by implicitly demonstrating how ideology, the imaginary relationship of individuals with the real conditions of their existence, operates to interpellate individuals as subjects, positioning them through the apparently natural and commonsense practices of everyday living.[31]

Mill's model also includes what later theorists have called a safety valve mechanism. He sees the ideological hegemony of the periodical press as, in part, sustained by a kind of repressive tolerance, by means of which gaps are left for oppositional voices and oppositional discourse. '[O]ccasionally, from various motives . . . the periodical press displays exertions both in opposition to the opinions which tend to confirm abusive powers in the hands of the few, and in favour of the opinions which tend to rescue from these powers the interests of the greater number.'[32]

This aspect of Mill's analysis may be compared with Barthes's view of the 'innoculation' effect in mass culture, by which an institutional discourse admits the possibility that the institution is liable to criticism, but the criticism actually functions to reinforce the *status quo*,[33] or with Foucault's work on competing discourses within a particular discursive formation.[34]

Mill also analyses the style, content and tone of the *Edinburgh* as a means of assigning it to a specific genre of periodical publication, to which the *Quarterly* also belongs. He uses this generic identification, and further rhetorical and textual analysis in an attempt to demonstrate that the much-vaunted diversity of these two periodicals in fact masks an essential identity. Mill also attempts to reconstruct the readership of this sector of the periodical press by analysing the mode of address of the *Edinburgh* and *Quarterly*. His analysis constitutes this readership as a specific discursive community, rather like Foucault's idea of a fellowship of discourse, 'whose function is to preserve or . . . reproduce discourse, but in order that it should circulate within a closed community, according to strict regulations'.[35] Mill goes on to describe the particular discourse of his chosen periodicals, analysing the 'vague language' used and deconstructing, or unpacking particular words and phrases, such as 'the country' (which habitually denotes the aristocracy), 'despotical', 'anarchical', 'democratical', and so on. Similarly, in his later article on the *Edinburgh*, J. S. Mill examines certain keywords like 'liberty' and 'constitution', and gives them their specific *Edinburgh Review* meaning.[36]

Mill's analysis of the language of the *Edinburgh* and the *Quarterly*, and its role in their ideological functioning may again be compared with Foucault's idea of discursive practices.

> Discursive practices are characterized by the delimitation of a field of objects, the definition of a legitimate perspective for the agent of knowledge, and the fixing of norms for the elaboration of concepts and theories. Thus each discursive practice implies a play of prescriptions that designate its exclusions and choices.[37]

Through the close reading of several extended passages James Mill, in particular, not only provides an analysis of the discourse of a particular periodical, but also attempts to locate that discourse within a pattern of discursive practices, and within a wider discursive community which he locates within a specific economic and political structure.

Of course, Mill has his own ideological purpose. His reading of the two great quarterlies is undertaken on behalf of an oppositional politics which seeks to challenge their hegemony. Knowledge of this fact must play a part in our understanding of his essay, but does not, I think substantially affect my attempt to use his methods (with the poststructuralist inflections which I have given them) as a broad theoretical model for a systematic study of the periodical press.

Clearly an important part of Mill's project is his attempt to reconstruct the reader from the pages of the *Edinburgh*. Just such a reconstruction of the reader, specifically from the pages of the *British Controversialist*, was also one aspect of Wolff's project in 'Charting the Golden Stream'. More recently, Brian Maidment has done some very interesting work on the address or discourse of magazines of popular progress, in which he attempts 'to bring together format and content by deducing the implied reader of a magazine from its tone, opinions, and rhetoric'.[38] Maidment's interest, like James Mill's, is in the mode of address of a particular group of periodicals, and particularly in the ways in which those periodicals position their readers. In short, he is concerned with the question of mediation, with the way in which periodicals and periodical writing function as social discourse, rather than as direct 'social statement'.

The reconstruction of the reader of a particular periodical cannot, however, be a matter of merely formal analysis that attempts to 'read off' the readers' consciousness from the text. Rhetorical and formal analysis must be accompanied by attempts to gain knowledge of the actual as well as the implied readers of periodicals. And, indeed, both Mill and Maidment attempt to bring together rhetorical analysis of text and empirical evidence about the social composition of the contributors to, and readers of, their chosen periodicals. Michael Lund's attempt to combine reader-response criticism of serial fictions with an investigation of the actual historical readers of those fictions also provides a useful pointer here.[39]

However, notwithstanding his movement in the direction of real historical readers, and his acknowledgement of the 'speculative' nature of his own enterprise, Maidment explicitly situates his own attempt to read content ('expressed opinion') in complex relation to form ('formal and generic aspects') as a 'necessary corrective to those historians who seek to use literary sources pre-eminently to illustrate ideological formations widely perceived in other kinds of economic and cultural formations'.[40] We have come full circle to Michael Wolff's original claim (see p. 5) that we should regard periodicals as 'primary research materials', rather than as providing 'secondary confirming evidence'. The essays by Maidment and Mill (as re-read above) offer some suggestions about the methodologies appropriate to the interpretation and analysis of this primary research material.

Taking these two essays as models I would want to argue the case for the importance to periodicals study of the close reading of text. First I would want to emphasise textual analysis in order to underline the importance of the redirection of attention towards the formal properties of media discourse which has come from the structuralist, semiological and linguistic analyses of texts, and from the central concern of these approaches with systems and processes of signification and representation. However, I would also want to emphasise that we should think of 'Text' in its Barthesian sense as a methodological field. This concept of Text, and the concepts of discourse and discursive communities, reinstate history, economics and sociology in a new interdisciplinary formation which would avoid the problems that Tony Bennett has noted in, for example, the Althusserians' tendency towards 'purely formalist "readings" or "deconstructions" of the signifying mechanisms of media forms, which paid scant regard to the conditions of their production or to the real history of their reception by different sections of the audience.'[41]

Such an approach would avoid the colonisation of periodicals study by a purely literary or formal methodology, while, at the same time, it would challenge those historians who refuse to regard the history of cultural forms, such as writing and its particular genres, as a central part of 'general history'. It would require them to adopt a view of history and of writing, in which cultural practices are seen as 'not simply derived from an otherwise constituted social order' but as in themselves 'major elements in its constitution'.[42]

Notes

1. James Mill, 'Periodical Literature', *WR*, I (1824) 206.
2. Joanne Shattock and Michael Wolff (eds), *The Victorian Periodical Press: Samplings and Soundings* (Leicester, 1982) p. xiii.
3. Michael Wolff, 'Comments on AHA Panel', *VPN*, no. 11 (1971) 14.
4. See Raymond Williams, *The Long Revolution* (Harmondsworth, 1965) pp. 65–70
5. Michael Wolff, 'Charting the Golden Stream', *VPN*, no. 13 (1971) 23–38.
6. Wolff, 'Charting', 26–7.
7. Wolff, 'Charting', 26–7.
8. Walter Houghton (ed.), *The Wellesley Index to Victorian Periodicals*, vol. I (Toronto and London, 1966) p. xv.

9. John North, 'The Rationale – Why Read Victorian Periodicals?', in J. Don Vann and Rosemary T. VanArsdel (eds), *Victorian Periodicals: A Guide to Research* (New York, 1978) p. 4.
10. Williams, *Long Revolution*, p. 69.
11. Tony Bennett, 'Media, "reality", signification', in Michael Gurevitch *et al.* (eds), *Culture, Society and the Media* (London, 1982) p. 287.
12. *VPN*, no. 11 (1971) 15.
13. Shattock and Wolff, *Samplings*, pp. xiv–xv.
14. The statement quoted also raises a number of other questions. It seems to represent the press as a (the?) determinant of consciousness, and begs the question of the economic, structural and ideological determinants of the press.
15. *VPN*, no. 13 (1971) 24.
16. Tony Bennett *et al.*, (eds), *Culture, Ideology and Social Process* (Milton Keynes, 1981) p. 14.
17. 'Culture is Ordinary' is the title of an early essay by Raymond Williams, in Norman MacKenzie (ed.), *Conviction* (London, 1958). See Stuart Hall in Bennett *et al.* (eds), *Culture, Ideology and Social Process*, p. 21.
18. Raymond Williams, 'Crisis in English Studies', in *Writing in Society* (London, 1983) p. 210. See also his *Marxism and Literature* (Oxford, 1977).
19. Williams, *Long Revolution*, p. 58.
20. Raymond Williams, 'The Press and Popular Culture: an historical perspective', in George Boyce, James Curran and Pauline Wingate (eds), *Newspaper History from the Seventeenth Century to the Present Day* (London, 1978) p. 41.
21. Williams, *Long Revolution*, p. 61.
22. Stuart Hall provides a critique of Williams in a very interesting comparison of the culturalist and structuralist approaches in British cultural studies. See 'Cultural Studies: Two Paradigms', in Bennett *et al.* (eds), *Culture, Ideology and Social Process*.
23. Bennett *et al.* (eds), *Culture, Ideology and Social Process*, p. 12.
24. Stuart Hall, quoted in Gurevitch *et al.* (eds), *Culture, Society and the Media*, p. 9.
25. See Williams's essay in Boyce *et al.* (eds), *Newspaper History*.
26. See, for example, 'The Study of the Media: Theoretical Approaches', in Gurevitch *et al.* (eds), *Culture, Society and the Media*.
27. *VPN*, no. 13 (1971) 27.
28. Roland Barthes, 'From Work to Text', in *Image, Music, Text*, trans. Stephen Heath (London, 1977) pp. 155–7.
29. *WR*, I (1824) 206.
30. *WR*, I (1824) 209.
31. Althusser defines ideology as 'a system of representation . . . perceived-accepted-suffered cultural objects' which negotiate the '"lived" relations between men and the world'. See *For Marx*, trans. Ben Brewster (London, 1969) p. 233.
32. *WR*, I (1824) 209.

33.   Roland Barthes, *Mythologies*, trans. Annette Lavers (London, 1973) p. 150.
34.   See, for example, Michel Foucault, 'Orders of Discourse', *Social Sciences Information*, X (1971) 7–30.
35.   Foucault, 'Orders of discourse', 18.
36.   J.S. Mill, 'Periodical Literature', *WR*, I (1824) 505–41.
37.   Michael Foucault, 'History of Systems of Thought' in D.F. Bouchard (ed.) *Language, Counter-memory, Practice* (Ithaca and Oxford, 1977) p. 199.
38.   Brian Maidment, 'Magazines of Popular Progress and the Artisans', *VPR*, XVII (1984) 85.
39.   Michael Lund, 'Novels, Writers and Readers in 1850', *VPR*, XVII (1984) 15–28.
40.   Maidment, 'Magazines', 86.
41.   Tony Bennett, 'Theories of the Media, Theories of Society', in Gurevitch *et al.* (eds), *Culture, Society and the Media*, p. 53.
42.   Raymond Williams, *Culture* (London, 1981) pp. 12–13.

2

Towards a Theory of the Periodical as a Publishing Genre

MARGARET BEETHAM

I

Periodicals are among the most ephemeral of printed forms. Read today and rubbish tomorrow, each number of a periodical becomes obsolete as soon as the next comes out. Nor is this particular relationship to time accidental; it is, as the name indicates, the defining characteristic of the genre.

Yet, while individual periodicals are ephemeral, the form has proved immensely resilient and self-renewing. It has developed from the eighteenth, through the nineteenth, and into the twentieth century as *the* characteristic modern form of print. It is not just that it has been enormously prolific.[1] It is also that the periodical has occupied a crucial place in the development of urban industrial societies. It has been important in the evolution of print technology and communications networks generally, in the dissemination of information and ideas, in literary history and in the growth of liberal political democracies.

Of course the generic term covers a range of types and kinds: newspapers, journals, reviews and magazines. The expensive quarterly reviews of the early nineteenth century differed substantially in price, content and tone from the penny publications which offered sensation fiction to a largely working-class readership. Since the emergence of a mass press, the periodical has appeared in ever more various shapes. But all these diverse types share that particular relationship to time which gives the periodical its name and its distinctiveness as a literary or publishing activity.

It therefore seems legitimate to talk of *the* periodical and to seek to define its formal qualities and to ask how they relate to its success as a publishing genre. Though I focus on the nineteenth century, the argument is relevant today.

Historians, including literary historians and critics, have long since recognised the special value of the periodical press in researching the recent past. Nineteenth-century magazines and newspapers are prime sources on economic, political and literary matters. However, a periodical is not a window on to the past or even a mirror of it. Each article, each periodical number, was and is part of a complex process in which writers, editors, publishers and readers engaged in trying to understand themselves and their society; that is, they struggled to make their world meaningful. I describe it as a 'struggle' because in modern societies the processes of making meaning – both individually and socially – are difficult and cut across by conflict. At the social level different groups have different, often conflicting, interests and therefore have different and conflicting ways of making sense of their world. In this contest some groups have more power than others to 'make their meanings stick'.[2] Those who owned, edited and wrote for the nineteenth-century periodical press had more power to define their world and 'make their meanings stick' than did their readers, whose most important power was the choice of whether to buy or not.

The formal qualities of the periodical and especially its time-extended nature meant it was peculiarly embedded in these processes. This makes isolation and definition of the form difficult. However, it is also the key to understanding it. In what follows, then, I will be focusing on the formal qualities of the periodical but always in the consciousness that the periodical press was and is part of a wider process of negotiation and struggle over meaning.

II

What is a periodical? How can we define it and delimit it? These questions are not easy to answer. To begin with, there is the problem of defining the basic unit which constitutes the text. For most students and academics, nineteenth-century periodicals are a quarry or mine from which they can dig isolated articles. But to describe the periodical as a collection of articles is obviously unsatisfactory. The whole issue or number seems a better unit of definition. However, it may equally well be argued that the periodical text is the whole run of numbers from start to finish. Even at this basic level, therefore, it is difficult to define 'a periodical'.

One way of approaching this problem is to define it in terms of the economic system. Periodicals are commodities or 'products'. Like other products (shoes, for example), they are produced and marketed by a specialist sector of the economy. Their production depends on developments in technology and on the work of producers both of hand and brain: printers, photographers and artists, writers, editors and publishers as well as advertisers, distributers and so on. The industry needs investors to provide capital in the expectation of profits. In short, the periodical press as we know it developed within capitalism and is impossible to understand unless it is situated within the economic system. The success of the periodical in the nineteenth century, and since, is partly to be explained by its convenience for producers. In theory the consumer of the periodical is not so much satisfied as stimulated to return at regular intervals to buy the next number of the product. As the first date-stamped commodity, the periodical was designed both to ensure rapid turnover and to create a regular demand.

However, periodicals cannot be completely explained by describing them in these terms. There is evidence that profit was not the only, sometimes not the most important, motive for those involved in production.[3] The exercise of the power to make one's meanings stick, the desire to educate the readers – whether in religious truth or political knowledge – could be as powerful as the desire for profit. It is true that these motives could not be indefinitely sustained against economic loss. But they cannot be simply discounted either. For the reader, of course, the periodical is not only a product to be consumed. It also enters into the processes of signification or meaning-making. To put that another way, reading a periodical is itself a productive process and what is produced is meaning. It is this dimension of the periodical which I have in mind when I describe it as a 'text'.

I would accept the argument that this distinction is not special to periodicals. To the consumer, many – perhaps all – products can have both a material aspect (they are objects we use or consume) and a signifying aspect (they enter into the construction of meaning). The shoes we wear, for example, are clearly both material objects which keep our feet dry and part of a system of meaning which can itself generate conflict and debate, as anyone who has overheard parents and teenage children in a shoe shop knows. Shoes are texts when we treat them as part of the system of meaning called 'fashion'.

Periodicals, however, are not just the same as shoes. After all, they deal in language, the medium of consciousness and the most sophisticated signifying system we have developed. Saussure argued that all other meaning systems or signifying practices could be understood as functioning like language, and Lacan argues that even the unconscious is structured 'like a language'.[4] Language, in its commonsense meaning, is the basic model of all signifying or meaning systems and language is the stuff of periodicals. This means that their signifying function is their primary function. It is this which distinguishes them from shoes.

If we start to argue that the important thing about periodicals is that they are made up of words, we are in danger of invoking a rather different kind of definition of the text from that given above. To describe something as a 'text' has traditionally meant not just that it is words but that it is authoritative words or even that it is 'The Word', the truth of God. Set texts on a course of study are self-explanatory units which are there by virtue of their authority and value in their own right. Their boundaries are clear. However, the periodical is a form which it has been extremely difficult to accommodate to the idea of the text as authoritative and self-explanatory. This is one of the reasons, I believe, that the study of its formal or generic characteristics has been neglected. That alternative definition of a text, which draws on structuralist accounts of language as a system of meaning, may, therefore, provide a more useful way into theorising the periodical as a genre.

The best way to begin this process of theorising is to remember that we are dealing with material objects. Because they are relatively cheap, periodicals have been printed on cheap paper and with paper rather than board covers. Indeed, with certain notable exceptions, the materials of which periodicals are made have been designed for speed of production and cheapness rather than durability, and the connection between the development of a mass periodical press and the technology for producing cheap paper, for example, is a close and dynamic one.[5] Where particular periodicals have departed from this, it has always been a matter worthy of note or even – as with the 'little magazines' of the 1890s or the 'glossies' of today – a central part of their definition. Indeed, the material characteristics of the periodical (quality of paper, size of the pages and lack of hard cover) have consistently been central to its meaning.

The modern reader of nineteenth-century periodicals is, however, confronted with a paradox. The physical objects with which we have to deal are likely to be the bound volumes on the library shelves. The nineteenth-century middle-class habit of binding favourite periodicals in volume form has ensured that vast numbers still survive, though the crumbling paper inside the covers bears witness that stay of execution is only temporary. However, it is these volumes which provide our texts.

This is the paradox. A periodical, by definition, appears in single numbers separated by time. Putting several numbers into one bound volume changes all this, not least by suggesting that *really* the periodical is a kind of book and the numbers are incomplete sections of the whole. Putting covers round the pages has ensured that they survive, but the survival is bought at the price of the form of the text.

Equally important is what does *not* appear between those stiff covers. Binders tended to think that end-papers and advertisements were not part of the periodical and so left them out of the bound versions. However much modern readers may disagree with this definition, we cannot retrieve the missing advertisements once they have been removed from the volume. Even more important is the absence from the bound volumes of whole categories of reading matter. The cheapest serials and periodicals were not usually considered worth binding at all. They were presumably passed from reader to reader until they fell apart or were thrown away.

Similar arguments can be made about the effect of the microfilm version of nineteenth-century periodicals, which fail to convey those aspects of texture, size and weight which are so important to what a periodical means. Even this brief sketch suggests the complex and dynamic relationship which exists between materiality and meaning or signifier and signified. The material character of the text decides its meaning but is also the product of definitions about its meaning. Whether we are concerned about a single text or bodies of literature our understanding is mediated to us by earlier definitions of the text. We may want to resist this tradition but we cannot escape it. Later generations will deal with the problems of our definitions and our modes of preservation.

Just as the material qualities of the volumes are produced historically and both constitute and are affected by the definitions of what a periodical is, so are the formal qualities. Here, too, the periodical is beset by problems of boundaries. It is amoeba-like; a genre marked by heterogeneity rather than consistency.

III

Periodicals are heterogeneous in that they are made up of different kinds of material. Many mix text and pictures. Indeed the relation of blocks of text to visual material is a crucial part of their meaning. Even where it does not use visual and literary material together, the periodical is still characteristically a mixed form.

Of course, some periodical types are more homogenous than others. The early nineteenth-century reviews, like the contemporary academic journal, were at one end of the spectrum, consisting almost entirely of long review articles, unillustrated and relatively consistent in tone. However, even in these, the heterogeneity of the form had to be asserted in terms of variety of voice. Some early numbers of the *Edinburgh Review* and *Blackwood's Edinburgh Magazine* may have been, as rumour had it, written by one prodigiously energetic writer. But the point is that the articles had to be presented as *though* by different writers. The rumours had to be denied.[6]

At the other end of the spectrum were the magazines, which became more important later in the century. These mixed together photographs, line drawings, fiction, articles, advice columns, advertisements, poems, jokes and letters pages in an apparently random manner but one governed by formulae which are still evident in magazine publishing. It might be argued that as the nineteenth century went on periodicals tended towards the more mixed rather than the relatively homogeneous. Certainly it was the mixed forms of the (illustrated) magazine and newspaper which emerged into the twentieth century as the characteristic periodical forms.

However, if the range of genres which appeared in the periodical had been contained by it, the problems of definition would be less acute. In fact these genres often lead an independent and vigorous literary existence. Serialised fiction, for example, was a staple of the magazine and an important part of many newspapers in the late nineteenth century. However, it is the book and not the serial which inevitably becomes the 'text' of the novel. Fiction is only a periodical form in a limited and contingent sense. Poetry also characteristically appeared and appears in periodicals, from which a selection is then preserved in volume collections. Even the forms like the essay and the article, which developed in the periodical, emerged into independent literary life in volume editions as collections. Some of the most influential prose of the late nineteenth century comes into this category, including Matthew Arnold's *Culture and Anarchy*, Ruskin's *Unto this Last* and Pater's *Renaissance*.

I have already suggested that translations from periodical to volume always involve a redefinition of the text, even if – most unusually – every word is the same in the two versions. The changes of format from serialised to volume novel or from single article to collection are significant because they always signal the rescue of the text. This has two aspects: rescue into the book form, which is physically more stable, and – equally important – rescue from the periodical into a recognised genre, i.e. fiction or poetry or essay.[7]

All this not only makes it hard to separate the periodical out from the other genres of which it is made up. It is also by implication a denial of importance as a literary form to the periodical. It then becomes not so much a form in its own right as an enabling space, a kind of nursery in which certain kinds of development in other forms can take place.

The heterogeneity and blurred boundaries of the genre are evident also in terms of the producers of the periodical. One way of identifying a text has traditionally been to situate it in the *oeuvre* of a particular author. However, the concept of authorship becomes problematic in relation to the periodical, where typically even one number involves several writers, the editor, perhaps the proprietor, perhaps the artist or engraver and the printer. Nor can the disappearance of the author as the only source of the text be compensated for by substituting the figure of the all-powerful and creative editor. It is true that the editor or proprietor will try to enforce a certain consistency of style and position but the tight editorial control and policy of rewriting contributions which Dickens followed in *Household Words* was and is exceptional.[8] Editors, too, are involved in processes of negotiation between authors, proprietors and readers.

Most important of all, there is the question of how the formal

qualities of the periodical are shaped by its particular relationship
to time. Obviously this means that it must be read diachronically
along the time line of its production as well as synchronically in
terms of the single issue or number. Since the periodical depends
on ensuring that the readers continue to buy each number as it
comes out, there is a tendency in the form not only to keep
reproducing elements which have been successful but also to link
each number to the next. This can be done through running a
series of articles, through constant reference to past and future
issues, through advertising, through readers' letters and through
serialisation. The spread of the serialised novel from magazines to
newspapers at the end of last century was undoubtedly due to the
success of the serial in ensuring that readers kept on coming back.[9]
The form is, therefore, not only characteristically self-referring but
is by definition open-ended and resistant to closure.

It is easy to see why the periodical has been difficult to
accommodate within the traditional taxonomy of literary forms. It
is so awkward to theorise in terms of the 'text' defined as 'The
Word', precisely because it always presents itself as part of a
system of meaning. The date and the issue number on the front of
every periodical spell out its contingent claims to truth. It always
points beyond itself – to other numbers of the same periodical, to
other words and texts which give it meaning, to other periodicals,
books or entertainments. (It is no accident that it is in the periodical
that book reviews and television and radio programme notices
appear.)

The tendency of periodical forms to re-appear in volume publications is evidence of another important characteristic. The form is
such that it invites a variety of readings. It may be argued that this
is true of all texts but, unlike other literary forms, the periodical
does not demand to be read from front to back in order. It is an
unusual reader of any periodical who reads every word 'from
cover to cover' let alone in the order in which they are printed.
Most readers will construct their own order. (Do you turn first to
the jokes, the letters page, the sporting tips?) The average reader
will also select and read only a fraction of the whole. The
periodical, therefore, is a form which openly offers readers the
chance to construct their own texts.

This last characteristic can also be related to that most important
quality of all, the way the periodical engages with its readers across
time. This means it involves them not just in the production of

their own individual readings but actually in the development of the text, taking that term to mean the whole run of the periodical. Reader response is fed back to the producers by sales figures but in addition many periodicals invite readers to intervene directly – by writing letters, comments and other contributions. This may help to account at once for the immense resilience and popularity of the form and for its intractability in terms of theories which think of texts as the results simply of authorial activity.

Although little work has been done in terms of theorising the forms of periodical literature, there has been such work on the serial forms of television and on other popular modes, especially those which employ narrative. Drawing on psychoanalysis to help to understand the way in which these cultural forms create meaning, critics have drawn a distinction between 'closed' and 'open' forms.[10] 'Closed' or 'masculine' forms are seen as those which assert the dominant structures of meaning by closing off alternative options and offering the reader or viewer only one way of making sense of the text and so, by analogy, of the world and the self. By contrast the 'open' form, the form which refuses the closed ending and allows for the possibility of alternative meanings, is associated with the potentially disruptive, the creative, the 'femi-nine'.

If we try to bring together this kind of theorising and the characteristics of the genre as I have described them, it seems that the essential quality of the periodical, its serial form and the other ways in which it seems to resist closure, can be read as a sign of its strength as a potentially creative form for its readers. In other words, we could argue that the difficulty of defining the periodical in terms of recognised genres and publishing modes is associated with a set of characteristics which make it a potentially disruptive kind of text. In the last section I turn to consider this argument.

IV

The concept of open and closed forms provides a way of explaining the relationship between the forms of texts, the psychic structures in which the individual self constructs meaning, and the structures of the social world. The description of 'closure' as masculine makes these connections explicit. The argument that the periodical characteristically resists closure and that consequently we should understand it as allowing its readers the possibility of alternative or even subversive readings is an interesting and potentially useful one. However, it needs qualifying.

Firstly, the account of the periodical which I gave in the last section is not inaccurate but it is incomplete. It omits another and apparently completely opposite set of qualities which are equally characteristic of periodicals but which are concerned with structure and closure rather than openness and fluidity.

The relationship to time is the central characteristic of the periodical but this means that the form has a deep regular structure. For some readers indeed the relationship between the periodical and calendar- or clock-time may be an important regulating mechanism in their lives. The nineteenth-century Sunday papers marked the pause in the week for those generations of working men who were being forced to adopt the particular discipline of work-time in an industrialised society.[11] The morning paper, the weekly magazine bought as a 'treat' may, in their different ways, function very similarly today. It is impossible to separate out the periodical from other structures by which in advanced industrial societies work and leisure have come to be regulated in time.[12]

This is the most important argument against the description of the periodical as open (and it applies equally to other kinds of serial, for example to those on television). However, there are others. The regularity of a periodical's appearance is matched by the continuities of format, shape and pattern of contents from number to number. The form is mixed and various but each individual periodical has to maintain a certain consistency of mixture. Every number is different but it is still 'the same' periodical. This consistency is necessary so that the reader keeps coming back to buy.

Maintaining a regular readership means offering readers a recognisable position in successive numbers, that is creating a consistent 'reader' within the text. The reader is addressed as an individual but is positioned as a member of certain overlapping sets of social groups, and this positioning is effected by all aspects of the periodical: price, content, form and tone. One magazine or newspaper, for example, will define its readers as male, middle class, Tory, Anglican, interested in formal politics; another as female, lower middle class, at home looking after children and therefore interested in domestic matters and child-rearing but not in politics, and so on. There is a relationship between this reader, invoked or positioned in the text, and the historical reader, who buys the magazine or newspaper and actually reads it, but it is not a direct or simple one. Letters from men to the 'women's magazines' which they claim to read illustrate the complexity of that relationship. The periodical, then, may offer its readers scope to construct their own version of the text by selective reading, but against that flexibility has to be put the tendency in the form to close off alternative readings by creating a dominant position from which to read, a position which is maintained with more or less consistency across the single number and between numbers.

In addition to the points I have already made, there is another problem posed by the serial or time-extended nature of the form. Every number of the periodical is the same in that it offers its readers a recognisable persona or identity and this is part of a recognisable pattern of contents and lay-out. But every number of the periodical is a new number which is different from all previous numbers. This means that each number must function both as part of a series and as a free-standing unit which makes sense to the reader of the single issue. Although it has elements of the serial, the periodical is therefore not a true serial. It is both open-ended and end-stopped. Indeed, although it may include true serials, most of the items in a single number will be characterised by closure.

The argument could be summed up by saying that the periodical is an open form in a number of ways: it resists closure because it comes out over time and is, in that respect, serial rather than end-stopped. Its boundaries are fluid and it mixes genres and authorial voices; all this in a time-extended form seems to encourage readers to produce their own readings. Yet, in complete opposition to these formal qualities are another set of qualities, which are equally characteristic. Each number of the periodical is a self-contained text and will contain sub-texts which are end-stopped or marked by closure. And each periodical positions its readers in terms which construct for that reader a recognisable self.

Any periodical will display both sets of characteristics, although each will mix them differently. This general account may be useful in providing a typology of the form. Specific periodicals can be located on a spectrum between those which emphasise its open, serial qualities and those in which each number is more self-defined. This is one way of returning the generalisation to the particular. However, any attempt to theorise the form must take account of both aspects for, Janus-like, the periodical looks two ways.

This means that the role of the periodical in relation to its readers is complex. The success and vitality of the form must in part be explained because it satisfies *their* needs and aspirations. At the same time it is convenient for producers and all with a stake in the dominant order. This is not just because of its qualities as the first date-stamped commodity. It is also because of the particular balance of closure against openness which is the form's character-istic mode. Readers are returned to the social and linguistic order even as they explore the possibilities of alternative readings. Nor are these two aspects, openness and closure, to be too easily lined up with the two groups, consumers and producers. For many – perhaps most – readers the desire to be confirmed in the generally accepted or dominant discourse may be a more powerful need than the dream of a different future or the desire to construct alternatives. The appearance of the periodical at regular intervals of time both asserts the importance of a time-regulated society and promises that this is not the end, there will be another number.

In conclusion, I would argue that to describe the process of the periodical as repressive or characterised by closure is as much an oversimplification as to describe it as potentially subversive or open. The periodical both offers and withholds the possibility of what we may call 'polymorphously diverse' readings. Neverthe-less, the dominant way in which it works can, I believe, best be described as that of deferred gratification. I would even argue that it is formally more likely to be conservative and repressive rather than disruptive and liberating, but this is a proposition which must be tested by readings of specific periodicals.

Those specific readings have also to address the limitations of this proposition, namely that it is concerned only with form and not with content or with the power relationships in which the forms are used. I cannot pursue this set of problems here. However, any account of these other aspects of the periodical which ignores the formal qualities must be impoverished. We need, therefore, to develop a theory of the periodical as a genre. This will, I believe, enrich not only periodical study but our understanding of other genres and forms.

Notes

1. M. Wolff, J. North and D. Deering (eds), *The Waterloo Directory of Victorian Periodicals, 1824–1900: Phase I* (Waterloo, Ontario, 1976) identifies roughly 24 600 periodicals. See also J. North, 'The Waterloo Directory of Victorian Periodicals: A Report', *VPN*, VIII (1975) 69–78, which suggests a further 20 000 titles may be still waiting to be identified. See also Scott Bennett, 'Prolegomenon to Serials Bibliography: A Report to the Society', *VPR*, XII (1979) 3–15.

2. John Thompson, *Studies in the Theory of Ideology* (Oxford, 1984) p. 4. See also discussion of this phrase in Deborah Cameron, 'What is the Nature of Women's Oppression in Language?', *Oxford Literary Review*, VIII (1986) 82–4 and the general argument in Deborah Cameron, *Feminism and Linguistic Theory* (London, 1985), to which I am indebted.

3. For example, the importance of motives other than profit in relation to the Manchester press is extensively evidenced in F.Leary, *History of the Manchester Periodical Press* (1903), unpublished MS in Manchester Central Reference Library Archives. See also discussion in A.J. Lee, 'The Management of a Victorian Local Newspaper', *Business History*, XV (1973) 140.

4. Ferdinand de Saussure, *Course in General Linguistics*, rev. edn, trans. Wade Baskin (Glasgow, 1974) especially p. 17. Jacques Lacan, *The Four Fundamental Concepts of Psychoanalysis*, trans. Alan Sheridan, new edn (Harmondsworth and New York, 1986) p. 20.

5. Marjorie Plant, *The English Book Trade: An Economic History of the Making and Sale of Books* (London, 1974) shows clearly how developments in print and paper technology were pioneered in the periodical press. See especially pp. 274, 283, 289.

6. See for example, V. and R. Colby, *The Equivocal Virtue: Mrs. Oliphant and the Victorian Literary Market Place* (New York and London, 1966, 1970) p. 199 on Mrs Oliphant and *Blackwood's Edinburgh Magazine*.

7. See Brian Maidment, 'Readers Fair and Foul: John Ruskin and the Periodical Press', in J. Shattock and M. Wolff, *The Victorian Press: Samplings and Soundings* (Leicester, 1982) pp. 29–58.

8. On Dickens as editor see John Sutherland, *Victorian Novelists and Publishers* (London, 1976) pp. 166–87; on the limits of editorial power see J. Shattock, 'Editorial Policy and the Quarterlies: The Case of the *North British Review*', *VPN*, X (1977) 130–9.

9. Amy Cruse, *After the Victorians* (London, 1938) p. 198.

10. This discussion draws on debates about narrative and other aspects of popular culture in the works of Roland Barthes, Umberto Eco and the French feminists, especially Luce Irigary. In Britain this debate is associated with the journal *Screen*. I have found the formulation by Tania Modleski in relation to soap opera especially useful, see T. Modleski, *Loving with a Vengeance: Mass-Produced Fantasies for Women* (New York and London, 1982) pp. 85–109.

11. Raymond Williams, 'The Press and Popular Culture: An Historical Perspective', in George Boyce, J. Curran and P. Wingate, *Newspaper*

History from the Seventeenth Century to the Present Day (London, 1978) pp. 41–9.

12.   E.P. Thompson, 'Time, Work-Discipline, and Industrial Capitalism', *Past and Present*, XXXVIII (1967) 56–97.

3

Popular Narrative and Political Discourse in *Reynolds's Weekly Newspaper*[1]

ANNE HUMPHERYS

In G. W. M. Reynolds's best seller *The Mysteries of London* (1846–8), the arch-villain Anthony Tidkins, known throughout the novel as the Resurrection Man, is drinking one night in a 'boozing ken' with several acquaintances, including one called The Cracksman. Waiting for a contact to appear, they engage in conversation with the waiter.

> 'Ah! there's many things that has struck me since I've been in the waiter-line in flash houses of this kind,' observed the paralytic attendant, shaking his head solemnly; 'but one curious fact I've noticed, – which is, that in nine cases out of ten the laws themselves make men take to bad ways, and then punish them for acting under their influence.'
> 'I don't understand that,' said the Cracksman.
> 'I do, though,' exclaimed the Resurrection Man.[2]

And as a way of making meaning of the flunkey's remark, he narrates 'the history of my own life'.

The making of meaning by the telling of stories is one of the oldest and perhaps most recurrent cognitive devices human beings possess. If I am puzzled by a series of events I witness on the street, I am likely to try to make sense of them by fitting them into familiar 'narrative' patterns such as those involving domestic arguments, or those of sudden violence or of betrayal and obligation. 'You'll never believe what happened today' is usually a prelude to a 'story' which turns out to be believable precisely because it is a recognisable narration of events with a beginning, middle and end, linked together through conventional patterns of cause and effect.

What we are doing when we make meaning of events in this way is 'plotting', that is imposing a familiar order on selected phenomena through narrative patterns.

The structures of these narrative patterns are likely to be known ones – those of fairy tales, Biblical parables, or of romance, either domestic, chivalric or gothic. Reynolds's Resurrection Man, for example, tells a story of a child mistreated by individuals and by institutions who becomes, as a result of his early experiences, a criminal. This interpolated narrative is as familiar to us in its pattern of events, in its suggestion of causes and effects as is the narrative of Oliver Twist which demonstrates the opposite – that goodness is indestructible and Cinderellas will eventually find their rightful places in society.

But we do not just begin with 'facts' and then make meaning of them through narrative models. It is equally the case that the stories that we use to 'explain' events may have actually shaped what we perceive to be the original 'facts'. For example, Elizabeth Gaskell and Charles Kingsley, having read Henry Mayhew's interviews with needlewomen in the *Morning Chronicle*, used Mayhew's 'facts' in their novels *Ruth* and *Alton Locke*. But it is also true that popular fictions themselves helped determine what Mayhew saw in the first place in his forays into the East End of London and certainly gave him the narrative models in which to report his experiences in the columns of the *Morning Chronicle*. For example, the distressed needlewoman motif popularised by Thomas Hood in 1843 predisposed Mayhew to see the needle-women he visited in a particular way, and the language of Hood's 'Song of the Shirt' is part of the language of Mayhew's reports.[3] My point is not that Mayhew was culpable in reporting the facts in fictional narrative structures, but that it almost always happens this way. The minute we interpret two events (Aristotle says it takes three actions to make a plot) we begin to construct a narrative. As Fredric Jameson has said, narrative deconstructs the fictive and the non-fictive.[4]

Nonetheless, such a deconstruction goes against a fundamental dichotomy in post-Kantian thought, that is, the opposition of 'fact' and 'fiction'. The dominance in our culture of technology and science has reinforced an adherence to this dichotomy and led, among other things, to the attempts in the social sciences particularly to mathematise the investigation of human experience.[5]

It is in the 'news' of the periodical press as against the novel that the opposition between fact and fiction appears most obvious. However, in the beginnings of both genres in the late seventeenth century, there was little if any recognisable boundary between fact and fiction, between the novel and the news.[6] 'Serialized fact and fiction, available cheaply to the publishers by simple piracy, and the sorts of criminal biographies and dying words which figured prominently in street literature rapidly became the content staples of [the popular] newspaper press.'[7] This mixture continued into the nineteenth century.

Despite this, the separability of 'fact' and 'fiction' was axiomatic in the Victorian period, the newspaper being preferred to the novel in many quarters precisely because it was 'not fiction'. This is one of the reasons fiction writers of the period, most of whom also wrote for and edited organs of the periodical press, tried to validate their fictions in terms of their 'factuality'. Dickens insisted in the prefaces to *Oliver Twist* and *Bleak House* that events in his novels were 'TRUE', and that all he did was dwell on 'the romantic side of familiar things'.[8] Needless to say, given the anxiety about the value of fiction as opposed to fact, there was no discussion of the role narrative might play in the reporting of the facts.

The most cursory investigation of the pages of many popular Victorian journals and periodicals, however, will turn up not only 'fiction' clearly labelled as such, but also a variety of 'true' stories and reports that are strongly similar to the clearly designated fictional contributions in event, structure and language. The department labels, such as 'letters from correspondents' or 'news from court' are helpful in determining what the editors of a given journal considered fact and what they considered fiction. But ignoring them may be equally helpful in determining to what degree the Victorian letter press may belong to a single discourse. Such a discourse would be a complex and varied one, of course, with the bare 'facts' of chronology and isolated event at one end of a spectrum and the self-consciously 'fictional' story at the other. But much of this journalistic discourse would share narrative characteristics, including a beginning, a middle and an end, and plotting strategies for linking separate phenomena.

An example of what we might learn by such an approach can result from looking at several examples in *Reynolds's Weekly Newspaper*, one of the many projects of G. W. M. Reynolds, the most popular writer in Victorian England.[9] *Reynolds's Weekly Newspaper*, along with *Lloyd's*, its main competitor for the working class

readership (*Lloyd's* always had a larger circulation though
Reynolds's lasted longer), essentially invented the format of the
mass media. In its early days *Reynolds's Weekly* was a combination
of political commentary, news of various sorts with a special
interest in the activities of the working class, sensational stories of
bizarre events, crimes and gossip, plus several standard departments such as news at court, notices to correspondents and
advertisements.

Reynolds's political ideas are found throughout commentary of
various sorts in each issue of *Reynolds's Weekly Newspaper*, most
directly in the front-page article signed by him.[10] In the beginning
the paper's political purpose was to support the six points of the
People's Charter. But more generally the politics of the paper
tended toward a verbally heated republicanism which Reynolds
had learned in France in the 1830s and which identified the old
aristocracy as the source of social, economic and political wrongs.
Today, Reynolds's politics as expressed in *Reynolds's Weekly Newspaper* can seem old-fashioned, and most historians identify his
position as one of an 'old analysis';[11] that is, his political writings
do not acknowledge that power had shifted from the agrarian
aristocracy to the industrial/financial sector. Nonetheless, in his
own time his politics were considered the 'reddest of the red', and
in any event I think the case for the reliance in *Reynolds's Newspaper*
on the 'old analysis' has been overstated.[12]

It comes as no surprise that Reynolds's political discourse is also
found in many of his fifty-odd novels; *The Mysteries of London*
contains long passages which inveigh against various specific
social crimes such as censorship or capital punishment, and others
which insist on the rights of the working class to a fair share of the
economic wealth of the country. Reynolds himself said later that
his purpose in writing the novel was 'to show up Royalty and
Aristocracy in their true light' (*Reynolds's* [11 July 1875]).

It takes a readjustment of our expectations about the separability
of fact and fiction, however, to recognise the narrative structures
and the language of his fictions in the political discourse of his
periodical writings. Berridge notes that the language of the political
discourse in *Reynolds's Weekly* is similar to that in the theatre and
popular fiction. But this connection serves in her analysis only to
demonstrate the 'easy and familiar assessments [which] helped
insure the commercial prosperity of the paper'.[13] I think the
interplay of popular politics and popular literature is more compli-

cated than that. The connections are more than language, and the effects go beyond commercialisation. The very structure and thought of the political discourse have roots in popular fiction, particularly in the dominant mode of narrative in Reynolds's own novels, namely melodrama.

Melodrama as it appears in Reynolds's novels, whether about the army (*The Soldier's Wife*, 1852–3), the city (*The Mysteries of London*, 1846–8), or the romantic worlds of Italy or Turkey (*Agnes, Beauty and Pleasure*, 1855–7 or *The Loves of the Harem*, 1855), has a similar structure:[14] a hero or heroine begins in a low state but is desirous of a useful and fulfilled life. This desire is checked by an evil 'blocking agent'. In the course of this struggle the virtuous protagonist is 'misprized', his or her virtue misconstrued, though at the end she is recognised for the incorruptibly good person that she really is. The blocking agent's motivation and weapons are a combination of sex and money, the demonstration of the former being the source of the strongest outrage expressed at Reynolds's novels by his contemporaries. (When the sexual motivation in theatrical melodrama, where the villain wants to possess both the heroine's body and her property, is incorporated into the novel, it is probably the uneasy relationship to realism in the novel that makes the role that sex plays in the pursuit of power more unacceptable.)

Nearly everybody who has written on the Victorian popular press has remarked on the prominence of the 'notices to correspondents' in these journals. In this column, we have the editor(s)' answers to all sorts of queries about law, history, literature and statistics as well as personal questions about love, work and etiquette. (This standard feature of the popular press in the nineteenth century continues today, though not in the 'letters to the editor'; rather the intimate exchange of the nineteenth-century 'notices to correspondents' survives in our time fragmented into 'advice' columns on love, health, law or business.) In the nineteenth century, to save space, the queries themselves were not printed, so that a characteristic set of entries reads:

AN ODDFELLOW: – not being enrolled, you cannot recover.
M.T.B. – The order is quite right; you had better send the money to save further expenses.
J.F.G. – The eldest son can take all the goods, he being the heir, in default of a will otherwise disposing of the property.

W.D.R. – The mother can make him pay. – Lord Byron had a defect in one foot.

(*Reynolds's* [11 March 1855])

Periodically, the text displays not answers to such queries but rather little stories, told to make a point about some injustice. In these cases, the narratising in the journalistic discourse is at its most overt. Whatever 'really happened', the meaning of the story is created by structuring the events as a conventional popular melodrama. For example:

> We continue to receive countless letters from attorneys' clerks, complaining of the hardships they endure. . . . One instance we are cognizant of, where a lawyer's clerk, having been thirty years in the offices of a flourishing firm, the principals of which, through indolence or incapacity, were compelled to consult with him on every occasion, so much so, indeed, that although they advised with their clients, and charged them with the same, the moment the latter's backs were turned, the confidential clerk was summoned, and it was he who undertook and settled the matter in question; his salary was twenty-five shillings per week; the income of the firm was full five thousand a year: it had he been doubled through the exertion, application, and ability of this indefatigable clerk. He modestly requested an advance after thirty years faithful service, of ten shillings a week! This request was not only denied, but he was given to understand that his services could be dispensed with, as a younger man was needed, who could do the same duties at a cheaper rate. The poor fellow was dismissed; his occupation was gone; he was out of his element; for thirty years the office had been to him his world; he was fitted for nothing else, or for no other place; all his life had he been remarked for his sobriety, the neatness of his attire, and the regularity of his habits; suddenly he became a drunkard, a sloven, and a vagabond; and may now be seen haunting the public-houses frequented by the law fraternity, shoeless, penniless, and lost. The clients of the firm, who knew the poor fellow, and appreciated his industry, politeness and ability, felt his loss, and would often express regret that their business was not transacted by him, who was so thoroughly conversant with it. When these observations reached the ears of the principal, he would coolly exclaim 'Ah, but the old fellow is turned such a tippler, that he is good for nothing!'

(*Reynolds's* [11 March 1855])

Undoubtedly there were, prior to this narrative, certain 'facts' – a once neat lawyer's clerk is seen shoeless in a popular lawyer's pub – but the text makes meaning of these 'facts' through a melodramatic narrative: the misprized hero; the evil blocking agents; the ironic reversal of fortune; the attempted intervention by helpers. The closure, to be sure, is not in accordance with melodrama since the hero is not restored to his rightful place, but to the degree that closure in melodrama demands merely the recognition of misprized virtue (heroes and heroines do sometimes die) this desire *is* fulfilled by the account of the fellow's 'true' character in the mass media. This must be the reason why, as a reader of this text, I do not feel the need for any further information or action. The sense of closure is underlined, moreover, by the verbal flourish of the deliciously ironic speech of the principal at the very end.

The narratising in such an example is relatively clear. But even in the drastically attenuated 'notices', where the editor's response is in a few words or a single sentence, the same process operates, except that in these cases the reader must do the story-telling, make the meaning: 'the eldest son can take all the goods, he being the heir, in default of a will otherwise disposing of the property'. That story sounds familiar to me, or at least I make it familiar by telling a story to myself similar to those in many popular texts. In one version, I posit a younger brother, disinherited by an elder son; a father dying before the lawyer can get there; I picture the writer of this letter – a sweetheart of the distraught younger son – desperately looking for help. Whether or not the original letter-writer narrated the situation in these melodramatic terms (not to mention what the original events might have been), the editor, in writing up the response, has selected language and structure that adumbrate the melodramatic structure.

The real power of the 'notices' to attract and keep readers for the newspaper, it now seems to me, is not just, as I have said in another place,[15] the closeness they generate between the editor and reader but rather the pleasure they provide the reader who can recognise in these 'factual' fragments familiar stories of desire, betrayal and reward. The pleasure that even the most sophisticated twentieth-century reader can have in reading the advice columns surely is the same; that is the pleasure of making meaning through the telling of familiar 'stories' about the 'facts' of life.

Of course the subjects of the 'notices', as of the advice columns, are the stuff of 'fiction', particularly melodrama: blocked desire, frustrated love, wills and inheritances, questions of deportment

and the law. What about the directly political discourse in
Reynolds's Weekly Newspaper, the columns and editorials which
promulgate Chartist and republican analyses of public events? I
think that in many of these pieces we can also see melodramatic
narrative patterns in terms of the structure as well as the language
that the text uses to 'make the news' from the public events.

Consider, as an example, the lead article, signed George William
Macarthur Reynolds, on page 1 of *Reynolds's Weekly* for 7 July 1850:
'The proletarian's career, from the cradle to the grave'. This piece
tells how at every stage of his life a worker is exploited by the
aristocratic abuse of power, especially as this power is exercised by
the lackeys of the aristocracy, the 'moneyocracy' – *Reynolds's
Weekly*'s term for the bourgeoisie. The piece ends with the following passage:

> How immense are the abuses which render our social system
> abhorrent to the humane man and terrible to the thoughtful one!
> – how undeserved are the honours, the luxuries, and the
> blessings which the favoured few enjoy – and how tremendous
> are the woes, the wrongs, and the cruelties which the millions
> endure! But what is to be the end of all this? No maudlin mock
> philanthropic Societies will alleviate the evils with which the
> poor man groans: no piddling, puny, milk-and-water measure of
> reform will reach the hideous gangrene which is devouring the
> heart's core of society. One wholesale annihilation of the abuse,
> on the one hand, and one unlimited acknowledgement of rights
> on the other, can alone save this country from chaos – from
> anarchy – from ruin. The People's Charter, as the means towards
> the reconstruction of the social system, is the only panacea, the
> only remedy.

As with the previous story of the law clerk, this text enables us to
understand power arrangements in Britain in the mid-nineteenth
century by narrating them in a familiar structure, namely that of a
Manichean struggle between good and evil. That is, the political
story is a melodrama. A heroic working class, misprized and
denied its birthright waits to be recognised and rewarded for its
goodness in the face of repeated efforts to block this end by the
villainous aristocracy. There is no middle ground in this story;
there is, as in all melodrama, an 'excluded middle'.[16] Efforts at such
a middle way, at philanthropy, are 'piddling, puny, milk-and-
water'.

The language of this piece, furthermore, comes from the same discourse as do Reynolds's novels of social melodrama. It is the language of excess. The 'woes, the wrongs, and the cruelties' suffered by the hero are 'tremendous'; the system of power arrangements is a 'hideous gangrene'. The abuses of the one must be annihilated 'wholesale' while the other must receive 'unlimited' acknowledgement of its rights. This heated language of melodrama tries, in Peter Brooks's words, 'a total articulation of the grandiose moral terms',[17] by bringing 'states of being beyond the immediate context of the narrative, and in excess of it . . . to bear on it, to charge it with intenser significances'.[18]

The grammar itself can contribute to the melodrama of politics as one can see in the way the many rhetorical questions operate in the text:

> To adopt another system of reasoning, it may be asked, who have rendered the masses so demoralized as they are represented to be? Have the higher orders set them a good example? Have they in their capacity of legislators sought to educate the millions? Have they fostered intellectual improvement? or, on the other hand, have they not done all they could to keep the masses ignorant?
>
> (*Reynolds's* [1 October 1854])

These rhetorical questions, like the abbreviated 'notices to correspondents', force the reader into the text; we must 'answer' them in order to make meaning of the utterance. And again, as in the 'notices', we tend to answer the questions by story-telling, especially in this text by telling melodramatic stories. 'Have the higher orders set them a good example?' is answered not only by our telling the story of villainous excess but also by actual 'news' stories found in other parts of the paper, especially in the legal and gossip columns, which detail the private lives of the upper classes, consisting of sexual promiscuity, conspicuous consumption, disregard of human feelings and other familiar traits of the upper-class melodramatic villains. (These 'news' stories about aristocratic misdeeds, of course, are also products of narratising, that is, in the 'news from court' or other 'news' stories, the predisposition to melodrama has shaped both the details that are chosen and the language that is used in description.)

Such a juxtaposition allows us to examine in a different way the apparent contradiction in *Reynolds's Weekly Newspaper* between heated attacks on the excesses of the ruling powers and an obsessive fascination with the details of the same excess. As the villain's desire provides the energy for the melodramatic action, so the details of upper-class life provide the energy for the political melodrama of the newspaper's politics.

Melodrama, however, does not operate solely to make the news textually. It also actually helps invent the popular political thought that precedes the text. It is here that my analysis of the connections between popular literature and popular politics diverges some-what from that of other commentators. While I agree that the language and structures of popular literature make the politics more accessible to the readers, I want to consider a prior question, that is, why melodrama? What is it in the structure and language of that form that has the power to 'explain' the political situation?

Popular political thought in all times and places tends to be melodramatic – that is extreme and Manichean – whether it is a case of Reynolds's aristocracy versus workers, Disraeli's 'two nations', Marx's capital versus labour, America's democracy versus communism, or simply everyone's them versus us. In fact melo-drama and politics have been linked since the beginnings of the form in France during the revolution. The process continues today. As Brooks says 'the melodramatization of modern politics suggests ... that Robespierre and Saint-Just are the ultimate models of reference, in their increasingly manicheistic struggle of virtue ... against vice'.[19] The persistence of this binary structure in political thought suggests to me that its origins are probably psychological, maybe in the infant's earliest sense of itself in terms of me and not me. And, of course, language itself tends towards the binary, words being defined in terms of their opposites. These fun-damental psychological and linguistic forces may be part of the reason the Manichean vision has such an appeal as an explanation of power relationships and also why narratising in popular politi-cal discourse tends so often to the melodramatic model.

The connection between politics and the melodramatic story, furthermore, may also be a result of the loss in public life of an earlier narrative structure by which the meaning of power rela-tionships could be understood hierarchically, namely the Biblical story. 'In a post sacred era' as Brooks says, 'melodrama becomes the principle mode for uncovering, demonstrating, and making operative the essential moral universe.'[20]

Let us take two examples from *Reynolds's Weekly* where we might see melodrama shaping political thought. The first is the interpretation of the role of Queen Victoria in the current political scene. Given the violence of the attacks on all aspects of the aristocracy in *Reynolds's Weekly*, it comes as something of a surprise to discover that the Queen herself is excluded from this argument.[21] I think melodramatic narratising is partly responsible for this seeming contradiction. In melodrama, a woman is the evil, blocking force when she is motivated by sexual energy. But since there was no way Victoria could fit that role, she had to fill the only other female role available to her in melodrama, namely that of innocent victim. And that is how Reynolds's texts, both novels and journalistic, tend to portray her: a passive, loving soul, duped by her ministers and her German husband, who can be saved by the knowledge her people can bring her. She is ignorant of profligacy around her (*Reynolds's* [30 November 1851]); on the death of Prince Albert she is praised for her moral life and role as mother. Is it too outrageous to suggest that one of the reasons Britain did not have a revolution in the nineteenth century was because there happened to be such a woman on the throne, and the story necessary to motivate and justify political action against the social order she represented could find no role for her in the plot but a benign one and that as a result revolutionary fervour was blunted?

Another example of the action of narratising in the political thought in *Reynolds's Weekly Newspaper* is in the solutions the text offers for the problems it points to. All the political pieces in the early years of the *Weekly* have a similar closure. Each time, whether the subject be the Preston strike, the Crimean War or a change in government, the text describes the situation in terms of its melodramatic excluded middle and Manichean opposition of good and evil, and then poses some version of the question 'What is to be done?' Surprisingly, given the totalising description of the problem, the resolution is not strong direct action, though *Reynolds's Weekly* always supported working-class actions, however strong, once they were in progress. That in melodrama the hero and heroine do not always take action against the forces of evil arraigned against them but are rescued by events or outside forces may support the text's reluctance to call for strikes or other organised worker action as a response to the exploitation so stridently narrated. For example, in the quotation I gave above, the solution to the devastating Career of the Proletariat is simply 'the People's Charter' – a set of principles not a set of actions. This resolution is, of course, completely in accord with Reynolds's political views, as well as with other trends of nineteenth-century British thought, and furthermore it is not inconsistent with my own liberal politics.

But in the reading of this text, I find myself disappointed by this 'liberal' resolution of the particular political story that preceded it. I expected another kind of closure to this story. Up until the very end, I have been reading melodrama; the closure of melodrama demands that the villain be routed and punished. But at the last moment, the ending of another story from another discourse has been substituted, that is, some form of comedy, the reconciliation of opposites rather than the punishment of evil and the reward of good. In my disappointment at the ending of this text I am reacting to the narrative not to the politics.

Moreover, the many vociferous critics of *Reynolds's Weekly Newspaper* were probably also responding to the narrative rather than the politics. Critics attacked the paper for its 'violent' opinions. *Mitchell's Newspaper Directory*, for example, described the newspaper in 1851 as having 'news and literary departments ... respectably conducted; and, but for its violent politics, it might be characterized as a good family paper'. But however excessive the language and however reductive the analysis of the problem is in the political discourse of *Reynolds's Weekly Newspaper*, the solution is usually benign. The critics have substituted the way the story 'is supposed to end' for the actual closure.

There is a way, however, that the closure of melodrama, which can be deeply problematic, is consistent with the seeming contradiction in *Reynolds's Weekly* between revolutionary analyses and liberal resolutions. However untenable the political system which has given rise to the power of the villain and the oppression of the hero and heroine may seem in melodrama, at the end the social order is not really different from that at the beginning. The evil have certainly been punished, but though the good are rewarded, they are so through their integration into the old order. The final result of melodrama is a kind of liberal utopia – a reconstitution of the old order in a better way where misprized virtue is given its due. Perhaps part of the reason for the prominence of spectacle at the end of theatrical melodramas (fires, floods and earthquakes) was to displace a seemingly inevitable revolutionary closure set up by the previous action onto special effects.

This dissolution of the expectation of revolutionary change in a reconstitution of the old order, further, may be another element in the power of melodrama in popular politics. The political discourse in *Reynolds's Weekly* divides and totalises the political 'facts' into implacable evil and unbeatable good. But while it validates the struggle between these two forces, it denies the inevitability of any final social disruption. It promises us that the triumph of good can be achieved without revolution. The discourse thus meets universal contradictory needs, namely the desire to sweep everything away and begin anew, and the fear of change which makes us long for stasis. The melodramatic political discourse ennobles the struggle, and denies the consequences. No wonder Marx thought Reynolds a 'scoundrel'.[22] Ultimately, however, the huge increases in circulation for *Reynolds's Weekly*[23] seem to indicate that melodramatic politics were probably more truly popular than were those involved in the romance of revolution.

Notes

1. The research on which this essay is based was supported in part through travel grants awarded by the PSC/CUNY Research Awards Program in 1984, 1985, 1987 and 1988, and by an NEH Summer Stipend Award in 1986.

2. G.W.M. Reynolds, *The Mysteries of London*, vol. I (London, 1846) p. 191.

3. See T.J. Edelstein, 'They Sang "The Song of the Shirt"': The Visual Iconology of the Seamstress', *Victorian Studies*, XXIII (1980) 183–210.

4. In a lecture on postmodernism at the Graduate Center of City University of New York, 15 May 1987.

5. Virginia Berridge's work on *Reynolds's* is an example of this effort, in this case analysing the content of newspapers by turning it into numbers. See 'Content Analysis and Historical Research on Newspapers', in Michael Harris and Alan Lee (eds), *The Press in English Society from the Seventeenth to Nineteenth Centuries* (London and Toronto, 1986) pp. 201–18.

6. Lennard J. Davis argues that the 'news' and the 'novel' both come out of the same discourse in the late seventeenth century. See *Factual Fictions: The Origins of the English Novel* (New York, 1983).

7. Harris and Lee (eds), *Press in English Society*, pp. 20–1.

8. See his remarks on Nancy's devotion to Sykes in the Preface to *Oliver Twist* and his comments on Krook's spontaneous combustion in the Preface to *Bleak House*. The quotation is also from the latter text.

9. *Bookseller* (1 July 1868) 447.

10. *Reynolds's* began 5 May 1850. From that date until 10 October 1853 Reynolds himself wrote both a front-page signed article and the first leader each week. In 1853 he stopped writing the leader, though he continued contributing the signed front-page pieces until 3 August

1856. He remained actively involved with the newspaper, however, until 1876, three years before his death. The paper itself lasted until 1967.

11. This is Virginia Berridge's position in her dissertation 'Popular Journalism and Working-Class Attitudes, 1854–86: A Study of *Reynolds's Newspaper, Lloyd's Weekly Newspaper* and the *Weekly Times*', University of London, 1976, and in 'The Language of Popular and Radical Journalism: The Case of *Reynolds's Newspaper*', *Bulletin of the Society for the Study of Labour History*, XLIV (1982) 6–7. See also Berridge, 'Popular Sunday Papers and Mid-Victorian Society' in G. Boyce, J. Curran and P. Wingate (eds), *Newspaper History: From the Seventeenth Century to the Present Day* (London, 1978) pp. 249–64.

12. There is evidence in *Reynolds's* of the 'new analysis'. See for example the front-page signed article for 7 November 1852: 'When the rule of the Birth Aristocracy passes away, God help the working classes if they are to be crushed beneath the power of the Money Aristocracy'. See also the front-page article on 14 November 1852, and the notices for 24 January 1858.

13. See Berridge, 'The Language of Popular and Radical Journalism', 7. In this article she also refers to a comment by Raphael Samuel to the effect that *Reynolds's* drew on a common stock of popular feeling which one also finds expressed in theatre and elsewhere.

14. I am indebted for my discussion of melodrama to Peter Brooks, *The Melodramatic Imagination: Balzac, Henry James, Melodrama, and the Mode of Excess* (New Haven, 1976). See especially Chapter 1, 'The Melodramatic Imagination' and Chapter 2, 'The Aesthetics of Astonishment'.

15. 'G. W. M. Reynolds: Popular Literature and Popular Politics', in Joel Wiener (ed.) *Innovators and Preachers: the Victorian Editor* (New York, 1986) pp. 16–18.

16. Brooks, *The Melodramatic Imagination*, p. 15.

17. Ibid., p. 8.

18. Ibid., p. 2.

19. Ibid., p. 203.

20. Ibid., p. 15.

21. Berridge probably oversimplifies *Reynolds's* position when she says the 'criticism [of the role of monarchy] was harsh and continuous' in 'Popular journalism and working-class attitudes', p. 333. The newspaper does question the institution of monarchy and also attacks Prince Albert personally, mainly for being a presumptuous German. After his death, the newspaper also chides the Queen for her seclusion, insisting that royalty has its obligations as well as its privileges, a position the newspaper shared with middle-class journals of opinion. But the paper does not attack the Queen. The first negative reference I have found that might actually refer to her, is on 9 July 1876 in a report of an accident involving the Queen's boat, 'an occurrence which in all its incidents displayed the selfishness, the heartlessness, and the proud imperiousness of royalty'. More characteristic is the comment on the death of Albert that there

is no reason to mourn for the nation on Albert's death but rather for the Queen 'who is a truly noble lady – who is the first of our monarchs who never conspired against the interests of the people – the first occupant of the British throne whose private life never outraged the laws of morality – the first wielder of the royal sceptre whose conduct as a wife and mother constitutes a proper model for British matrons – the first of our Sovereigns who, as a woman, has a just claim to the respect and affection of her subjects'. (*Reynolds's*, 22 December 1861).

22. In a letter to Ferdinand Lassalles, 28 April 1862, Marx complained that the only 'big organ' the working class had in England was 'the scoundrel Reynolds's *Newspaper*'. See Saul K. Padover (ed.), *The Letters of Karl Marx* (Englewood Cliffs, NJ, 1979) p. 465. Marx, like others, seemed to consider Reynolds a careerist.

23. After the abolition of the stamp duty in 1855, circulation rose from 50 000 to 150 000 and stabilised at between 200 000 and 300 000 after the repeal of the paper duty in 1861. Circulation figures for newspapers in the nineteenth century are difficult to determine exactly. These come from Berridge, 'Content Analysis and Historical Research on Newspapers', p. 208.

4

Newspapers and Periodicals in Historical Research

EDWARD ROYLE

Among the first questions which any student of history needs to ask of his or her source material are: who wrote it? when? and why? These questions pose immediate problems for the reader of any newspaper or periodical article, for the answers are neither obvious nor easily discovered. Yet the content of the press can only be interpreted with confidence once answers, however inadequate, have been found. In this essay, I should like to exemplify the problems and go some way towards answering these three basic questions, by discussing nineteenth-century newspaper and periodical literature in general but with special reference to the periodical literature of radicalism and freethought with which I am most familiar. I shall then go on to discuss examples of some general problems in the use of newspaper and periodical content.

Who wrote it? In the case of periodicals the answer is sometimes clear. The editor's name is frequently emblazoned across the title page, if not included in the title itself: *Cobbett's Political Register* (1802–36); *Reynolds's Newspaper* (1850–1962). Even this information, though, should be not taken at face value: *Sherwin's Political Register*, for example, was edited in its closing stages not by W.T. Sherwin but by Richard Carlile; and *Reynolds's* continued to bear its founder's name long after his death.

But proprietor/editors have not always been so forthcoming as was Cobbett. The *Voice of the West Riding* (1833–4), produced in Huddersfield to advocate political reform and factory legislation, was anonymously produced. Joshua Hobson, the printer and publisher, is frequently claimed to have been the founding editor until his imprisonment relieved him of the post in favour of the Leeds Owenite John Francis Bray. In fact, there is no hard evidence that Hobson was ever the actual editor of the paper. Historians have assumed that he was, and it seems likely that he was, but we do not know.[1] The same problem affects even so well known a source as the Chartists' *Northern Star* (1837–52). The editor was never formally declared in the paper itself, so we have to glean from reports within the paper who was, in fact, the editor for most of its comparatively long life: William Hill to July 1843; Joshua Hobson until November 1845; George Julian Harney until August 1850 – approximately. But then who? William Rider appears the most likely candidate, succeeded sometime the following spring by George Alexander Fleming. These were two very different men and a knowledge of who the editor was can influence the way one regards the paper. Rider was a West Riding militant, likely to have wanted a strongly independent Chartist line at a time when compromise was in the air; Fleming, by contrast, was an ex-Owenite moderate more in tune with the times. One has to turn to the internal evidence of style, with all its dangers of proving only what one had first assumed.

Such problems recur on many occasions. Two further examples from much later in the nineteenth century come from very minor papers, freethought periodicals from the 1890s at a time when G.W. Foote, the President of the National Secular Society, was under increasing attack from what was termed 'the awkward squad'. The latter published their thoughts in a monthly periodical, *Secular Work*, between May 1896 and May 1897: at no point was the identity of the editor disclosed, though it may well have been the lecturer, printer and publisher, George Standring, who was a noted freethinker, advocate of birth-control and supporter of Fabian socialism. If it were Standring, that would be significant, for Foote was a Liberal individualist and so any clash of personalities would also represent a clash of ideologies. Another paper, in which the issues were not quite so serious, was the *Jerusalem Star*, running monthly from June 1895 to September 1896. This was a spoof paper reporting Old Testament news as though it were current, edited by Le Vitty Cuss – as indeed he was; only in the last issue did W. J. Ramsay, printer and one-time prisoner for blasphemy along with G. W. Foote, own up to being the man behind the pun.

More seriously, it is not always obvious who the editor of a local newspaper was. This is especially a problem in the earlier nine-teenth century, when editors were active participants in local political life and in part creators of the very news which they reported.

Here the technique has often to be a close scrutiny of reports in the hope that a name is let slip. Most fruitful can be the reports in a rival paper, in an age in which local newspapers could rarely resist the descent into personal abuse.[2]

Even more of a problem is finding out who was behind the editor. With many small radical periodicals, the editor or publisher was responsible, but with larger papers – especially the provincial press – a nameless group of proprietors hid behind the editor, representing an alliance of political and religious forces in the locality. If no company records survive, their identity can remain uncertain. Again, the historian has to hope for one of those monumental rows which erupted from time to time in the best of circles, when some – if not all – was revealed in the opposition press.

Beyond the proprietors and editors, we have the problem of the identities of the journalists themselves. In the periodicals articles were often signed – though sometimes with pseudonyms; in the newspaper press anonymity was the rule. The provincial journalist has sometimes to be dug out of the census returns, Post Office directories or poll books. The periodical writer often emerges only in his obituary notice. Some remain concealed for ever. Even when we have a considerable amount of information, the identity of a journalist can remain but a shadow. Who was Malfew Seklew – and was that really his name? Only a considerable amount of detective work could establish the identity of this 'amusing and lively prophet of the new Egoist–Materialist–Libertarian–Socialist School', as the *Labour Annual* put it in 1900. Born in 1863, he had worked on the *Nottingham Journal*, spent fifteen years in the USA and stood for Congress; in 1903 he was running the Chicago Lunch Bar at 24 Manchester Road, Bradford. But we cannot yet consult the Census Returns for 1901 to check his name and find out more about him; and the Rate Books for Bradford were pulped during the war. Yet he must be one of the easier cases, for at least we have an identity, an address and what might conceivably be his name. Patient, local detective work is sometimes the only way to provide a satisfactory answer to the question, who wrote it?

If we cannot take for granted whose opinions we are reading in the press, at least we know when they wrote their pieces – or do we? The weekly press was usually dated from a Saturday or Sunday, but printing of long runs had to begin earlier in the week and a provincial edition might date from as early as the preceding

Tuesday. This can be important. For example, if one turns to the issue of *Punch* (15 April 1848) – dated shortly *after* the Chartist meeting on Kennington Common on 10 April – one finds a cartoon which takes the Chartist petition seriously. This is because the cartoon was drawn and printed *before* the world had decided that the meeting was a fiasco and the petition bogus. For the true reaction of *Punch* to these events one has to go to the issue of 29 April. Some periodicals are not even dated at all, and one has to guess to the nearest week or month. The *Lancashire Beacon* (3 August 1849 to 4 January 1850), did not carry a single date and one has to calculate when the issues appeared from certain fixed points suggested by internal evidence such as advertisements for and reports of lectures. And seldom can a periodical have been as eccentric as the *Truth Seeker*, issued in Bradford between April 1894 and sometime in 1915, but with increasing irregularity and frequently undated from 1907, with some issues simply repeating earlier issues, comprising blasphemous cartoons without text when other copy was short.

Why they wrote is the easiest question to answer, providing one reads the editorials carefully – and is prepared to believe them, which is not always the wisest thing to do. One of the joys of the relatively minor periodical press is that one gradually gets to know the editor/owner/principal or sole journalist over the years. As Charles Bradlaugh wrote of his *National Reformer* in 1886: 'The *National Reformer* has, for these last twenty-six years, been a sort of personal diary in which those who cared had companionship in our life'.[3] What emerges with such an editor over the years is a mixture of motives: a desire to speak the truth – at least as he saw it; to campaign for a right cause; self-publicity and glorification; an addiction to the printed word.

Having established, to the best of one's ability, who wrote a piece of journalism, when and why, the historian can begin to read the press for its content, discovering what the periodicals and newspapers actually said, week by week and month by month. Often one turns first to the editorial or leading article of the week. Here one gets opinion – erudite, outraged, biased, self-righteous and combative according to the mood, the material and the circumstance. This is especially valuable when one is looking either at the development of policy within the group represented by the editor and the paper, or the reactions of the group to outside events. The weekly *Freethinker*, for example, provided an essay from G. W. Foote, the founding editor, almost every week from 1881 to his death in 1915, in which he gave his own liberal, freethought perspective on national and international issues: war and peace, Mr Gladstone and Cardinal Newman, socialism and imperialism, women's rights and vegetarianism. This is a characteristic of the periodical form, which lent itself to the considered essay. The subject matter of the newspaper is usually more ephemeral, especially the daily newspaper which became increasingly common from the 1850s, though the weekly newspaper often retained or developed some of the characteristics of the periodical, as readers of the *Newcastle Weekly Chronicle* during W.E. Adams's long editorship in the later nineteenth century will know.

One also looks to the newspaper for news: sometimes as a major source, sometimes for confirmation of information or events found elsewhere. Here the relative quality of the sources is important. Good journalistic reporting in the nineteenth century could be very good indeed. *The Times*, for example, is for much of the nineteenth century a better source than *Hansard* for parliamentary debates – *Hansard* did not even employ its own reporters until 1878, and was taken over by Parliament in 1909 because of the inadequacy of its reports at that time.[4] Indeed, one can do far worse when studying the story of Charles Bradlaugh's parliamentary and legal struggles in the early 1880s than to rely upon the reports in his own *National Reformer*, which provided parliamentary and legal reports with meticulous detail in lengthy weekly supplements to the main paper.

In studying the history of an unpopular, minority movement such as some small or highly personalised branches of radicalism and freethought, using the 'in-house' press can present problems. The freethought press, for example, was always prone to exaggerate, both consciously and otherwise, the importance of its movement. But there is little alternative available to the historian. The ordinary press was even more likely to underestimate freethought or to ignore it completely. Many local newspapers deliberately refused to publicise freethought meetings by reporting them; and when a local paper did report local happenings, some eager supporter usually sent a clipping in for insertion in the freethought press, either because the report was favourable, or because it was an outright lie needing exposure. One rapidly becomes conscious that the freethought press, therefore – despite one's initial and correct suspicions – is actually an unrivalled source for what was going on. Yet reliance on such a single source can rapidly dull the critical faculties as one begins to take the writers at their own valuation. Historians of the many small radical groups which proliferated in the nineteenth century will doubtless share the relief one feels when some bitter quarrel explodes the calm surface of reported success and growth, enabling one to read in the accusations and counter-accusations what might really have been going on beneath the surface.

All this is obvious. But periodicals and newspapers also yield important information in their less obvious features, such as their advertisements. To some extent these tell one, by their number and range of products, the likely nature of the readership. A middle-class paper, for example, like the *Manchester Guardian*, carried more commercial advertisements than its more radical rivals which were aimed more towards a financially poorer market. As always, though, one has to be careful, lest one assumes, for example, that all readers of the Chartist *Northern Star* were constipated hypochondriacs, judging by the number of advertisements for patent medicines. Nevertheless, one can assume that the advertisers had target readerships and that their advertisements can therefore be informative. Sometimes, though, an advertisement may not be all it seems. When William Armitage, seed merchant of Huddersfield, advertised his wares in the *National Reformer*, one suspects he did so less because he believed freethinkers to be avid gardeners than because, as president of the local Secular Society, he wanted a way of alleviating the perennial financial crisis of a periodical which he supported. Here the value of the advertisement lies in what it tells one about the advertiser himself, in that it gives the historian the occupation and status of a man with a very common name in his town who could not otherwise have been so surely identified.

A major use of the periodical press, and to some extent the newspaper press as well, is to identify the lesser members of a movement. The *Northern Star* has been widely used in recent years by historians of Chartism in search of the ordinary membership: lists of nominees for each locality of the National Charter Association, which usefully contain occupations; letters to the editor; reports of local activities from and about local activists; details of prisoners for the cause and subscribers to 'victim funds'.[5] All but the first of these also featured in most radical periodicals throughout the century. Lists of names can easily be compiled; not all are helpful, but sometimes names can be traced between different periodicals and over a number of years, establishing both skeletal biographies and evidence of radical continuities. Some names can then be further identified in sources such as Post Office directories. In these days of computer-held databases, one can make considerable progress in understanding the nature of the lesser membership of a popular movement in this way. Obituary notices are also an important source, particularly in periodicals which have a long run. Both Susan Budd and I have analysed several hundred names derived from the freethought press.[6] The historian of radicalism cannot ignore the *Newcastle Weekly Chronicle* which became something of a graveyard for worn-out radicals in the 1880s and 1890s, with letters from and about them, appeals to support them, autobiographical snatches and eventually obituary notices.

Letters to the editor can be valuable if used with caution. Some letters were not only to, but pseudonymously from, the editor; and genuine letters were selected in accordance with editorial opinion. The most famous case of a letter to the editor is probably Richard Oastler's correspondence in the Leeds press on the question of 'Yorkshire Slavery' – that is, child labour in worsted factories – in 1830–1. Oastler's first letter went to the *Leeds Mercury*, controlled by the Baines family. Edward Baines (senior) had been a friend of Oastler's father, and together they had formed part of a Leeds delegation which had visited New Lanark to report on Robert Owen's work in 1819. Edward Baines (junior), who actually ran the paper, could hardly refuse to insert the letter.[7] Yet, as the correspondence grew increasingly bitter, he could hardly afford to accept it either, for fear of alienating his readers and advertisers who were drawn from the West Riding industrial capitalist employer class. Eventually he cut Oastler's fourth letter, which was then promptly printed in full in the rival *Leeds Intelligencer*.[8]

It is always important to remember that newspapers in the nineteenth century, even more so than today, were party organs. Their owners and editors were participants in many of the events which they reported. The struggle between the factions represented by the Leeds papers – the *Mercury*, Whig and for parliamentary reform, against the *Intelligencer*, Tory and for factory reform – was violently contested. When the operatives campaigning for factory reform in the West Riding made a great pilgrimage to York at Easter, 1832, they were accompanied by the editor of the *Leeds*

Intelligencer but not by his rival of the *Mercury*. This did not prevent the latter describing the demonstrators as a drunken rabble. In response an angry mob of National Anthem-singing workers burnt Baines in effigy outside the *Mercury* office. On a banner the demonstrators displayed the words which William Cobbett had recently applied to the *Mercury* and its editor – words which should always serve as a caution to all readers of the press in every age – 'The great Liar of the North'.[9] The golden rule for all historians using the press – or, indeed, any other source – is to assume that, until you have reason to believe otherwise, it is not telling the truth. Newspapers were propaganda.

Bias in reporting, whether deliberate or otherwise, is a major problem with any newspaper. If one cannot believe what was reported, how can one find out what actually happened? An example to illustrate this problem can be found in reports of events which took place in Manchester on 8 March 1842 when Feargus O'Connor was due to lecture at the Owenites' Hall of Science on the Repeal of the Act of Union. A riot broke out, allegedly the work of Irishmen in the pay of the Anti-Corn Law League. O'Connor's *Northern Star* reported (in O'Connor's own words) 'The missiles now began to fly in all directions at those on the platform, when I went to the front, took off my hat, and cheered the Chartists on' and he had to be forcibly removed to safety by his lieutenants. The hostile *Manchester Guardian*, which supported the Anti-Corn Law League but had little time for O'Connor, failed to mention the allegations implicating the League and reported, 'Mr O'Connor, it is said, made a prompt exit through a back door, on the beginning of the fray'. A third account appeared in the radical *Manchester and Salford Advertiser*, whose reporter was knocked unconscious in the riot.[10] The historian has to exercise judgment in a case like this. Imaginative historical experience is needed to decide the probable truth of the matter, but even so in the end different historians will themselves betray their own bias in the conclusions which they reach.

If a healthy scepticism is needed in the historian who relies heavily on newspaper reports, then the following lengthy account should encourage it. It comes from the memoirs of William Harrall Johnson, an ex-Methodist freethinker, an admirer of Ernest Jones, who later served ten years for obtaining money under false pretences, and then provided the material for a libellous biography of Charles Bradlaugh. The memoir was published in the *Agnostic*

A GREAT DEMONSTRATION.

Mob-Orator. " Tell me, Minion ! Is it the intention of your proud masters at all hazards to prevent our Demonstration ? "

Magistrate (blandly). " Yes, Sir."

Mob-Orator. " Then know, Oh Myrmidon of the brutal Whigs, that I shall go home to my tea, and advise my comrades to do the same ! "

FIGURE 4.1

Journal in 1892–3 when Johnson was fifty-nine, and probably in need of money. That supplies the answers to who wrote it, when and why. In the extract which follows, Johnson was recalling events in 1856 when the Chartists of Lancashire and Yorkshire, led by Ernest Jones, celebrated the return of the exiled John Frost with a great meeting on Blackstone Edge. The reader should treat this evidence as highly suspect, and compare this account with that in Jones's *People's Paper*, 30 August 1856. This shows that Johnson's recollections were not based on a re-reading of the *People's Paper* for there are a number of minor factual errors.[11] Nevertheless one must not assume that, because the two accounts have very little in common, the later one is necessarily always wrong. For example, Jones's speech is far less dramatic in its *People's Paper* form, but this could have been because (as in Johnson's recollection) Jones had been carried away into seditious utterances and so may have decided to tone it down in print.[12] If one compares Johnson's version of Jones's Byronic hyperbole instead with that satirised in a *Punch* cartoon of 24 June 1848 (Figure 4.1), one might conclude that Johnson was not entirely making the story up:

There might have been 2,000 when we left Todmorden. Ernest Jones assured me the bulk of the people had taken advantage of the gleams of sunshine to get a good position on Blackstone Edge. The procession moved slowly; but we saw that the delegates sunk over the ankles into the slush of the moor. Mr Frost looked wistfully round to count the numbers who were present. In vain I tried to cheer him. Ernest Jones, as we neared the trysting spot, asked how many he should say were present. With an eye to effect, I suggested that we might say 10,000, if only to encourage John Frost. Mr Jones was at that time canvassing Nottingham, which had been represented by Feargus O'Connor. When we got to the platform the rain descended in torrents; but Ernest Jones was indignant at the friendly shelter of an umbrella. He took off his hat and spoke in a strain of classic oratory, when, suddenly, rising to the height of his theme, he informed his audience that in six weeks he should be the member for Nottingham, and he would then tell the corrupt, the brutal, and the perjured House of Commons that, unless the six points of the People's Charter were granted, Her Majesty would be cashiered, and those who called themselves the representatives of the people would have to start from the gilded hall of St

Stephen's. He then called upon the audience, with one heart and voice, to swear that they would never cease agitating, until the Charter was the law of the land. Solemnly, like an officiating priest, he bent his knee to swear himself the oath, and commenced by invoking the 10,000 stalwarts who stood around him to register that vow before high heaven.

In the meantime, I had noticed a few dozen more join the audience. When *sotto voce* I whispered to the orator, '15!', he at once grasped the situation, and reverently uttered these words: 'I swear before these 25,000 people here present not to rest, eating or sleeping, until every adult shall have the franchise. Within six weeks of this day I shall be the representative of Nottingham, and I will demand on the floor of St Stephen's the enfranchisement of the people;' and with solemn acclamation the audience re-echoed the words of the speaker. Still John Frost was not satisfied. He again estimated the numbers present, and intuitively knew that he was an extinct volcano. The *Manchester Guardian*, with brutal frankness, estimated the number present at 2,000. The rival journal was more liberal, and said there might be 20,000 people at the meeting. This reporter's optics were rendered more acute by the gracious words he received from Ernest Jones. On the return Mr Jones asked me to write a report for the *People's Paper*. I had taken no notes, and suggested this as an insuperable difficulty. This objection was brushed aside at once by Mr Jones saying: 'Finlen and I will write our own reports; you write the speeches of the rest. Don't trouble to recollect what they said; send me three or four columns of what they ought to have said.' I did so on this and many such occasions; and the country delegates were well satisfied on reading their supposed addresses. When the report did appear it was accompanied by a leading article, which magnified the numbers present to 100,000, and stated that, had the weather been fine, there would not have been less than a quarter of a million present. Political history is still frequently written with equal imagination.[13]

Notes

1. See S. C. E. Cordery, 'The Voice of the West Riding: Joshua Hobson in Huddersfield and Leeds, 1831–45', MA thesis, University of York, 1984.

2. For a general discussion of proprietors, editors, journalists and

printers in a provincial setting, see N. Arnold, 'The Press in Social Context: A Study of York and Hull, 1815–1855', MPhil thesis, University of York, 1987.

3. *National Reformer* (3 January 1886).
4. G. Kitson Clark, *The Critical Historian* (London, 1967) pp. 77–8.
5. D. Thompson, *The Chartists* (London, 1984) ch. 5.
6. S. Budd, *Varieties of Unbelief* (London, 1977) pp. 94–8; E. Royle, *Radicals, Secularists and Republicans* (Manchester, 1980) pp. 127–30.
7. See *Leeds Mercury* (16 October 1830) for Oastler's letter and some editorial tight-rope walking in response.
8. *Leeds Mercury* (19 March 1831); *Leeds Intelligencer* (24 March 1831). Note that, as the papers were published on different days of the week, the *Intelligencer* could usually get in before the *Mercury*, but then had to wait longer to reply.
9. *Leeds Intelligencer* (3 May 1832); *Leeds Mercury* (5 May 1832); C. Driver, *Tory Radical: The Life of Richard Oastler* (New York, 1970) pp. 161–2.
10. *Northern Star* (12 March 1842); *Manchester Guardian* (9 March 1842); *Manchester and Salford Advertiser* (12 March 1842). The *Guardian's* report was much more cursory than that of its rivals, but this may have been because the paper would have been going to press as the incident happened and it did not have its own reporter there.
11. For example, it was the *Manchester Guardian* which gave the sympathetic account of numbers and the rival *Examiner and Times* which did not, instead of *vice versa*. The latter partly retracted its own report after receiving a letter from one of the Chartists, though his estimate was based on the assumption that the density of the crowd was nine people per square yard, which seems over-optimistic.
12. Instead of an attack on the monarchy and 'the gilded hall of St Stephens', Jones's own account states: 'For my part, I expect to be in Parliament before many months. Rally round me then, and I'll either shake the house about the ears of the rats, or drive the rats out of the house'. He deliberately *wrote* house not House, though this would not have been apparent to his *hearers*. The substance of the text here, though, is impressively recognisable in Johnson's recollection.
13. *Agnostic Journal* (1 July 1893). Although Jones had appealed for an impartial Chartist reporter for the meeting, he evidently had not found one, for the speeches were reported by different people and some of the lesser speakers were scarcely reported at all. Finlen's had not arrived by the time the paper went to press (Thursday, 2.30 pm for Saturday) and had to be added the following week. This could mean he had not finished writing out what he had said, although Jones implied that it was some reporter's fault.

Part II
The Diversity of Victorian Journalism

5

Local Journalism in Victorian Political Culture

ALED JONES

The Victorian newspaper and periodical press may be characterised above all by its abundant variety, in subject matter, political allegiance and geographical distribution. The peculiar vigour of nineteenth-century journalism has commonly been attributed to the influence of the dual processes of economic growth and technological innovation, but the energies released by Victorian politics, both high and low, central and local, also played their part. Political institutions and organisations encouraged and sustained a lively and heterogeneous press, and the emergence of reformed political and administrative systems were the subjects of intense scrutiny and speculation by journalists and their readers throughout Britain. But the contribution made by journalism to Victorian political culture in general was complex and paradoxical. While it is true that the variety of the press was impressive, certainly by modern standards, its diversity nonetheless was constrained by strict political limitations, and if in its range and perceived responsibilities it could be described as 'democratic', it was so in a political system that did not allow for full democratic electoral participation in government. Within these limitations, however, popular Victorian journalism contained elements that encouraged readers' engagement with a participatory, though in many instances an extra-parliamentary, political process. The diversity of this journalism signifies above all the richness and expansiveness of Victorian political culture.

The language conventionally used to describe and to situate the Victorian press, however, inadequately expresses the extent of this diversity. The terms 'the provincial press' and 'the national press', particularly when applied to the early- and mid-nineteenth century, are anachronistic and highly problematic constructions. A national press, itself a term contested by the Irish, the Scots and the

Welsh, could hardly be said to have existed anywhere in Britain before the last decade of the century, and the growing dissimilarity between county and town newspapers renders untenable the terms provincial as anything but a very general description. Though there can be no doubt that such newspapers as *The Times* or, increasingly, the Sunday papers, circulated widely throughout Britain, and that magazines emanating from London were read in homes and public institutions across the country, it remains true that in general the simple dichotomy between a provincial and a national press in this context and at this time is misleading.

In contrast, much advantage may be gained by drawing greater attention to the Victorian local press. The term avoids the implied uniformity and pejorative overtones of the word 'provincial', and applies equally to papers in London and in other large urban centres, as well as to those in smaller towns and rural areas. It also enables individual titles to be considered principally in relation to their immediate concerns and markets, however large or small they might be, rather than to their location *vis-à-vis* the national political and economic institutions in London.

Without doubt, the relationship between journalism and the state is vitally important in terms of political attitudes and access to information. But many local newspapers were as preoccupied with national and international news as were the London-based national papers, and there is little evidence to suggest that interest in world affairs meant that readers of the local press did not share a keen concern for local matters. Often, the one was a key to the proper understanding of the other. The relative increase in local content itself assured a certain degree of diversity between titles, but the orientation towards the local did not imply that attention was being diverted away from more general concerns, nor from the activities of the Government and the debates and rumours of the Commons. A news diet that comprised both local and national coverage in the local press satisfied the political and cultural appetites of readers who were living through, and negotiating, a period of intense political and administrative restructuring that was to transform traditional relationships between central government and the localities.

The accretion of political power, particularly over social policy, by a secular state was a complex process that involved extending the administrative machinery of government at both central and local levels. The subsequent growth of local as well as central state structures provided Victorian political journalism as a whole with its principal *raison*, and ensured that journalists in different localities were attentive, in the first instance, to the activities and conflicts of the local state, including the incorporation of boroughs, levels of local taxation, education policies and the costs of administering welfare schemes or the building of new town halls. The growth of organised political parties and constituency organisations, as Maurice Milne and others have shown, further strengthened the economic foundations of the local press. These were not isolated, parochial developments but the stuff of the 'Victorian revolution in government' that reshaped so many features of the nineteenth-century British state. The liveliness and diversity of the Victorian newspaper press owed much to the growth of the local state and its resulting municipal rivalries.[1]

In an important sense, the great majority of early- and mid-Victorian newspapers were local. Newspapers were clustered in constellations around specific nodal points, among which the local state figured prominently. But journalism could be local to a widely scattered ideological constituency as well as to a place, to a movement as well as to a town. Religious denominations, political parties and pressure groups, cultural formations and language groups cut across geographical boundaries and provided further locales for the nineteenth-century press. A major characteristic of the diversity of Victorian journalism was its capacity to 'narrowcast' messages to a readership that was highly fragmented into social, geographical and ideological groups.

The variety of Victorian journalism was personified above all by the editors of newspapers and magazines. These individuals were, as often as not, leading public figures in their own right, well-known in the communities among which they endeavoured, often in the face of furious competition, to carve out their markets. Edward Baines in Leeds, William Byles in Bradford, Joseph Cowen in Newcastle upon Tyne or John Jaffray in Birmingham proudly regarded themselves, as Ian Jackson has observed, as 'intermediaries between political, economic and social theorists and particular local readerships',[2] and each publicly aspired to be 'the uncrowned king of an educated democracy'.[3] Not content with interpreting the world, they also did their best to change it. Many Victorian editors were political activists in pressure groups and political parties, and for an influential minority journalism was a means of gaining local political office or a seat in Parliament. The enormous political significance of editors across Britain in the second half of the nineteenth century has rightly been emphasised by Joel H. Wiener, who has argued that 'the editor was situated at the nucleus of the Victorian world: he typified both the transformations that were making Britain an urban nation and a stable society'.[4]

If editors may be said to have embodied the political diversity of the Victorian press, then it has to be admitted that the extent of that diversity had very clear limitations. Though many editors were Liberal in politics and radical in sentiment, few, with the qualified exception of G. W. M. Reynolds,[5] could be described as being heirs to the unstamped or Chartist traditions of popular oppositional journalism. The diversity of the late-Victorian popular press did not include within its compass much space, for example, for the socialist or republican left. On the contrary, the 'middle ground' of politics which so many journalists shared with the representatives of the main parliamentary parties effectively marginalised the political press which had flourished in the 1820s and 1830s. The solid, bourgeois respectability of so many Victorian editors, along with the spiralling costs of production and the interests of shareholders and advertisers, imposed their own constraints on the freedoms of the press. The integrity of the notion of a Fourth Estate has in recent years been ably and deservedly demolished, and its continued use by journalists and historians is distinctly unhelpful. Nevertheless, as one Conservative critic of the politicisation of newspapers published outside London complained in an article in the *National Review* in 1886, 'During the last fifty years ... the opinionated journal has become the rule, the pamphlet has become almost extinct, and although there are still a few newspapers that do not profess to have any political creed, their pretended neutrality is really a cloak for mild Radicalism'. If the years between 1855 and 1918 were not the much vaunted 'Golden Age' of the British press, they were, nonetheless, years in which journalism developed a singularly conspicuous presence in political life. For although editors struggled in journalism's pre-eminently 'Liberal Age' to reach and to influence an educated, and therefore a propertied and limited, 'democracy', it is quite evident that the enfranchised middle class was not their only clientele.[6]

Despite its political limitations, and the urgent imperative to re-establish social control over a traumatised and undisciplined industrial society, much of the Victorian press allowed its readers to be informed about, and perhaps to share in the making of, a process of change. Political life in the nineteenth century was in flux, electoral change was firmly on the agenda, and administrative reforms, many of which were articulated in the first instance by utilitarian social theorists, were gradually being implemented. Information was an essential commodity in this changing political climate, and for the most part journalists supplied knowledge in a form best suited to stimulate informed discussion. If much reporting revolved around parliamentary politics, the state of the parties, the speeches of political leaders and election results, a considerable amount of attention was paid also to matters that lay outside this narrow definition of the political. Victorian political news included extensive coverage of the meetings of pressure groups, trade unions, friendly societies and popular campaigns, and in many cases such detailed accounts and minutes of meetings are the only surviving records of large numbers of transient and peripheral popular institutions.[7]

Above all, public involvement in political issues was encouraged by the 'open space' offered in the readers' letters columns, a close reading of which reveals not only the extent of public interest in political affairs, and the inordinate lengths at which certain issues were allowed to be discussed by indulgent editors (often for many months, and across several local newspapers), but also the great variety of the social and occupational backgrounds of the correspondents. Political awareness, and the need to be involved in the political process, were not dulled by the denial of the franchise to large numbers of newspaper readers but were probably sharpened by the competition between titles within localities, and the resulting articulation of conflicting political attitudes towards the important issues of the day. It is difficult to measure the extent of their political influence, but there can be little doubt that editors and journalists were in the main acutely aware of their responsibilities in this direction.

In the absence of universal suffrage Britain enjoyed a press that was, within certain limits, politically diverse, and which encouraged a participatory political culture. It is ironic that, with the broadening of the franchise in 1884, 1918 and 1928, the political heterogeneity of the popular press was correspondingly reduced. Between the 1890s and the end of the First World War, much of the distinctive variety of the local press was undermined by a combina-

tion of economic and technological developments, including the
concentration of ownership, the growth of newspaper chains and
huge increases in the circulations of the popular papers, that left
their mark on the political functions of journalism as they had been
performed in the Victorian years. Political journalism became
increasingly preoccupied with the vicissitudes of party leaders and
the affairs of prominent individuals, a change in style represented
most clearly by the growing popularity of the newspaper inter-
view. Relations between reporters and politicians were recon-
structed after a failed Fenian bomb attack on the Commons in 1884,
and in the course of the following year were formalised in the
exclusive lobby system which allowed selected journalists privileged access to Parliament and, crucially, to 'unattributable
briefings' with government ministers and senior civil servants.[8]

Such developments marked a shift in the balance of British
journalism towards a national press, and London, simultaneously
the heart of an empire and an increasingly important publishing
centre, began in the late nineteenth century to exert its remarkable
dominance over the British press.[9] In the course of this transition,
the size, structure and functions of the local press were radically
transformed. The ranks of the local weeklies had been thinned by
the early twentieth century, and F. K. Gardiner could mourn also
the passing of the local Victorian morning papers that had 'led
many a reform, helped to foster local patriotism, stimulated
cultural progress and been a friend and guide to millions', attribut-
ing their demise to 'the ever-growing pressure of the national
popular papers'.[10] The growth of a national press affected the
content of the surviving locals by disturbing the balance of their
news reports, and the emergence of evening papers in the larger
urban centres had by 1900 introduced a broad division of labour
between the political news of the national mornings and the local
industrial, social and cultural reports of the local evenings, and set
the pattern for twentieth-century newspaper coverage.[11]

Changes in newspaper economics, and the time factor in the
flow of news, were largely responsible for these developments, but
the distinctive characters of local and national papers were con-
ditioned also by changing definitions of the target readership and
of the political functions of the popular press. The new mass
national newspapers of the early twentieth century, published
almost exclusively in the metropolis, unlike the leading Victorian
locals owed much of their startling success to the fact that they

relied on no clearly identifiable social, geographical or ideological market. The withering of the variety of the local press in the first half of the twentieth century resulted also in a marked decline in the belief that one of the prime functions of journalism was to educate and to involve the public in a political *process*. Spenser, Robert B. Parker's sardonic sleuth, lamenting the absence of 'substance' in modern American political journalism, observed that 'The question was of performance, of errors made, of runs scored, of wins and losses. Rarely was the question of substance discussed. . . . Even the editorials tended to judge politics in terms of a contest, or victory and defeat'.[12]

Much of modern British journalism has been in the same vein, but it is not a failing for which the great majority of Victorian editors could be held responsible. The local newspapers that remained in place after the late Edwardian period flourished, and continue to do so, but they operated in a changed social climate, with less local competition. Mergers, buy-outs and incorporations carved out larger markets for the survivors, who, in consequence, functioned politically in new ways.

Local Victorian journalism may not have lived up to the standards of plurality and public service dreamed of, if not set, by the activists of the unstamped. But it did make a distinctive contribution to political life within and outside Parliament, and it was in practice considerably more accessible and representative than it had been in the previous century, or was to become in the twentieth. Knowledge of the Victorian local press, however, is uneven, and many areas of its fascinating history remain hidden. Much can be learnt from new local studies, and the following essays on the Victorian press in Wales and London, and the emergence in the late nineteenth century of a national journalism, map important parts of this previously little explored terrain.

Notes

1. Keith Robbins has explained how the discourse of a British nation emerged in the late nineteenth century through the simultaneous occurrence of processes of integration and diversity in political, social and cultural life, and in similar vein it is possible to argue that the local press for much of the middle of the nineteenth century was able to maintain its diversity precisely through its integration with the British state at the local level. Keith Robbins, *Nineteenth-Century Britain, Integration and Diversity* (Oxford, 1988). For studies of Victo-

rian state 'Collectivism' see William Graham, 'The Collectivist Prospect in England', *The Nineteenth Century*, XXXVII (1895) and A.V. Dicey, *Lectures on the Relation Between Law and Public Opinion in England during the Nineteenth Century* (London, 1905). Further contemporary accounts of political change may be found in Barbara Dennis and David Skilton (eds), *Reform and Intellectual Debate in Victorian England* (London, 1987). For the press and local politics, see Maurice Milne, 'The Survival of the Fittest? Sunderland Newspapers in the Nineteenth Century', in Joanne Shattock and Michael Wolff (eds), *The Victorian Periodical Press: Samplings and Soundings* (Leicester, 1982) p. 214. Local government reform was effected chiefly by the Municipal Reform Act of 1835, the Metropolis Management Act of 1855 and the Local Government Act of 1888.

2. Ian Jackson, *The Provincial Press and the Community* (Manchester, 1971) p. 11.

3. W. T. Stead, 'The Future of Journalism', *Contemporary Review*, L (1886) 663–79.

4. Joel H. Wiener (ed.), *Innovators and Preachers: The Role of the Editor in Victorian England* (Westport, Conn., 1985) p. xiii.

5. Recent studies of Reynolds include Virginia Berridge, 'Popular Sunday papers and mid-Victorian society', in G. Boyce, J. Curran and P. Wingate (eds), *Newspaper History from the Seventeenth Century to the Present Day* (London, 1978) pp. 247–64, and Anne Humpherys, 'G. W. M. Reynolds: Popular Literature and Popular Politics', in Wiener (ed.) *Innovators*, pp. 3–22.

6. A Conservative Journalist, 'Why is the Provincial Press Radical?' *National Review*, 7 (1886) 678. These and related issues are discussed in A.J. Lee, *The Origins of the Popular Press in England 1855–1914* (London, 1976), and in essays by George Boyce, Raymond Williams and James Curran in Boyce *et al.*, *Newspaper History*. Useful critical observations on the 'Fourth Estate' debate may also be found in Brian Harrison, 'Press and Pressure Group in Modern Britain', in Shattock and Wolff (eds), *Samplings*, pp. 261–96.

7. See, for example, the minutes of national and regional conferences of the Amalgamated Association of Miners in the *Wigan Observer* and the *Western Mail* between 1869 and 1875.

8. Peter Hennessy, *What the Papers Never Said* (London, 1985) pp. 1–11.

9. The centralisation of political power was, if Marshall McLuhan is right, itself dependent on the creation of a highly centralised newspaper press. 'Socially, the typographic extension of man brought in nationalism, industrialism, mass markets, and universal literacy and education', Marshall McLuhan, *Understanding Media: The Extension of Man* (New York, 1964) p. 157.

10. F. K. Gardiner, 'Provincial Morning Newspapers', in *The Kemsley Manual of Journalism*, with introduction by Viscount Kemsley LLD (London, 1952) pp. 204–5.

11. John F. Goulden, 'Provincial Evening Newspapers', in *The Kemsley Manual*, pp. 210–11.

12. Robert B. Parker, *The Widening Gyre* (Harmondsworth, 1988) p. 54.

6

Welsh Periodicals:
A Survey

BRYNLEY F. ROBERTS

Periodicals have always been a barometer of public concerns and interests, but in Wales consideration of the way in which they may reflect cultural, religious or political life has been complicated by the bilingual nature of society. English and Welsh have signified different social classes, aspirations and attitudes, and the two languages have represented two monoglot groups with an expanding bilingual section between them. In modern Wales the monoglot Welsh population has disappeared but it nevertheless remains true that the languages represent distinct separate cultures both for monoglots and bilinguals.

For various historical reasons Wales has not enjoyed the political and administrative developments which have given rise to the modern nation-states. Though there have been local or regional centres there has never been a natural centre which might combine those administrative and commercial roles which help to create the cultural and social ambience of a capital. The designation of Cardiff as capital city in 1955 was a recognition of its size and pre-eminence within the populous industrial region, but all the Welsh national institutions are nineteenth-century creations which have a wide geographical distribution – a National Museum in Cardiff but a National Library in Aberystwyth, a federal national university of six constituents in five towns and a peripatetic national eisteddfod. In the eighteenth century there was no single centre of learning, no pre-eminent commercial centre, no political focus. Though the overwhelming majority were monoglot Welsh-speakers, there had developed a polite society of gentry and middling sorts who were monoglot English-speakers or bilinguals. The ability to use English with a fair degree of fluency put one into this latter group, for whom the universities and London provided cultural and social foci. For these English-speakers in a non-Welsh society, Welsh

71

culture became a defining agent, representing those aspects of their lives which were recognisably Welsh and which were given substance in societies and publications. In the context of daily living their perception of Welsh culture was conservative, academic, backward-looking, essentially defensive. This is not to belittle their interests, merely to describe them, for they have an honourable history, from the antiquarians of the seventeenth century and the remarkable labours of the only Welsh *virtuoso*, Edward Lhuyd, to the work of the London-Welsh societies and the publication of volumes such as the collected poetry of Dafydd ap Gwilym (1789), the *Myvyrian Archaiology of Wales* (1804) and the county histories. For monoglot Welsh-speakers literary and historical culture was traditional, oral and unselfconscious, but even bilinguals tended to see traditional popular literature as at best quaint, at worst uncouth, and they sought out an older medieval literature which they could equate with classical forms and represent in augustan modes, or which they could view as primitive epic or romance.

When the monolingual Welsh-speakers became literate the motivation for their periodicals is seen to be basically different from that which gave rise to those produced by and for the English-speaking group. The periodicals as they appear in the eighteenth and early nineteenth centuries clearly reflect these different cultural needs. The English journals are intended to express an awareness and definition of Welshness which is non-linguistic and mainly antiquarian. Welshness, however, is implicit in the use of the Welsh language and thus the Welsh periodicals have as their aim the education and winning of minds and hearts. Paradoxically, therefore, the Welsh periodicals are not as regional in appeal as the English (or Anglo-Welsh) and they have a deeper awareness of an external world than those intended for English-speaking society which can draw upon a wider range of periodicals for matters not specific to Wales. To a greater or lesser degree this has been true of the English and Welsh periodicals produced in Wales down to modern times. It is not surprising that Welsh-language periodicals appeared before Welsh-orientated English ones and that they are radical, political publications whereas the other group is antiquarian and literary–historical in content. The former were produced in Wales, the latter in London.

The first of these was the *Cambrian Register* (published by E. & T. Williams, The Strand, edited by William Owen Pughe): three volumes appeared, 1795 (in 1796), 1796 (in 1799) and 1818. William Owen Pughe was an energetic, erudite writer and editor who clearly saw himself as an heir of the learned antiquarian tradition established by Edward Lhuyd and continued with greater panache but less scholarship by Lewis Morris, the eighteenth-century civil servant of many parts. This tradition was historical, literary and archaeological/topographic, and laid stress on original documents, transcripts of manuscripts, literary remains and so on, but as the eighteenth century progressed the academic discipline of those who followed these paths grew weak and scholarly attitudes waned so that much of the work is uncritical, sometimes bizarre. Pughe was such a scholar – both knowledgeable and gullible, immensely productive but uncritical, full of ideas but a dangerous theoretician of language development. His *Cambrian Register* is very well organised into specific sections – history of Wales (texts of Geoffrey of Monmouth with English translations of the *Mabinogion*), ancient laws, parochial histories (inspired by Edward Lhuyd), topography, Welsh poetry and notices of manuscript collections, correspondence of scholars and antiquaries of the past.

Pughe's aim, he says, was to produce volumes 'of Cambrian remains' and to bring out the vast treasure of ancient memorials in Welsh preserved in manuscripts and oral tradition, and capable of being visually presented in contemporary engravings and prints. He was no doubt inspired by his feelings of cultural nationalism, his respect for the memorials of the past and the desire to ensure that they might be preserved, not simply as a record of the past but as an inspirational motivation for the continuance of this ancient culture in the future.

Love and zeal for Welsh culture deeply rooted in the past ensured that Pughe's *Cambrian Register* was followed in 1819 by the three volumes of the *Cambro-Briton and General Celtic Repository* (1819, 1821, 1822) edited by John Humffreys Parry and again published in London. It was intended to succeed the *Cambrian Register*, but though the editor acknowledges his debt to some of the same patrons and helpers named earlier in the *Register*, there is nevertheless a subtle deterioration here. The journal was under the patronage of a popular London-Welsh society, Y Gwyneddigion, which had been responsible for some notable literary ventures in the late eighteenth century but which was now in decline and less interested in matters of substance. And in spite of the journal's association with the grandiloquently titled Metropolitan Cambrian

Institution, the quality of what is written, and any real awareness of scholarship, have weakened.

The name Cambro-Briton, the Celtic in the title, the emblem of Stonehenge are all reminders that we are in the age of Celtomania and in Wales of a Celtic romanticism corrupted by the bardic fantasies of that most gifted of forgers and inventors of tradition, Iolo Morganwg. Together with the historical documents and traditional triads we now find 'bardic effusions' and Iolo's faked triads: the essays on poetry, music, biography, laws, antiquities and topographical notices now jostle with an essay on the 'Elementary Character' of the Welsh language, a description of the elemental features of this most ancient and original tongue.

The defensive aim of the journal is still to justify Welshness, 'to diffuse amongst Strangers a knowledge of the history, manners, genius of Wales and the fame of these literary treasures'; cultural nationalism, perhaps cultural justification for one's existence, is still the motivation but the foundations have become less secure.

The *Cambro-Briton* was followed, or rather continued, in 1822 by *Transactions of the Cymmrodorion Metropolitan Cambrian Institution*, (1822–8, pt 4, 1843, volumes 1 and 2), the journal of the revived second Cymmrodorion Society of 1820, which was edited by J. Humffreys Parry, the editor of the *Cambro-Briton*, and which continued the antiquarian tradition. From 1829 to 1833 there appeared the five volumes of the *Cambrian Quarterly Journal and Celtic Repertory*, yet another London-published journal which hoped to preserve 'native lore', to cater for antiquarian tastes and to create interest in Wales, but which also published a higher proportion of poetry and reviews than its predecessors. But the significant successor to these antiquarian journals was *Archaeologia Cambrensis* which appeared in January 1846.

The second Cymmrodorion Society had come to an end in 1843, but in June 1846 the Cambrian Archaeological Association was established. Its aim was to study and to preserve the national antiquities of Wales. It was firmly rooted in the geography and terrain of Wales as its objects of study were physical artefacts and remains together with their documentation, rather than the literary tradition. It derived its pattern and inspiration from England, from societies like the Archaeological Institute of Great Britain and Ireland, but without its local Welsh roots it could never have flourished. It adopted *Archaeologia Cambrensis* as its journal and from its inception it has published scholarly articles on archaeological remains, inscriptions, genealogies, and has attempted to publish plans, drawings and collections of documents relating to the history of castles, religious and lay houses and their architecture, manuscripts and so on, together with valuable supplements and accounts of the association's activities, excavations and field trips.

The society and its journal still thrive today, but in 1853 one of the founders of the Cambrian Archaeological Association, John Williams ab Ithel, an Anglican clergyman but a scholar *manqué*, completely lacking in any appreciation of academic discipline, finding the more rigorous approach of the association irksome, set up a rival society, the Cambrian Institute for 'the promotion of Celtic and Welsh literature and the advancement of the arts and sciences'. No meetings of the institute were held outside London but its *Cambrian Journal* appeared from 1854 to 1864 in six volumes. The institute attracted some figures of substance and the *Journal* published articles on the Celtic languages, on biography, topography, traditions and legendary lore, parochial accounts, in the tradition of the other antiquarian periodicals which preceded it, without forgetting its commitment to the sciences, for example, mining, botany and medicine.

The antiquarian theme has been a thread which runs through these nineteenth-century English periodicals. When the third Cymmrodorion Society was set up in 1873 times had changed and social issues joined the cultural ones, so that its two journals, the *Transactions* and *Y Cymmrodor* ('The Native'), reflect the standards of a new educated age and of new academic disciplines which ensured that these became valued scholarly periodicals. The more popular, local history, amateur antiquarian tradition, however, continued in journals like *Byegones Relating to Wales and the Border Counties* (printed and published by the *Oswestry Advertiser* from 1871 onwards) and bearing its motto 'I love everything that's old: old friends, old times, old manners, old books, old wine'. It retained its character (notes and queries, short excerpts from documents, local history, dialect, lore, families, worthies) until its demise in 1939, and these same characteristics define the nature of *Old Wales: Antiquities of Wales and the Border*, edited by W. R. J. Williams, 1905–7, an interesting assiduous compiler and transcriber of lists which are still useful reference works.

These English periodicals of the late eighteenth century, the nineteenth and early twentieth centuries are semi-learned, polite in readership, antiquarian in outlook. Such interests are also to be found in a few Welsh periodicals of the first part of the nineteenth century. Amongst the members of the London Gwyneddigion Society were some important contributors to the *Cambrian Register* and the *Cambro-Briton*, and the society had itself promoted valuable literary projects, so that when it published under its own auspices its Welsh periodical *Y Greal* ('The Grail', nine volumes, 1805–7), it is not surprising that its tone is similar to the contemporary English journals in its interest in antiquities, history, topography and also agriculture, horticulture and mining.

Significantly, however, it gave prominence to poetic meetings and eisteddfodau, not only because these were actively encouraged by the Gwyneddigion but also because, one suspects, a Welsh-language publication could not omit reference to the contemporary literary scene. Indeed, the first Welsh publication which can be regarded as a periodical, *Tlysau yr Hen Oesoedd* ('Gems of Past Ages', edited by the publisher Lewis Morris at Holyhead, 1735)[1] is a collection of literary excerpts. It was motivated by the editor's enthusiasm for Welsh literature and his desire to encourage anglicised and bilingual Welshmen to regain their cultural heritage.

The tradition was continued by Josiah Rees's *Trysorfa Gwybodaeth: Neu Eurgrawn Cymraeg* ('The Treasury of Knowledge: Or Welsh Magazine', fifteen fortnightly issues, 1770). In this period, *Y Greal* and *Trysorfa* sit more easily in the English context than the Welsh, for the contemporary Welsh periodicals were, in general, fiercely radical in outlook.

Though the London–Welsh societies had amongst their members pamphleteers with a high level of political and reformist awareness, the radical strain in Welsh life was neither new nor foreign. The older Nonconformity, and Unitarianism especially, had always contained those questioning, free-thinking social elements which were inevitably to lead to concern for the human condition in the present world, and Welsh radicalism has never lacked religious motivation. The Baptist Morgan John Rhys brought out his *Y Cylchgrawn Cyn-mraeg (Cymraeg)* ('The Welsh Magazine') in 1793 and maintained it for five numbers. He preached against the slave-trade and advocated parliamentary reform, freedom of conscience and saw the French Revolution as a new dawning of Liberty, but his *Cylchgrawn* was not wholly political or secular and even in its early numbers it reveals the religious basis of the editor's radicalism, while the appearance of biographical material, literary discussions and poetry underline the cultural dimension which cannot be divorced from writing in Welsh. Rhys emigrated to America in 1794 but even more overtly political and radical periodicals were to appear in 1795 and 1796, the *Miscellaneous Repository: Neu y Drosorfa Gymmysgedig*, which, like Rhys's *Cylchgrawn*, had articles on literature, language and Welsh Indians but which made its political stance more unequivocal. Its inspiration could not be made any clearer than when it published a Welsh translation of the *Marseillaise*.

London society had a role in the ideas and opinions put out in these periodicals, but it is significant that they were printed and published in Wales. They are in a different world from the Cambrians and Celts of the contemporary Anglo-Welsh press for whom 'strangers', rather than compatriots, were an important element in their readership.

It seems, however, that such full-blooded political commitment could not be sustained in the Welsh press. Any such commitment requires an educational, instructional campaign if converts are to become zealots, and the 1800s were not a good time to proclaim the virtues of France and her Revolution. At home, Wales was now attempting to restructure society and to reorganise her life following the earthquakes of the Methodist revivals from 1735 onwards which had instilled new sets of values, new concepts of human activities and new attitudes to the duties of believers to God and to Caesar as represented by divinely instituted temporal leaders. In all denominations one of the most obvious fruits of the Nonconformist emphasis on personal responsibility to learn what was necessary for salvation was a remarkable extension of popular literacy and the production of theological and moral literature for Sunday Schools, and personal reading for laymen and preachers. The boundaries between denominations became more sharply differentiated, along theological lines or rules of church government, though their dislike of the toryism and anglicisation of an established episcopal Anglican church was a common bond between them.

Religious periodicals soon proliferated. The Calvinistic Methodists were first in the field with *Trysorfa Ysprydol* ('Spiritual Treasury', 1799) which would ultimately develop into the 'official' *Trysorfa* of the new denomination in 1831. All the denominations acquired journals, the Wesleyan *Eurgrawn* ('Magazine', 1809), the

Baptist *Seren Gomer* ('Star of Gomer', 1818), the Congregationalist *Dysgedydd* ('Instructor', 1821) in north Wales, and *Yr Efangylydd* ('The Evangelist', 1830) in south Wales, the Unitarian *Yr Ymofynydd* ('Inquirer', 1847). There were very many more periodicals but these were the flagships. These were basically group journals, catering for a defined readership, providing mutually interesting items of news on one another's activities within the group, informing, educating, correcting, enlightening, confirming the identity of the group.

There are, of course, differences between them, but their broad general similarity is more characteristic. If they have a political attitude, it is broadly liberal, but more frequently politics and religion are mixed; though an editor such as William Williams, 'Caledfryn', had strong radical views, they veer far more to religion than economics or even social justice. The journals have a strongly didactic, informative, educational role, and have sections reserved for essays, reviews and poetry. They serve to create and confirm a Nonconformist view of life and inculcate Nonconformist values and mores, though the Baptist *Seren Gomer* had wider cultural and general interests than most of the others.

It is difficult to overemphasise the importance of these religious and denominational periodicals in any survey of Welsh cultural history. There are specialist publications for Sunday Schools, for temperance movements, for musicians, for sermon-makers, for foreign mission news and so forth. Some are important for their literary value, as the accepted medium for uplifting novels, and as the source of a new literary form, the biographical essay. For the vast majority of literary Welshmen these periodicals were the regular and staple bill of fare, but as Nonconformity created not simply avid readers but also, in conjunction with other popular cultural movements like the eisteddfod, an endless supply of writers, correspondents, poets and reviewers, it is no surprise that the golden era of Welsh Nonconformity is also the golden age of Welsh publishing in all fields.

These periodicals were in an ideal situation. They had an established readership based on group loyalty and group iden-tification, the chapels provided a distribution network, the editors were usually preachers for whom an itinerant ministry and invita-tions to preaching services provided a ready mode of rapport with customers. And the customers themselves were for the most part from the same social class – the ministers and deaconate tended towards the new middle class, but most chapel members were workers, craftsmen, miners, iron workers, farm workers, tenant farmers and quarrymen; all members of the same non-privileged group of largely monoglot Welsh-speakers. The Nonconformist culture which encouraged an interest in literature, theology and contemporary religious life, created a general interest in matters of the mind which was to be reflected in a major change in the nature of Welsh periodicals in the second half of the nineteenth century.

The break with the old radical tradition represented by *Y Cylchgrawn Cymraeg* and *Y Geirgrawn* ('The Magazine') was gradual. The old Nonconformists, Congregationalists, Baptists and Unitarians, did not deny their radical roots and individual editors took up firm positions. Indeed much of the strength of *Seren Gomer* came from the personality of its founder and first editor, Joseph Harries, and some of his successors, for it was not formally adopted as a denominational organ until 1880. But the clearest example of the continuing Nonconformist radicalism is the Congregationlist *Y Diwygiwr* ('The Reformer') of 1835. This and the Anglican *Yr Haul* ('The Sun') were born from a sense of dissatisfaction with *Yr Efangylydd*. David Rees created *Y Diwygiwr*, put the impress of his powerful personality upon it and used Daniel O'Connell's slogan 'Agitate!' as his own.

That same year, the erstwhile editor of *Yr Efangylydd*, a minister who had served his time with Baptists and Congregationalists, became editor of the Anglican *Yr Haul*. David Owen, 'Brutus', was a satirical writer of ebullient skills and for fifteen years the two journals, and to a lesser extent the two editors, contended, argued and expressed some very bitter relationships. Owen was the more personal and intemperate and therefore the more entertaining. Rees, however, was the better editor and it was he who created a journal which had a consistently militant point of view on social issues. *Y Diwygiwr* is of greater importance and in its day it had greater influence on public opinion because it spoke from conviction rather than pique. Rees's convictions were religious and reformist rather than strictly political. His journal had many of the common features of denominational periodicals – biographies, articles on morals, education, theology, Sunday Schools, poetry and reviews, but the leading article was a means of attacking and teaching, for its strength lay in the editor's clear idea of what his publication aimed to do. As he himself put it in 1865, his aim had been to teach Nonconformists their rights, to shake them from their inertia, and to give them fearless pride in being called political dissenters. It has an honourable place in Welsh social history.

Yr Haul, Brutus's Anglican paper, is by contrast polemical with little substance. It gave Welsh literature two good works of satire, but its mockery and attempts at scandal ultimately became self-defeating. Though it is striking testimony to the infantry battles of church and chapel in the nineteenth century, it is not, in fact, a true reflection of what the Welsh Anglican church had been and was capable of being.

In the spate of religious periodicals launched between 1809, 1818 and 1835 it is easy to miss the rather different *Y Gwyliedydd* ('The Sentinel') which appeared in 1823 and came to an end in 1837. This journal, edited and supported by a group of Anglican clergymen, is one of the most civilised publications of the nineteenth century.

There had been other 'church' periodicals and as R. T. Jenkins remarked, these tend to differ from 'chapel' periodicals, even the early *Seren Gomer*, in the space they give to general articles, to historical themes and to literature. This urbane air reaches its fullest flowering in *Y Gwyliedydd*, claimed by R. T. Jenkins to be the best periodical of its day from a literary point of view.

As Welsh Nonconformity of the 1830s and 1840s distanced itself from traditional Welsh culture, replacing it with its own chapel culture, and as Victorian utilitarianism verged towards philistinism, it providentially fell to the lot of a group of historically minded, traditionalist, literary Anglican clergy to nurture the best traditions of Welsh culture. They were open-minded, co-operative and ardent in their zeal for the protection of the cultural life of Wales. No longer could the London-based societies be expected to play the part of literary patrons, but the classical education and intelligent respect for the past learned at university by these clergy could be channelled to help the language, literature and history of Wales. The literary societies became Welsh regional societies from which grew a series of provincial and local eisteddfodau.

The literary competitions were ambitious and scholarly and created a new confidence in the real cultural roots of Wales after the excesses of eighteenth-century eccentrics; but the literary and bardic competitions gave Nonconformists an opportunity of returning to their own literary traditions so that by the end of the nineteenth century the national institutions would inherit the academic aspects of these years while the more popular involvement in linguistic culture could be taken up by the literate and thoughtful mass of the population, the chapel-goers. Ironic it may be, but the inheritance was preserved for these crucial years by those literary parsons, whose journal was *Y Gwyliedydd*, the bridge between the English-language antiquarian journals and the new Welsh literary journals of the early twentieth century.

There is, however, another bridge, equally important, but created by the Nonconformists themselves. This is *Y Traethodydd* ('The Essayist') founded in 1846 by Lewis Edwards, principal of a Methodist seminary at Bala. Directly inspired first by copies of *Blackwood's Magazine* which he chanced upon in 1827 and then by his experience of contemporary English writing in the reviews and magazines, he strove to wean Welsh Nonconformity from its distrust of secular reading to this wider world of classical and European literature while at the same time insisting that Welsh literature be subject to the same serious scrutiny. From the first, Edwards determined to be selective and to publish only work of the highest standards, and over the years he succeeded in extending the horizons of the Methodist societies presenting theology as an intellectual discipline and introducing Nonconformist clergy and schoolteachers to contemporary opinions in philosophy, science and literature in England, Germany and France. The ground had been laid by *Y Gwyliedydd* and the early *Seren Gomer* but *Y Traethodydd* was characterised by a firmer philosophical attitude, and modelling itself on the English and Scottish magazines it gradually established the literary critical review article as a literary form in Welsh. That such an uncompromisingly serious quarterly should have flourished is testimony both to the editor's skills and to the intellectual life of Welsh Nonconformity in the second half of the nineteenth century.

By the end of the century Nonconformity had established itself as the accepted pattern of social behaviour. It produced a generation of hardworking, thrifty , serious-minded folk, eager to present themselves as a cultured, moral and religious people, but equally intent on becoming a respectable middle class. Rooted in chapel life, its distinctive language was Welsh, which implied that no longer could 'the language of heaven' be the medium for the political dissent which David Rees had preached in 1835. Welsh was cultural, religious, non-political and non-utilitarian. These were not in themselves restricted fields and the periodicals serving these interests had a real function to perform. The uncertainty of role was a problem, rather, for the English-language periodicals.

Welshness, as it was perceived, was well and competently catered for in the Welsh-language press, and did not reside in political and social discussions, though these were now of the essence of the Welsh problem. The dilemma facing the English journals was how to define the purpose which they were attempting to fulfil, for the danger was that they might become so restricted in their attitudes as to be irrelevant for the audience they thought to serve.

The *Red Dragon: The National Magazine of Wales* (1882–7) attempted to meet the needs of non-Welsh-speaking people, but though it contained the old established fare of biographical sketches, folklore, gossip from Welsh colleges and resorts and so on, much of it was taken up with novelettes, dramatised and versified episodes from Welsh history and the like. It is a brave attempt, but one suspects the need it tried to meet did not exist. The real justification for Welsh periodicals in English was that they should look at the problems facing Wales, and for late Victorian and Edwardian Wales these were political questions relating to Welsh nationhood as expressed in issues like a disestablished church, education and national institutions.

Young Wales (J.H. Edwards, 1895–1904, the organ of Welsh national reform), and *Wales* (J.H. Edwards, 1911–14) addressed these matters, but the most ambitious and professionally conceived and edited was the *Welsh Outlook* (1914–33) which, though containing useful literary articles, placed its main emphasis on economic and political developments in postwar Wales. It had a progressive social attitude and sought to provide national guidance on social reform, education and industrial problems. It was consciously Welsh but strove not to be parochial so that it was always aware of the tension between Welsh and cosmopolitan outlooks and issues. Nevertheless, in spite of a highly professional commercial attitude it made a consistent financial loss.

The Anglo-Welsh periodical could be relevant only in its readership's terms, as an expression of its own awareness of a Welsh dimension which did not depend upon the Welsh language. O.M. Edwards had founded another *Wales* in 1894 with aims which were to be echoed forty-odd years later by Keidrych Rhys and Gwyn Jones. But whereas their journals arose from an emergent Anglo-Welsh culture, both nurturing it and being confirmed by it, Edwards's *Wales* originated in Welsh Wales and offered the English-speakers what he believed they needed; and this depended heavily on his own perception of Wales.

For O.M. Edwards, a crofter's son who became a Fellow of Lincoln College Oxford and Chief Inspector of Schools for Wales, Wales was a land of local communities peopled by the *gwerin*. The *gwerin*, more a concept than a social class, are common folk, not well endowed with material possessions but aristocrats in their ability to appreciate the things of the mind and the spirit. They were the upholders of Welsh culture and of all those virtues of high morals and self-education which Edwards believed were characteristic of Welsh life. His mission was to educate the *gwerin* in their own history and literature, and to achieve his aim he produced *Cymru* ('Wales') in 1891 which he edited single-handed (together with a children's periodical) until his death in 1920.

His high-minded ideals ('to revive the old country', by teaching the ordinary man his own history and literature) were achieved by means of skilful editing, meticulous attention to typography and illustrations, a relaxed style of writing and a constant regard for an active reader-relationship. *Cymru* succeeded in being lively, interesting and informative; it attracted, even created, a number of effective writers and retained its readership over two or three generations so that the culture which had been nourished by the London–Welsh societies, the provincial eisteddfodau and *Y Gwyliedydd*, was transmitted in an attractive contemporary form, to the *gwerin*.

Edwards's *Wales* was an attempt to serve the non-Welsh-speaking workers and middle class in a similar fashion, but his new periodical failed after only four volumes. He had little understanding of the people of English Wales, who he believed lacked the high-mindedness and aesthetic capabilities of the Welsh-speakers. Though his attempt to introduce non-Welsh-speakers to their own culture and industrial history was ahead of its time, his underlying aim of moulding the English populace of Wales in the pattern of his idealised Welsh-speaking *gwerin* doomed *Wales* to failure.

The *gwerin* were well served by *Y Brython* ('The Briton', 1859–63), *Cyfaill yr Aelwyd* ('Friend of The Hearth', 1880–94), *Cymru* (1891–1927), *Y Geninen* ('The Leek', 1883–1928) and *Y Ford Gron* ('The Round Table', 1930–4). Together with the more substantial *Y Traethodydd* and O.M. Edwards's *Llenor* ('The Littérateur', 1895–8), they remind us that the myth of the book-loving cultured Nonconformist *gwerin* has validity for they met the needs of their targeted audience while the English-language periodicals were still seeking theirs.[2]

Wales is still a land of two languages but the proportion of Welsh- to English-speakers is the complete reverse of the situation at the beginning of our survey. English is now the majority language, but the English-language periodicals suffer from that age-old difficulty that they must justify their existence by defining the need they aim to meet. It is not, in essence, a commercial problem, but rather a matter of the Welsh consciousness of English-speakers. The evidence of the periodicals is not encouraging, for if circulation figures say anything, they seem to indicate that Anglo-Welsh culture, and the recognition of a Welsh dimension to social, industrial or economic questions are of interest to a minority of that minority who use periodicals. The most successful contemporary Welsh-language periodicals are those that have strong sectional interests: *Llafar Gwlad* ('Folklore'), a magazine of folklore and tradition, *Barddas* ('Poetics'), discussion on poetry and *Y Casglwr* ('The Collector'), for collectors of anything and everything. These succeed because they fulfil the real role of periodicals, but what this situation implies about a Welsh Wales whose liveliest interests lie in traditional verse, rural folklore and relics, while English Wales reveals little interest in a Welsh dimension to society, politics and economics, is a disturbing thought as we face the challenges of the 1990s.[3]

Notes

1. Only one number appeared but the intention 'to carry on this Collection' and to publish it quarterly seems to justify regarding it as a periodical.
2. I have noted only the major titles: one should recall also that the denominational periodicals and the weekly newspapers have the same broad readership.
3. See further Huw Walters, *Y Wasg Gyfnodol Gymreig 1735–1900: The Welsh Periodical Press* (Aberystwyth, 1987); Huw Walters, 'Cyfarpar Llyfryddol Gwasg Gyfnodol Gymreig y Bedwaredd Ganrif ar Bymtheg', *National Library of Wales Journal*, XXV (1988) 411–44; Aled G. Jones, 'Y Wasg Gymreig yn y Bedwaredd Ganrif ar Bymtheg', in Geraint Jenkins (ed.), *Cof Cenedl III* (Llandysul, 1988) pp. 89–116.

7

Yr Amserau: The First Decade 1843–52

PHILIP HENRY JONES

Although nineteenth-century Welsh-language newspapers remain *terra incognita* to most historians outside Wales, *Yr Amserau* ('The Times') enjoys the distinction of being mentioned, admittedly in a footnote, in Professor H. J. Hanham's *Elections and Party Management* where it is characterised as a Liverpool-published fortnightly which exercised an 'extraordinary influence in its day' in making Welsh Dissenters and Calvinistic Methodists aware of their political disabilities.[1] While identifying accurately the paper's prime concern, this description obscures its true significance: as the first successful Welsh-language weekly the *Amserau* formed a vital link between the radicalism of the denominational magazines of Old Dissent and the Welsh-language newspaper press which flourished after 1855. Hanham's description also overlooks the *Amserau*'s important role in presenting continental nationalist movements to the Welsh in a favourable light: thus in 1850 a delegation from the Hungarian Committee visited Liverpool to thank the paper for publicising 'Hungarian sufferings' so effectively.[2]

Despite the importance of the *Amserau* there is no full and reliable published study, even in Welsh, of its history.[3] One reason for this is the paucity of sources other than the almost 700 numbers of the paper which appeared between 23 August 1843 and 28 September 1859. A further reason is undoubtedly the confusion arising from the publication of several versions of the paper's early history by its co-founder and first editor William Rees[4] (better known by his bardic name 'Gwilym Hiraethog' and henceforth referred to as Hiraethog). His later accounts of the *Amserau* were heavily coloured by an acrimonious dispute in 1856 with its proprietor, John Lloyd, and it is regrettable that it was one of these versions which found its way into *Llenyddiaeth Fy Ngwlad*,[5] a mine of well-intentioned misinformation which remains the only comprehensive survey of Welsh-language newspapers and periodicals.

This study of the *Amserau* during Hiraethog's editorship (1843–52) discusses why the paper was founded and how it survived successive crises until a marked increase in advertising in the early 1850s together with a substantial expansion of sales during the Crimean War placed its finances on a potentially firmer footing. Certain commonly accepted assertions made by Hiraethog concerning the duration of his editorship and his remuneration will also be shown to require considerable revision.

On moving to Liverpool from Denbigh in May 1843 to take charge of Tabernacle Welsh Independent Church, Hiraethog resolved to found a radical Nonconformist paper which would fill the gap left by the death of the monthly *Cronicl yr Oes* ('Chronicle of the Age') in 1839. Liverpool had been the economic capital of much of north Wales for many years, its status being reinforced as coastal steamers and subsequently the coming of the railway strengthened its links with that area. It contained a substantial Welsh immigrant population possibly amounting to 12 000 or more by the early 1840s, many of whom enjoyed a moderate, if precarious, measure of prosperity as craftsmen, shopkeepers and clerks. Largely isolated by their language and religion, an isolation intensified by a tendency towards residential segregation, the Liverpool Welsh formed a compact and ethnically aware concentration of Welsh-speakers such as could be found in few areas within Wales itself. Their potential as the core of support for a Welsh newspaper was enhanced by the spread of political radicalism amongst sections of the community and by the existence of Welsh printing-offices in the city.

One of these printers, John Jones (1790–1855),[6] co-founder and first publisher of the *Amserau*, had been a prominent figure in the Liverpool Welsh community since the early 1820s. Although a Calvinistic Methodist preacher from 1821 onwards, and despite being a close friend of the arch-reactionary Methodist leader John Elias, Jones was a man of broad and liberal sympathies. Able, active, an effective if sarcastic public speaker, he appeared to be destined to assume a dominant position in local Methodism until disciplined for accepting a bribe of £30 during the by-election of 1830. Although readmitted to membership on refunding the bribe, he was not allowed to resume preaching. His supporters believed that he had been punished too severely and that local leaders of the denomination, in particular the unamiable autocrat Samuel Jones, had taken advantage of what was, by the standards of Liverpool politics, a trivial lapse in order to neutralise a dangerous liberal. Their suspicions were reinforced by the refusal to appoint Jones a deacon in 1836, despite his having secured sufficient votes. When finally expelled early in 1838 (for defaming a chapel treasurer), Jones joined the Independents, remaining a prominent member of that denomination for about a decade. Late in 1838 he flaunted his new allegiance by publishing *Yr Ysbryd a'r Briodasferch*, Hiraethog's sermon on *Revelation* 22:17 which had offended many Calvinistic Methodists for allegedly denying the person and operation of the Holy Spirit.

Hiraethog's accounts of the *Amserau*'s origins imply that he and Jones decided upon the project only after his move to Liverpool,[7] but the rapidity with which the paper was launched suggests that there may have been earlier discussions. A prospectus was distributed before the end of July 1843 and the first number would have appeared in early August had the necessary stamped paper arrived in time. Although the ultimate objective was a weekly paper, the only practicable course initially was to publish the *Amserau* as a four-page threepenny fortnightly. Jones undertook to bear all the costs, deal with readers' letters and market prices, and savage inexperienced versifiers, while Hiraethog wrote the leaders and edited the paper. 'Editing' proved to be a euphemism for translating and condensing from English newspapers virtually all the *Amserau*'s news in return for no more than his editorial expenses. Hiraethog clearly hoped that income from the *Amserau* might eventually supplement his stipend of £150 a year but his prime motivation in devoting long hours to the stultifying task of providing copy was propagandist. His objectives were summarised in the prospectus of the paper which emphasised its support for Free Trade, its intention of exposing 'injustice and oppression', its opposition to the 'superstitious, unchristian and papist' practices of the Oxford Movement and, above all, its support for voluntaryism in religion. Hiraethog, like many younger leaders of the Welsh Independents, had become a strong believer in disestablishment by the early 1830s,[8] participating in 1839 in the publication of a short-lived disestablishmentarian periodical *Tarian Rhyddid a Dymchwelydd Gormes* ('The Shield of Freedom and Overthrower of Oppression'). While the *Amserau* would devote considerable attention to the great issues of the day – the Corn Laws to 1846, education in 1847, foreign affairs in 1848–9 – its constantly reiterated message was the necessity of disestablishment throughout Britain.

The choice of *Yr Amserau* as title had a twofold significance. Firstly, it recognised the pre-eminence of its English namesake, while maintaining that *The Times* (like Lord Brougham) currently served as a dreadful warning of the way in which great talent and reforming zeal could be perverted.[9] Secondly, it reflected Hiraethog's apocalyptic world-view: the paper bore as a motto *Matthew* 16:3 'Oni fedri di arwyddion yr amserau?' ('Can ye not discern the signs of the times?'). The first fifteen numbers expounded a providential interpretation of history: nothing happened by chance, forthcoming events being prefigured in the scriptures and by prior happenings. Those who paid proper attention to current affairs could hope to identify links in the chain of events, comprehend God's plan and forecast forthcoming occurrences such as the imminent overthrow of that diabolical institution, the papacy. Hiraethog later claimed that the flight of Pius IX verified his predictions, the revolutions of 1848–9 clearly representing the opening of the sixth seal and partial emptying of the seventh vial of wrath.[10]

Although sales rose steadily from 400 to over 1200 by mid-May 1844[11] each number still incurred a loss of several pounds. A major problem, which was to trouble the *Amserau* throughout its existence (and which was responsible for the premature demise of many nineteenth-century Welsh periodicals), soon became apparent, namely a general reluctance to pay for the paper. Publication had to be suspended between mid-May and late June 1844 while debts were collected to provide the five pounds or so required to purchase stamped paper for each number.[12] After the first few months, advertisements made virtually no contribution to the paper's finances: indeed, several numbers published in the spring and summer of 1844 contained none. Few could have been surprised when the *Amserau* ceased publication because of mounting losses on 19 September 1844.

After a few weeks of indecision, John Jones was persuaded by David Morgan of Llanfyllin,[13] an Independent minister, fervent liberal and author of a church history which traced voluntaryism back to the Apostles, that the *Amserau* could be revived provided supporters of its principles assumed responsibility for underwriting its costs.[14] Following a meeting at the paper's office on 8

November 1844, at which it was resolved to recommence publication,[15] potential supporters were circularised and 'some scores' purchased the 400 shares on offer. These were probably £1 shares, 10s. paid, to yield an initial capital of £200.[16] Jones transferred his rights in the paper to the company without charge[17] but remained actively involved in its production, editing and management until August 1845. Hiraethog continued as chief editor, assisted by a former collaborator on *Tarian Rhyddid* and fellow Independent minister, Hugh Pugh.[18] Pugh assumed responsibility for editing news reports from unpaid local correspondents in Wales as well as contributing news snippets, short notices and the occasional humorous article.

Hiraethog subsequently described the *Amserau* as being sustained from 1845 onwards by 'patriotic Liverpool Welshmen'.[19] All the officials and virtually all the members of the successive committees responsible for the paper to mid-1848 can be identified.[20] Their religious affiliations suggest that while patriotism was undeniably important, a strong belief in disestablishment was of greater weight. Thus the company's treasurer, the wealthy Independent draper William Evans, was one of the four delegates representing Liverpool's Welsh Independents at the conference in London in April 1844 which led to the founding of the British Anti-State-Church Association (later the Liberation Society).[21] The other three delegates, the Independent ministers Thomas Pierce,[22] Robert Thomas ('Ap Vychan')[23] and Hiraethog himself, all served on the 1845 *Amserau* committee. Although other prominent Independents such as John Ambrose Lloyd,[24] the company's secretary, were associated with the *Amserau*, it received sufficient support from Baptists and the more liberal Calvinistic Methodists for it to be regarded as a Dissenting publication rather than one associated with a particular denomination. Since this was vitally important to its survival, editorials frequently emphasised the *Amserau*'s denominational neutrality.[25] The discussion of narrowly sectarian issues was discouraged and readers' letters which might damage Nonconformist unity were excluded, their writers being firmly directed to the appropriate denominational magazines.[26]

The two years following the relaunch of the *Amserau* in mid-January 1845 were superficially successful. Sales rose from some 1250 to over 2000 in the course of 1845,[27] despite a halfpenny price increase in mid-August to cover the cost of expanding the paper, and continued to rise to about 2500 during 1846.[28] By late spring

1845 official distributors had been appointed in some fifty-five places in Wales, including fifteen or so centres in the industrial south.[29] Despite surprising gaps in coverage, and although several of the smaller distributors were to drop out, almost forty of these places (including the majority of the centres in industrial South Wales) still had *Amserau* distributors in 1850.[30]

From 1845 onwards a more determined attempt was made to obtain advertisements despite their unpopularity with readers. While a typical issue in 1845 might contain six or seven, by 1846 the number ranged from a dozen to twenty or more: indeed, in mid-March 1846 the paper filled a whole page with advertisements for the first time. But the *Amserau* still relied on a limited range of advertisers, with many advertisements being inserted by its supporters or reflecting their influence on bodies with which they had some connection.[31] Since the paper was not regarded as a worthwhile advertising vehicle by most Liverpool concerns until the early 1850s, the persistent shortage of advertisements led to a dangerous reliance on income deriving from sales.

When John Jones moved to Wales in August 1845 to ghost the conclusion of an exposition on the Old Testament,[32] the task of printing the paper was transferred to the Liverpool partnership of M. J. Whitty[33] and W. Ellis. As only one of their compositors could understand Welsh,[34] Hiraethog's editorial work became even more time-consuming. The carelessness of the pressmen, 'children of Hengist', resulted in damaged copies of each number having to be sent to subscribers.[35] But by far the most serious consequence of Jones's absence was the lack of business experience in dealing with the paper's accounts. Long-standing debtors remained undisturbed while other subscribers were affronted by being pressed to settle bills which they had long since paid.[36] Despite a substantial improvement in sales and advertising, the *Amserau* continued to lose so much money because of outstanding debts that shareholders had to make a third payment of 5s. per share in March 1846.[37] Eventually, in December 1846, John Lloyd (former publisher of *Cronicl yr Oes*) was appointed at Hiraethog's suggestion to take charge of the accounts.[38]

1847 was a disastrous year, sales falling by a fifth to about 2000 and the number of advertisements decreasing to some ten per issue. By mid-June the *Amserau* claimed (probably with some exaggeration) that its debts exceeded £600, largely because of the dishonesty of its debtors.[39] Since even this failed to shame them into paying, publication had to be suspended, despite the imminent general election, from early July to mid-August while sufficient ready money to continue was scraped together. A further factor in the paper's decline was the commercial crisis of 1847 onwards which affected Liverpool particularly severely. Many Welsh people left the city,[40] some returning to Wales while a growing number, including at least two members of the 1845 *Amserau* committee,[41] emigrated to the United States.

The decline in sales may have been checked to some extent by publication in the *Amserau* from December 1846 onwards of Hiraethog's 'Llythyrau 'Rhen Ffarmwr' ('The Old Farmer's Letters'). Employing the persona of an irascible elderly farmer, Hiraethog commented in the letters on current affairs in ingeniously misspelt dialect Welsh. This popular journalistic innovation soon inspired many imitations and Hiraethog's assertion that many bought the *Amserau* solely on account of the letters was probably not unfounded.[42]

By late 1847 sales and advertising had fallen back to mid-1845 levels and the accumulated burden of debt rendered the paper's prospects far less favourable than they had been two years earlier. However, towards the end of November 1847 Liverpool Welshmen became aware of English newspaper summaries of the reports of the Welsh Education Commission of 1846–7.[43] Even those who normally shunned political activity were incensed by what they regarded as a gratuitous, Anglican-inspired attack on the 'morality and religion of Wales'. A protest meeting held at the Portico on 14 December 1847[44] resolved that the *Amserau* should be transformed into a weekly in the New Year in order to defend Wales and diffuse 'useful knowledge' in that country. The additional funding required to support weekly publication was to be raised by forming a new company with a capital of £500 in 200 shares of £2. 10s. each. 'Many' shares had been taken up by the end of the year,[45] and in late January or early February 1848 the *Amserau* was transferred to its new owners. Its size was increased in mid-January by a change of format from four to eight (rather smaller) pages, but enthusiasm then cooled as it was realised that the publication of each number added six pounds[46] to an accumulated debt of several hundred pounds.

Transferring production of the *Amserau* to the Isle of Man came to appear increasingly attractive since publishers both there and in the Channel Islands were, by virtue of the special constitutional status of these territories, free from the fiscal burdens imposed upon the press elsewhere in Britain. At the same time the islands enjoyed the right, formally endorsed in the 1840 Penny Post legislation, to send newspapers printed there post-free to mainland Britain.[47] This privilege, intended for purely local publications, came to be systematically abused by proprietors of mainland temperance and radical journals, a development noted by the *Amserau* which commented upon Bronterre O'Brien's activities at Douglas[48] and subsequently carried an advertisement for *Cronicl Cymru* ('The Chronicle of Wales'), a Jersey-published Welsh weekly.[49]

In June 1848 it was finally decided to transfer the *Amserau* to Douglas in the hope that the lower selling price consequent upon a reduction in costs would expand sales and thus make possible weekly publication. To facilitate matters the paper was sold to John Lloyd for £100,[50] the proprietors granting him credit for part of the price since Hiraethog agreed to continue editing the paper in Liverpool[51] while Lloyd supervised its production in Douglas. John Jones, who had resumed editing the paper's correspondence on his return to Liverpool in mid-1846,[52] agreed to act as general manager once again.[53]

After a month's break in publication, the first Manx-published number appeared on 28 July 1848 under the modified title *Yr Amserau Wythnosol* ('The Weekly Times'). Its printer was the redoubtable Manx radical, Robert Fargher,[54] a temperance enthusiast and specialist in printing works for mainland distribution. Freed from stamp duty, the *Amserau*'s price was reduced from 3½d. to 2d., leading to a rapid increase in sales from 2000 a fortnight to about 3000 a week.[55] Advertisement rates were also lowered from a minimum of 2s. 6d. (itself a late-March 1848 reduction from 3s. 6d.) to 1s.[56]

The *Amserau*'s stay in Douglas was to be brief. North Wales Tories and churchmen were alarmed by the paper's change to weekly publication and incensed by the means adopted to effect it. Within a fortnight, the 'Bangor Anglican fortnightly *Y Cymro* ('The Welshman'), founded at the beginning of 1848 to counteract the *Amserau*'s influence, commenced a vigorous campaign against the paper and its supporters. Two main themes predominated: that the move was illegal, rendering the *Amserau* 'smuggled goods', and that by resorting to a known haunt of Chartists the paper had revealed its true colours.[57] The *Amserau* replied equally forcefully that there was nothing illegal about the move to Man: an official at

Douglas Custom-House who had attempted to delay the paper had actually received an official reprimand for his pains.[58]

Lloyd was, however, anxious about developments in London. The *Amserau*'s move had been brought to the notice of the authorities following a meeting of clergy and gentlemen in Bangor at the beginning of August. Their account of the paper's circulation was clearly exaggerated – according to the *Cymro* the Chancellor of the Exchequer believed that 20 000 copies a week were being sent into Wales – and its political views were probably also misrepresented.[59] Governmental suspicion of Welsh-language papers and the general mood of crisis which prevailed during the summer of 1848 prompted swift legislation to block the legal loophole exploited by the *Amserau*, with the Postage on News-papers (Channel Islands) bill receiving its third reading on 29 August 1848. The act (11 & 12 Vict. cap. 117), designed to end what the Chancellor of the Exchequer stigmatised as 'a fraud perpe-trated on the Revenue' which subjected newspaper proprietors to 'most unfair competition', withdrew the islands' privilege of free postage on newspapers.[60]

After number 9 (misnumbered 8) of the new series had appeared on 22 September 1848 the paper returned to Liverpool, resuming publication there on 26 October as a stamped 3d. weekly, printed by Lloyd himself on a decrepit machine. At the higher price sales fell to below 2500 by mid-November[61] and then to 2000.[62] A list of copies sold through distributors was published in mid-November which, though not wholly accurate, provides a fair conspectus of the geographical distribution of *Amserau* subscribers.[63] Over a third of the *Amserau*'s sales were in industrial south Wales; distributors in Glamorgan and Monmouth were without exception located in industrial centres (particularly iron-works towns) rather than in the rural hinterland. Similarly, thirty of the thirty-four copies sent to Breconshire went to the Beaufort works and six of the fifty-two sold in Carmarthenshire to the Amman Iron Works. The impor-tance of south Wales sales to the *Amserau* is underlined by the fact that more copies were sold in Merthyr (134, excluding Dowlais which accounted for a further fifty) than in the whole of Merioneth. In the predominantly rural counties of north Wales sales also tended to be concentrated in industrial centres: thus sixty of the 132 copies sold in Merioneth went to the quarrying centre of Ffestiniog. Even where the *Amserau* had penetrated rural areas, many small towns remained without a distributor: as one indignant Merioneth correspondent demanded, where were the Nonconformists of Maentwrog, Harlech, Dyffryn Ardudwy, Barmouth, Tywyn, Aberdyfi, Corris and Llanegryn?[64]

Despite repeated attempts to induce readers to pay for the paper in advance or at least to settle their accounts regularly, by the end of 1848 unpaid debts once again threatened the paper's existence. In early March 1849 Lloyd claimed that the paper could clear its production costs of £18 per week[65] only if everyone paid punctually. Since the 1d. stamp and ½d. per copy paid to distributors left only 1½d. per copy towards producing the paper the decline in circulation made necessary a price rise to 3½d., paid in advance, from the beginning of April 1849 onwards.[66] Within a few weeks of the increase sales fell by a further 300 to 1700.[67]

The paper's well-publicised difficulties prompted well-wishers to send donations and organise events such as lectures and tea-parties to help it meet its liabilities. In all, £78. 18s. 9½d. was raised, reducing the old company's debt to some £271,[68] which the shareholders (or possibly trustees) eventually honoured. All these activities were intended to reduce the old *Amserau* debt and, as Lloyd was later to complain, did nothing to alleviate his chronic shortage of working capital.[69] He gained some relief by adopting a harder line towards recalcitrant debtors. Following repeated threats, the names of three absconding debtors were published in early August 1848[70] with others following at irregular intervals. From 1849 onwards legal proceedings were initiated against defaulting distributors but all too often they could not be traced or had emigrated, like Emanuel Jones of Rhymney who owed no less than £10. 4s. 6d.[71] From time to time the names of defaulting subscribers were also published at the request of local distributors.[72] In order to ensure that subscribers could no longer maintain that they were unaware that their subscription had expired, the penultimate copy of each subscription from the beginning of 1850 onwards was posted in a distinctive yellow wrapper rather than in the customary white one.[73]

A further factor tending to depress the *Amserau*'s sales in the late 1840s and early 1850s was Lloyd's persistent inability to publish the paper punctually. North Wales farmers and merchants required reliable information on Liverpool market prices before attending local markets, normally held on Wednesdays or Thursdays. Lloyd recognised their need by changing the *Amserau*'s day of publication from Thursday to Wednesday in January 1850 but frequently failed to ensure that the paper was ready in time to catch the Tuesday evening post to Chester. Repeated complaints from readers led to an illuminating explanation in late March 1850. Part of the paper (the inner forme) was printed in advance on Monday evening, the remainder having to wait until Liverpool market prices were received at 4 pm on Tuesday. Setting and imposing the prices required at least 90 minutes so that printing would normally begin at about 6 pm. Since it was impossible to print the whole edition before the post office closed at 7.15 pm, priority was given to printing and making up in bundles the thousand or so copies destined for north Wales to ensure that they were delivered on Wednesday.[74] The tight production schedule was easily upset by illness[75] or mechanical problems; when the machine broke down at the end of May 1850, it damaged a great deal of type and caused the paper to miss the Tuesday evening post.[76] Mechanical failure could no longer be used as an excuse from early October 1850 onwards since the paper then purchased a new press,[77] reverting from machine to hand-printing until the rise in circulation consequent upon the Crimean War necessitated the purchase of a steam-powered machine in August 1854.[78] What was characterised as Lloyd's lack of 'push'[79] also tended to delay the paper, but the most common reason for late publication remained lack of ready money. Stamped paper had to be ordered weekly from Manchester and paid for in advance. If the proceeds of the sale of one week's number had not reached the *Amserau* by that Saturday, purchasing paper for the next number would be delayed and production consequently disrupted.[80]

Even when the paper had been published on time readers sometimes complained of late delivery. Lloyd's response was to blame the Post Office, claiming that certain postmasters were delaying the paper until they had read it themselves.[81] In 1852 he offered a reward of three months' supply of the *Amserau* to anyone who could identify persons deliberately impeding the paper's transmission.[82] There is no mention of this reward being paid and the problem clearly persisted, since two years later Lloyd maintained that continuing delays were politically inspired[83] and offered an increased reward of £5 and six months' supply of the paper.[84]

Although Hiraethog remained the *Amserau*'s nominal editor until the end of 1852, from 1850 onwards he distanced himself from the paper, the regular editorial work being increasingly executed

by others. Readers were not informed of the change for fear of
damaging sales, the secret being so well kept that John Roberts,
'Ieuan Gwyllt', was startled to discover, on his appointment as
assistant editor in November 1852, that he was expected to do
virtually all the editorial work rather than merely assist
Hiraethog.[85] However, a few items in the paper's columns from the
beginning of 1850 onwards suggested some change in the editorship. As early as February 1850 Hiraethog and John Jones
formally announced that they had had no part in editing the
paper's correspondence column since the beginning of the year,[86]
a change which coincided with the introduction of several journalistic and typographical innovations. Letters from the Old Farmer
became so infrequent that one reader enquired in August 1850
whether he had emigrated to America.[87] Eleazer Roberts maintained that when he joined the *Amserau* at Lloyd's invitation at the
beginning of 1851 Hiraethog's links with the paper had become
very tenuous: he contributed articles occasionally but Lloyd
apparently acted as editor.[88] This may explain a cryptic statement
made in August 1851 that the owner and publisher of the paper,
and its chief editor were not Independents,[89] the most probable
interpretation being that all three offices were filled by Lloyd, a
Calvinistic Methodist. Why Hiraethog reduced his involvement
remains a mystery. He may already have quarrelled with Lloyd:
Eleazer Roberts hinted darkly at 'adequate reasons'[90] which he
refused to enlarge upon. Hiraethog's health had deteriorated, as
had relations with his congregation (he was to resign suddenly in
1853), new literary ventures in Welsh increasingly occupied his
time and he was also writing *Providence and Prophecy*, each page of
which, he claimed, took as long to compose as fifty pages in
Welsh.[91]

Although overseeing the paper's contents, Lloyd was not responsible for writing any part of it.[92] Much of the *Amserau* from
1849 onwards (if not earlier)[93] was the work of Thomas Manuel[94]
who, in addition to translating and condensing material from
English papers, was the author of a dialogue-series commenting on
current affairs '*Y Felin*' ('The Mill') which almost matched the Old
Farmer's letters in popularity. Manuel also contributed letters,
ostensibly from readers, under a number of pseudonyms such as
'Callestr' and 'Ysolyr o'r Fferyllfa'.[95] The drudgery of sustaining
the paper took its toll and Manuel succumbed to tuberculosis, was

compelled to resign at the beginning of November 1851 and died in late December.

Manuel's failing health may well have precipitated one of the gravest crises in the whole of the *Amserau*'s history. During the summer and autumn of 1851 the paper appeared to have lost its way: the new journalistic features faded out and a few controversialists were allowed to monopolise the correspondence columns, filling them weekly with lengthy and acrimonious debates on poetic and musical questions. Despite repeated complaints, these disputes were not terminated until the end of the year when it was belatedly recognised that they had so disgusted many readers that they had given up buying the *Amserau*.[96] The paper's conduct was particularly foolhardy since disaffected readers could turn to a new fortnightly competitor, *Seren Cymru* ('Star of Wales'),[97] which was attempting to win Baptist readers from the *Amserau* by claiming that the latter was the mouthpiece of the Independents.[98] The *Amserau*'s insensitivity to its readers' wishes combined with the emergence of an aggressive rival reduced its sales to a level – about 1400 in November 1851 – which put its existence at risk.[99] An urgent appeal to readers and distributors in late November[100] combined with the well-publicised end of the debates rapidly won back readers, sales recovering to over 2000 by late March 1852[101] before dropping back to 1850 in early December.[102]

Hiraethog, perhaps deliberately, created a great deal of confusion concerning his remuneration as editor. Later writers, wishing to stress the heroic nature of his achievement, have generally accepted his frequent assertions that his labours were unpaid.[103] His original agreement with John Jones was that he would simply be reimbursed his expenses as editor[104] but once the paper passed into company ownership in 1845 he clearly expected to receive some payment. In an editorial at the end of 1846 he described the tribulations of a Welsh newspaper editor, all suffered for 'less than a tenth' of what English editors received,[105] and complained once again in March 1847 of being poorly paid.[106] A report on the finances of the first company casts some light on the sums involved and suggests that as the paper's finances deteriorated Hiraethog could no longer be paid: amongst the 'old debts' is a sum of £100 due to the editor who had worked for three years without receiving any pay.[107] Arrangements following Lloyd's acquisition of the paper were only slightly less unsatisfactory. Hiraethog later maintained (and Lloyd made no attempt to deny) that he had never asked for money but had accepted what Lloyd offered him:[108] for four years' labour he had received what would have represented three months' pay for an English editor.[109] The 30s. a week offered to Ieuan Gwyllt as full-time assistant editor in late 1852[110] suggests that Hiraethog may have received a (notional) salary of some 10s. per week for his part-time editorship. No evidence has survived to indicate whether Manuel was paid a fixed salary or according to the quantity of material supplied. Eleazer Roberts, who was employed on the latter terms, received 2s. a column between 1851 and 1857; the sum due was assessed at roughly monthly intervals but payment was irregular since even during this more prosperous period Lloyd was frequently short of ready money.[111]

The *Amserau*'s fortunes from 1853 onwards can be only briefly outlined here. Under the editorship of Ieuan Gwyllt sales rose from an average of just over 2000 a week in 1853 to over 4500 in 1854,[112] an increase which the editor modestly attributed to Nicholas I rather than to his own powers.[113] Repeated denunciations of the Crimean War, most notably by Eleazer Roberts writing as 'Meddyl-iwr' ('The Thinker'), supposedly damaged sales,[114] but there is in fact no evidence of any decline: possibly the *Amserau*'s lavish coverage of war news (including letters from Welsh servicemen) offset the effects of unfavourable editorial comment.

The abolition of the duty on newspapers in July 1855 created a new environment to which the *Amserau* failed to adapt. By 1857 a new liberal penny weekly, *Yr Herald Cymreig* ('The Welsh Herald'), had attained sales of over 9000,[115] well over double that of the *Amserau*. Although there was still a place for a quality Welsh weekly, the *Amserau* seriously weakened its position by publishing from late 1855 onwards a series of anonymous attacks on Hiraethog which shook the loyalty of many readers and prompted Hiraethog to reconsider his refusal to assist any paper which might damage the *Amserau*. In November 1856 Thomas Gee[116] induced him to join the editorial team of a proposed threepenny paper, *Baner Cymru* ('Banner of Wales'), which was expressly designed to attract *Amserau* readers.[117] The appearance of the first number of the *Baner* on 4 March 1857 marked the beginning of the end for the *Amserau* since Gee, in addition to possessing the ruthless drive which Lloyd so conspicuously lacked, enjoyed sufficient resources to nurse his new title through its first few years while engaging the services of many of the leading Welsh journalists of the day.

The ability of the *Amserau* to resist this new challenge was fatally compromised by disputes between Lloyd and his staff. Ieuan Gwyllt resigned in November 1856 because of Lloyd's interference in editorial matters but was persuaded to resume the editorship until October 1858,[118] and Eleazer Roberts had departed by the end of 1857.[119] As the *Amserau* became increasingly scrappy, with perfunctory editorials and a reliance on detailed criminal reports of a kind which had been expressly excluded during its early years, Gee increased the pressure by launching a penny version of the *Baner, Udgorn y Bobl* ('The People's Trumpet') on 20 March 1858. The *Udgorn* pre-empted Lloyd's ultimate expedient, the reduction of the *Amserau*'s price to 1d. at the start of October 1858. *Udgorn* readers were offered a well-produced, coherent and respectable family newspaper rather than a poorly-printed compilation which had been reduced to including dubious medical advertisements. As both the quality and cheap ends of the *Amserau*'s potential readership fell increasingly into Gee's grasp, Lloyd cast about for alternative means of earning a living including the trade of emigration agent[120] and keeper of a temperance hotel, before selling Gee the paper for £300 on 1 October 1859.[121] Gee immediately merged the *Amserau* with the *Baner* to form *Baner ac Amserau Cymru* ('Banner and Times of Wales'), which became the leading Welsh-language organ of radical Nonconformity for the remainder of the century.

Notes

1. H. J. Hanham, *Elections and Party Management: Politics in the Time of Disraeli and Gladstone* (1959) p. 171, n.1.
2. M. H. Jones, 'Wales and Hungary', *Transactions of the Honourable Society of Cymmrodorion* (Session 1968, Pt. 1) 7–27, provides a detailed account of one aspect of the paper's interest in international affairs.
3. Two unpublished studies include useful discussions of the *Amserau*: T. Eurig Davies, 'Cyfraniad Dr. William Rees (Gwilym Hiraethog) i Fywyd a Llên ei Gyfnod', MA thesis, University of Wales (Bangor), 1931, and D.E. Jenkins, 'Cyfraniad y Parch. William Rees (Gwilym Hiraethog) i Fywyd a Llên ei Gyfnod', National Library of Wales, (henceforth NLW), MS. 12791C.

4. *DWB*. The Welsh biography by T. Roberts and D. Roberts, *Cofiant y Parch. W. Rees* . . . (Dolgellau, 1893) should be consulted in preference to E. Rees, *William Rees (Hiraethog): A Memoir* . . . (Liverpool, 1915).

5. T. M. Jones, *Llenyddiaeth Fy Ngwlad* . . . (Treffynnon, 1893) pp. 15–16.

6. *DWB* supplement (in Welsh only). Much information is scattered in the valuable (but unindexed) study by J.H. Morris, *Hanes Methodistiaeth Liverpool*, 2 vols (Liverpool, 1929–32).

7. T. Roberts and D. Roberts, *Cofiant* p. 235.

8. R. Tudur Jones, 'The Origins of the Nonconformist Disestablishment Campaign 1830–1840', *Journal of the Historical Society of the Church in Wales*, XX (1970) 39–76.

9. *Amserau* (23 August 1843) 1.

10. A detailed exposition of his views will be found in W. Rees, *Providence and Prophecy: Or, God's Hand Fulfilling His Word* (Liverpool, 1851).

11. *Amserau* (16 May 1844) 2.

12. *Amserau* (27 June 1844) 1.

13. *DWB*.

14. *Amserau* (16 January 1845) 1.

15. *Dysgedydd* (December 1844) wrapper.

16. *Amserau* (12 March 1846) 4 refers to a 'third payment' of 5s. per share.

17. For this and the remainder of this paragraph see the *Amserau* (30 December 1847) 4.

18. *DWB*. There is no modern study of this important figure.

19. *Baner ac Amserau Cymru* (5 October 1859) 3.

20. 1845 committee and officials, *Amserau* (13 February 1845) 5; 1846 committee and officials, *Amserau* (12 March 1846) 4; 1848 trustees, *Amserau* (28 March 1848) 4.

21. *Amserau* (16 May 1844) 1.

22. Pierce is not included in the *DWB* but a contemporary memoir, H. E. Thomas, *Cofiant* . . . *y Diweddar Barch. T. Pierce Liverpool* (Liverpool, [1864]) briefly notes his disestablishmentarian activities, p. 47.

23. *DWB*.

24. *DWB*.

25. *Amserau* (15 December 1847) 4; (20 August 1851) 2.

26. *Dysgedydd* (January 1856) wrapper p. 3.

27. *Amserau* (12 March 1846) 4.

28. Letter from William Evans to Thomas Stephens, 20 November 1846, NLW, MS. 965E ii. 375–6.

29. *Amserau* (24 April 1845) 8.

30. *Amserau* (23 October 1850) 3.

31. John Ambrose Lloyd, for instance, was almost certainly responsible for ensuring that an advertisement for Liverpool Mechanics' Institute was placed in the paper.

32. D. E. Jenkins, 'Esboniad James Hughes: Ei Orffennydd', *Drysorfa*, CII (1932) 95–9.

33. There is a useful article on Whitty, founder of the *Liverpool Daily Post*, in *Dictionary of National Biography*.
34. *Baner ac Amserau Cymru* (4 June 1862) 364.
35. *Amserau* (7 May 1846) 4. The problem arose because the authorities allowed no rebate on printed sheets damaged in this way.
36. *Amserau* (22 October 1846) 4.
37. *Amserau* (12 March 1846) 4.
38. *Amserau* (31 December 1846) 4; *Dysgedydd* (April 1856) wrapper p. 4.
39. *Amserau* (17 June 1847) 4.
40. Thus membership of the Tabernacle fell from 324 in 1846 to 249 in 1850 (T. Eirug Davies, p. 282) and the total number of full members of the Welsh Calvinistic Methodists from 1824 in 1847 to 1686 in 1849 (J. H. Morris, vol. I, p. 132).
41. Robert Littler and William Benjamin Jones.
42. *Amserau* (4 November 1847) 2. In his later accounts, Hiraethog maintained that the letters were responsible for a substantial increase in the circulation of the *Amserau*. This is not borne out by the sales figures.
43. *Amserau* (16 December 1847) 3 states that a summary published (with disparaging comments) in the *Daily News* on 24 November was reprinted in the *Liverpool Journal* on 27 November.
44. *Amserau* (16 December 1847) 1.
45. *Amserau* (30 December 1847) 4.
46. *Amserau* (5 March 1856) 3.
47. There is a useful summary of the position of the Isle of Man in W. Cubbon, *A Bibliographical Account of Works Relating to the Isle of Man*, vol. II (1939) pp. 1181–5.
48. *Amserau* (17 July 1845) 3.
49. *Amserau* (18 November 1847) 1.
50. *Amserau* (5 March 1856) 3.
51. *Dysgedydd* (April 1856) wrapper p. 4.
52. *Amserau* (30 December 1847) 4.
53. *Amserau* (29 June 1848) 4.
54. Fargher's career is outlined in W.T. Kneale, 'The Trials of a Manx Radical: the Life and Times of Robert Fargher, 1803–1863', *Journal of the Manx Museum*, VI (1959–60) 89–93.
55. *Amserau* (10 May 1849) 5.
56. *Amserau* (28 July 1848) 4.
57. *Cymro* (12 August 1848) 130–1; (26 August 1848) 140.
58. *Amserau* (25 August 1848) 4; (15 September 1848) 4.
59. *Cymro* (9 September 1848) 149.
60. The act received minimal coverage in *Hansard* and *The Times*: the most complete account (copied faithfully by the *Cymro* a week later) is in the *Carnarvon and Denbigh Herald* (2 September 1848) 2. The effects of the act are summarised in Cubbon, pp. 1183–5.
61. *Amserau* (16 November 1848) 4.
62. *Amserau* (10 May 1849) 4.
63. *Amserau* (16 November 1848) 5.
64. *Amserau* (7 December 1848) 6.

65. A figure very close to the rate of £9. 10s. per thousand copies quoted by J. T. Jones for printing *Ifor Hael* in 1850 and the *Gwladgarwr* in 1851, NLW, MS. 3231D.

66. *Amserau* (8 March 1849) 4.

67. *Amserau* (10 May 1849) 5.

68. *Amserau* (27 February 1850) 2, a full list of donations, including fifty individual contributions of 2s. 6d. or less.

69. He received none of the proceeds of the Liverpool tea-party and only two places in Wales sent him any money, *Amserau* (5 March 1856) 3.

70. *Amserau* (4 August 1848) 4.

71. *Amserau* (18 October 1849) 4.

72. Four Llandeilo defaulters named, *Amserau* (23 January 1850) 4.

73. *Amserau* (27 December 1849) 4.

74. *Amserau* (20 March 1850) 4.

75. *Amserau* (21 May 1851) 4 (two compositors went home because they were unwell).

76. *Amserau* (29 May 1850) 4.

77. *Amserau* (2 October 1850) 4.

78. *Amserau* (2 August 1854) 2.

79. Eleazer Roberts' expression, *Geninen*, XXV (1907) 239.

80. *Amserau* (15 January 1851) 4; (26 November 1851) 4.

81. *Amserau* (7 August 1850) 4.

82. *Amserau* (14 January 1852) 4.

83. *Amserau* (12 July 1854) 4.

84. *Amserau* (5 April 1854) 4.

85. J.E. Jones, *Ieuan Gwyllt* . . . (Treffynnon, 1881) pp. 38–9, 122.

86. *Amserau* (27 February 1850) 4; (28 May 1851) 3.

87. *Amserau* (21 August 1850) 2.

88. E. Roberts, 'Adgofion am Rai o Gymry Fu Lerpwl', *Transactions of the Liverpool Welsh Nationalist Society*, XII (1896–7) 55; *Geninen*, XXV (1907) 238; *Baner ac Amserau Cymru* (4 June 1862) 2.

89. *Amserau* (20 August 1851) 2.

90. *Geninen*, XXV (1907) 239. Ieuan Gwyllt also found Lloyd to be an infuriating employer (Jones, *Ieuan Gwyllt*, pp. 41–2).

91. D. Griffith, 'Y Diweddar Barch. William Rees, D.D.', *Traethodydd*, XXXIX (1884) 156.

92. *Geninen*, XXV (1907) 299.

93. Manuel may have had some connection with the paper as early as 1847 for in that year he contributed a 'Survey of the Welsh and Channel Isles Periodical Press' to the *Christian Witness*, IV (1847) 535–6, which commented very favourably on the *Amserau*.

94. For Manuel's early life see M. Fraser, 'Child Prodigies at Llanover', *Presenting Monmouthshire*, XVI (1963) 30–5. Details of his work on the *Amserau* are mainly drawn from his obituary, *Amserau* (31 December 1851) 4.

95. John Davies, 'Gwyneddon', maintained that Thomas Jones, 'Glan Alun', was 'Ysolyr' in his 'Llenyddiaeth Newyddiadurol Cymru', *Traethodydd*, XXXIX (1884) 179, but offered no supporting evidence.

His article is generally unreliable, while the identification of Manuel as 'Ysolyr' is made in the 1851 *Amserau* obituary.

96. *Amserau* (31 December 1851) 4.
97. *Seren Cymru* (13 August 1851–23 December 1852) is briefly discussed in R.D. Rees, 'A History of the South Wales Newspapers to 1855', Unpublished MA thesis, Reading, 1955, pp. 573–5. With sales of 1000 a fortnight it lost £200 in some sixteen months.
98. *Amserau* (20 August 1851) 2.
99. *Amserau* (3 March 1852) 4.
100. *Amserau* (26 November 1851) 4.
101. *Amserau* (31 March 1852) 4.
102. Jones, *Ieuan Gwyllt*, p. 39.
103. Thus F. Price Jones, 'Gwilym Hiraethog – Tad y Wasg Gymraeg', in A. Llywelyn-Williams and E. ap Nefydd Roberts (eds) *Radicaliaeth a'r Werin Gymreig* (Caerdydd, 1977) pp. 65–72, especially p. 67.
104. T. Roberts and D. Roberts, *Cofiant*, p. 235.
105. *Amserau* (3 December 1846) 2.
106. *Amserau* (17 March 1847) 4.
107. *Amserau* (10 May 1849) 5.
108. Letter from Hiraethog to Ebenezer Thomas, 'Eben Fardd', 5 March 1856, NLW, Cwrtmawr MS. 402B.
109. *Dysgedydd* (April 1856) wrapper p. 4.
110. Undated draft of letter from John Roberts, 'Ieuan Gwyllt' to Lewis Edwards (?), NLW, MS. 9918E (11).
111. *Geninen*, XXV (1907) 238.
112. These figures are based on the official returns of *Amserau* stamps purchased in 1853 and 1854.
113. Jones, *Ieuan Gwyllt*, p. 39.
114. T.M. Jones, p. 17. The circulation figures quoted here are extremely exaggerated.
115. R. Maldwyn Thomas, 'Hen Gefndir yr *Herald Cymraeg*', *Y Casglwr*, XXIII (1984) 10–11.
116. *DWB*.
117. T. Gwynn Jones, *Cofiant Thomas Gee* (Dinbych, 1913) pp. 161–3.
118. Jones, *Ieuan Gwyllt*, pp. 41–3.
119. *Geninen*, XXV (1907) 240.
120. *Amserau* (24 June 1857) 4.
121. The agreement was drawn up on 3 September 1859 and signed on 1 October, NLW, Thomas Gee MS. O 11.

8

London's Local Newspapers: Patterns of Change in the Victorian Period

MICHAEL HARRIS

Writing on the history of the English newspaper press is still very fragmented. It is almost inevitable, given the diversity of interest and approach, that there should be large gaps in the coverage and that major themes and periods should be under-represented. Among the most important tasks facing historians of the press at this stage is the construction of an effective bibliographical record. At one level this means continuing to assemble listings of titles and locations. However, as the practice of bibliography is itself re-defined in broader cultural terms, it also means identifying elements in the structure of the English press which help to reveal both its internal mechanisms and its external relationships. The aim of this chapter is to follow the second bibliographical objective and to discern the chronological and geographical development of the London locals. Alan Lee was the first modern historian to identify their interest and importance, and their absence from most views of the Victorian press seriously distorts the general picture.[1]

The papers themselves are highly elusive. Well over 600 titles were produced in the London area during the second half of the nineteenth century and no comprehensive finding list yet exists.[2] At the same time, although the volume of material held by the major libraries is considerable, the gaps in individual files can be striking. Establishing the relationship between rapidly changing titles is itself a highly complex activity, the problem being com-pounded by the wholesale destruction of publishers' archives. Over the last twenty years or so, as a remorseless process of empire building has taken place across the local press, much of the historical record has been irretrievably lost. Such difficulties, combined with the modest status of the local newspaper, whether as an institution or as an object of study, help to explain the absence of detailed research into the history of this sector of the press.

As a preliminary, it seems worth attempting a definition of the main structural elements. Firstly, the local papers categorised by Alan Lee, I think mistakenly, as 'parochial'. I have in mind those papers, usually but not always published weekly, which were geographically specific. Their target audience, unlike that of the 'class' papers of the Victorian period which catered for almost every specialist interest, was identified mainly in terms of place. Regions and districts of London provided the titles while the optimistic strings of locations which ebbed and flowed through the mastheads of the local papers offer a useful though not always reliable guide to distribution areas. There was an inevitable overlap between the different types of weekly publication. The locals sometimes assumed a political or class emphasis and the publications of local interest groups, Croydon cyclists for example, can be sufficiently ambiguous to undermine firm rules of identification. Harder still is the construction of an effective definition of London. As the process of population growth and physical expansion continued through the eighteenth and nineteenth centuries the notion of London shifted. By 1850 the idea of London had begun to extend well beyond the building line into outer areas which were increasingly described as part of 'Greater London'. Sell's newspaper directory in the 1880s used the conventional twelve miles from Charing Cross to define the range of the London suburbs, identifying sixty-six separate locations within the circle. It was clear even at the time that the boundaries of the County of London, as established in 1888, were going to exclude a good deal of what was considered to be part of London. In this analysis I shall be concerned with an area related to but not confined by the boundaries of the lamented Greater London Council.

Before 1850 newspaper coverage of the London area was organised from two district bases. Firstly, from London itself. Since the early eighteenth century the papers published in the centre had created, by way of a network of newsmen and agents, a form of exclusion zone for local publication. This was maintained into the nineteenth century and the home counties remained the heartland of the readership of the powerful metropolitan dailies and weeklies. Using increasingly sophisticated production and distribution techniques, these papers continued to dominate the upper levels of the market. Secondly, the London area was colonised by weekly newspapers based in the county towns which ringed the capital. Offering a diet of rather generalised local material, the proprietors of these papers established agencies across the area and were usually well represented in London itself.

In 1830 the *Kent Herald* received advertising, notices and news at eight separate addresses in central London. The county weeklies circulating through the region could be big business. This was clearly demonstrated in the case of W. E. Baxter of Lewes whose main publication, the *Sussex Express*, was produced in the early 1850s in conjunction with his *Surrey Standard* and *Weald of Kent Mail*. Baxter had a full-scale editorial office in Duke Street, Southwark where his papers were published and where material was received. In 1852 he stated that as well as employing 'two editors, five reporters and forty persons engaged in the printing offices', his staff included 'ninety-one regular weekly paid correspondents and agents, and thirty appointed correspondents', besides the irregular suppliers of news.[3] This substantial editorial establishment was costing Baxter nearly £2000 per annum. He also calculated that the *Sussex Express*, produced in editions of something over 4000 copies, was circulating, mainly through the post, to fifty market towns. The county papers for Kent, Essex, Hertfordshire and the other home counties meshed with the metropolitan publications, the whole structure being propped up by the system of taxation which effectively excluded cut-price competition.

Even so, the publication pattern of newspapers before 1850 was not entirely static. Centres of population within London's sphere of influence, such as Windsor, Deptford, Greenwich and Woolwich, sometimes offered special opportunities to the entrepreneur. In the period before the repeal of the newspaper taxes a number of new weekly papers were produced across the area, apparently with some success. Whatever the local circumstances, publication in the pre-repeal period was hard to sustain. The editor Charles Knight gave a graphic account of the problems facing the newspaper publisher in terms of production and distribution. However, as he makes clear, the main stumbling block was taxation. The dire financial results which this could produce were occasionally the subject of comment in the papers themselves. According to an editorial notice in the Greenwich-based *Kentish Mercury* in 1840, arrears of advertising duty had by themselves nearly ruined the proprietor and led to the seizure of much of his property.[4] Fear that repeal would remove the major constraint on local publication haunted the owners of the county weeklies and pushed them into the forefront of the opposition through such organisations as the Provincial Newspaper Society. W.E. Baxter was extremely anxious. 'I have no doubt', he wrote, 'that, as a mere matter of trade, every printing office will have its local sheet'.[5] However, he was wrong in anticipating the decay of the county weekly. In the event such papers continued to flourish, the *West Sussex Gazette*, for example, reaching a circulation of about 35 000 copies a week in 1880.

The timing of the first phase of local publication in the London area, extending into the 1870s, represented a direct response to the sequence of tax repeals. The removal of the advertising duty in 1853 prompted the first crop of papers and the end of the stamp in 1855 a second. The repeal of the duty on paper in 1861 had a less marked effect but still gave a worthwhile boost to the marginal finances of the small-scale weeklies selling at ½d. In 1860 the *King's Cross Mirror* was said to have cost its proprietor £30 per annum in paper duty alone.[6] Subsequently only the remnants of the old security system involving the registered proprietor in finding £800 lingered on as a financial threat. According to one commentator its rigorous application could have led to the 'virtual suppression of the local journals throughout the metropolis, which answer a harmless and useful purpose'.[7] However, very few cases seem to have been brought under the legislation and the outcry over the prosecution of the *Camden and Kentish Town Gazette* in the late 1860s suggests that it was rarely used.[8]

While the response to the repeals can be identified across the whole of Greater London it is possible, particularly during the first phase, to make a broad distinction between the activity in the inner and outer areas. In central London, with its erratically extending building line and massive population levels, the presence of a numerous and dispersed printing trade made the rapid development of local newspaper publication almost inevitable. W.E. Baxter's fears of repeal were centred on the printing office where the newspaper offered a number of traditional advantages – not least regularity of income and the opportunity of setting up a variety of commercial contacts. Such considerations had underpinned the primary burst of newspaper publication at the end of the seventeenth century and operated with equal force 150 years later. The

core of the printing trade extended through a broad band stretch-
ing from Clerkenwell in the north, through the City and across the
river into Southwark. At the same time, printers were scattered
through all the main centres of population to the west and east of
the City and consequently a large number of variably sized
printing and publishing businesses were available to support the
impulse to local newspaper production. At the lower end of the
scale the marketing of pre-packaged material in the form of
partly-printed sheets containing general news and routine forms of
fiction made it fairly easy to integrate a local paper with jobbing
work. John Evans of Clerkenwell who produced the halfpenny
North London Record continued to offer the usual range of cards,
billheads, handbills and so on, as well as 'Harper Twelvetrees Mice
and Rat Killer'. The benefits that pushed Evans into newspaper
production also had value at the other end of the commercial scale.
James Wakeham ran one of the largest printing businesses in west
London, employing forty hand-setting compositors at several
premises where he carried out a substantial amount of official
contract work.[9] This did not prevent him from launching the
successful *Kensington News* and from the 1870s his local paper
became a major component of the firm's output.

Although the burst of local newspaper publishing during the
1850s and 1860s presents a bewildering picture, it conformed to the
dominant inner structure of London itself. In its totality the
built-up area appeared an amorphous and undifferentiated mass.
However, within it were the intricate patterns of local development
by which individuals defined their relationship to the urban space.
The journalist James Grant in his *History of the Newspaper Press*
(1872) sliced London into four sections – North, South, East and
West – identifying one regional and seven local newspapers within
each. Eric Hobsbawm, on the other hand, in a modern analysis of
Victorian employment saw London as a tripartite structure – North
and East, North and West, and South – grouping the local
newspapers within this alternative framework.[10] Both attempts to
create manageable subdivisions blur at the edges but both emphasise the crucial distinction between region and district which must
be applied in any classification of the London locals. Grant and
Hobsbawm coincide in their sense that the area south of the river
presented the greatest regional coherence. As a journalist of the
1860s put it, 'The part of London which lies on the Surrey side of
the Thames . . . is of itself a great city'.[11] Although lacking an urban

focus it was in the south that the most active efforts at regional publication were made and in which one of the most successful regional papers, the *South London Press*, was established.

To the north of the river the regional wedges extending out from the centre of London through the large and densely populated metropolitan boroughs were less clear cut. Grant identified the papers which dominated his northern, eastern and western sectors as the *Clerkenwell News*, the *Eastern Post* and the *Marylebone Mercury*. These were regional publications with a status which placed them mid-way between the district locals, from which they had emerged, and the metropolitan dailies which they aspired to challenge. Below them the struggle for a place in the local market could itself be influenced by the character of the region. To the west, for example, conventional weeklies were supplemented by local papers which reflected the social and literary pretensions of the residents. The *West End News* selling at 2d. was not only published from the Oxford Street printing office but appeared simultaneously in Brighton and Paris.[12] An alternative form of social climbing was evident in the case of the *Kensington and Belgravia Gazette*. According to the *Newspaper Press* it was 'got up in an elaborate style on thick toned paper, and printed in clear bold type, with a red border to its pages, and we are informed that future numbers are to be scented'.[13] In spite of this sort of oblique regional influence most of the local papers published in the built-up areas of inner London had a clearly defined district character. Local government divisions, reconstituted and reinforced through the Metropolis Management Act of 1855, provided the geographical framework for much of the output of the first phase. At the same time the target area for local publication was sometimes considerably narrowed. The *Essex Road and Balls Pond Advertiser* claimed as its main selling point that 'every person reading an announcement in its pages, would be within walking distance of the advertiser', – 'a point of very great importance', added a sceptical commentator.[14]

In the outer areas the initial impulse to local newspaper publication followed a similar but rather slower trajectory. Strung out along the main roads around London were a variety of small coaching and market towns. Many, such as Barnet to the north-west and Bromley to the south-east contained populations which had levelled off at about 4000 or 5000. The most substantial of London's urban satellites was Croydon, located just beyond the southern fringe of the built-up area and containing in mid-century a population of about 50 000. Prior to the repeals these centres lay within the exclusion zone for local papers. However, the necessary condition for development in the shape of an extensive printing and publishing network was already in place. To take one example from Barnet, John Cowing had moved out from central London at the end of the eighteenth century, setting up a printing and bookselling business in the High Street.[15] By 1830 he was engaged in a variety of specialist activities including a certain amount of local publishing. His *Barnet List of Coaches to London*, for example, formed part of a miscellaneous jobbing output. He also ran a successful subscription library and acted as agent for a major county newspaper, the *Hertfordshire Mercury*. In 1845 his business was described as that of paper-hanger, bookseller, binder, copper plate and general printer, stationer and newsagent.[16] In the same year the entry in the *Post Office Directory* for Bromley in Kent included a printer and two booksellers and stationers, while the Croydon list contained the names of ten individuals with an interest in the book trades. The presence of potential newspaper publishers across the outer area provided a platform for the development of the local press. However, it required the conjunction of circumstances starting with repeal and extending through the coincident processes of population growth and railway construction to set things in motion. Railways and newspapers were locked together in outer London. This was partly a matter of publication as proprietors identified outlets along adjacent lines and made extensive use of station sales both locally and at the metropolitan termini.[17] But more than this, the railway provided rapid access to London for a variety of organisational purposes and at the same time supplied a basic component of readership appeal. The railway timetable became from the first an integral part of suburban newspaper content, sometimes delaying publication or extending into valuable advertising space.

The first phase of newspaper publication in outer London began in the 1850s. George Cowing launched his paper the weekly *Barnet Press* in 1859 having purchased a secondhand press for about £130 from William Eglington, a City printer.[18] He also arranged for Eglington to supply a partly printed sheet to which could be added local material worked off in a shed behind his High Street premises. He produced the paper in editions of 750 copies of which Eglington received 100 gratis. Publication of the *Bromley Record* in

1858 followed a different line. Apparently projected and owned by someone outside the trade, it was produced monthly at the printing office of Edward Strong and consisted of sixteen pamphlet-sized pages, the first being entirely filled with the London, Chatham and Dover Railway timetable. Here again newspaper production was slotted into the highly miscellaneous activities of a jobbing printer.[19]

I am not able at this stage to provide the sort of statistical account of the local press in London that evidently needs to be produced. However, using the directory entries and such useful but limited sources as the *Times Tercentenary Handlist*, it is possible to suggest a general shape to the initial development in terms of 'fresh starts'. From the mid-1850s into the early 1860s the number of new locals published each year across the region averaged about ten. A slight downturn in the mid-1860s when the average fell to about six was followed by a sharp upturn exemplified by the appearance of about thirty new locals in 1869. This sudden boom may have been generated by the build-up in suburban railway construction. From the mid-1860s new lines as well as improved access to the system were changing the character of such inner fringe suburbs as Kensington and also stimulating the development of new working-class communities away from the centre such as those at Enfield and Walthamstow. Through the 1870s the identifiable fresh starts again averaged around ten. Against this high level of activity has to be set the equally substantial failure rate. In May's newspaper directory for 1880, fifty-eight local titles were listed, of which only eleven had been in existence in 1860. Buying into the local press could be cheap enough. The copyright of the *St. Pancras Gazette* together with the press and type was sold in 1866 for £50.[20] It was the difficulty of maintaining publication which posed the real problem.

The extent to which the construction of limited liability companies under the legislation of 1856 and 1862 helped to stabilise the London locals is not entirely clear. Alan Lee calculated that some 420 newspaper companies had been formed nationally by 1885 and that one-third of these were based in London.[21] Although it is not possible to isolate the local press within these figures, it is clear that the build-up in newspaper output of the 1850s and 1860s was linked to, but not dependent on, the creation of these small-scale capitalist enterprises. The London and Provincial Newspaper Company Ltd, for example, established about 1862, was involved three years later in the publication of its main regional paper, the *West London Times*, and in the production of eighteen other titles circulating through the suburban districts all round London.[22] In fact, the papers were produced at the same printing office in the City and while the outer of the four pages were identical in each case, except for the masthead, the inner conformed to about four basic patterns. The construction of this chain of papers does not seem to have been a commercial success. In March 1866 all the subordinate titles were discontinued and only the *West London Times* lingered on until its final disappearance in 1869.

Part of the general expansion of the local press was achieved through the sort of chain-building undertaken by the London and Provincial Company. To the south of London a titanic struggle developed in the 1860s between George Bacon of Southern Counties Newspapers and W.E. Baxter now running South of England Newspapers. Both published a major Sussex-based paper, both had London offices in Southwark, and while Bacon had eleven titles in publication in 1867, Baxter was publishing twenty-four and was credited with owning the largest number of newspapers in the country.[23] Their spheres of interest extended well into the London area and both produced a regional paper aimed at a readership within the southern suburbs; Bacon the Liberal *South London Chronicle* and Baxter the Conservative *South London Journal*. On an altogether smaller scale the pragmatic process of expansion, which was in some respects a condition of survival, was demonstrated in north London by George Cowing. Finding his paper the *Barnet Press* not sufficiently profitable to support two members of the family, he opened a branch of his business in Tottenham and began to publish the *Waltham Telegraph*.[24] Development did not end there. Cowing's branch manager, E. H. Crusha, later took over this part of the firm and began to publish the *Tottenham and Edmonton Weekly Herald*. Success in the local newspaper business was mostly slow and doubtful, and the establishment of satellite publications could, as the editor of the *Croydon Advertiser* pointed out, add an element of stability to the central production.[25]

In spite of increasing competition between titles, local newspapers continued to proliferate. The number of fresh starts reached their highest level in the 1880s and 1890s and, according to the *Times Tercentenary Handlist*, averaged about seventeen a year – a total of over 350 titles. Underlying this striking acceleration was the continuing increase in population and its dispersal through

Greater London. On the other hand, the impulse to local publication was becoming more diversified, particularly through political
intervention. London locals had been established on behalf of the
Liberal or Conservative interest since the 1830s and many of the
companies concerned in this sector of the press had political
objectives. The cheapness, adaptability and close relation to the
readership of the local paper offered peculiar political advantages
which could be exploited by individuals as well as groups. Until
the passing of the Corrupt and Illegal Practices (Prevention) Act in
1883, such intervention could be of substantial benefit to both the
proprietor and the politician.[26] In central London this appeared
clearly in the case of Sir Edward Clarke who stood as Conservative
candidate for the Borough of Southwark in the General Election of
1880.[27] He approached the publishers of the *Kentish Mercury* with
the proposal that they should produce a local edition of their paper
under the title of the *Southwark Mercury*. The terms, as agreed, were
that the new paper should contain nothing but Southwark news
on its inner pages with a half column permanently available for
any political material Clarke should choose to insert. In return he
was to pay 1d. per copy on an issue of 2000 for two years, the
money to be raised by subscription. In the event Clarke had to pay
a substantial proportion of the £866 out of his own pocket. By
regularly sending a copy to each of the 800 public houses, beer
houses and coffee houses, he was able to reach sections of the
constituency which were not accessible through the usual public
meetings, lectures and appearances.

If such individual manipulation of the local press became less
evident, party engagement was extended during the 1880s and
1890s with the emergence of more radical forms of politics. Deian
Hopkin has listed and described the monthly publications of the
Independent Labour Party appearing in seven London suburbs
including Ealing, Clapham, West Ham and Woolwich.[28] In some
respects these publications were closer to the class papers than
they were to the generalist locals. However, their progressive
ideology also manifested itself with some force within the more
conventional output of the local press. Nowhere was the interaction between radical politics and local publishing more evident
than in the new working-class suburb of Walthamstow. With a
population which had risen from about 11 000 in 1871 to nearly
50 000 twenty years later, largely by migration from London's
desperately overcrowded and poverty stricken East End, Waltham-

stow was fertile ground for progressive ideas.[29] At the centre of the picture was the remarkable figure of J.J. McSheedy, former member of the Irish National League and friend of the prominent journalist T.P. O'Connor. Moving to Walthamstow to take up a job with the London School Board, McSheedy rapidly became involved with the members of the local progressive party which achieved a small majority on the District Council at the end of 1894. The previous October eight or nine of the group had set up a local paper under the title of the *Walthamstow Reporter* to be 'devoted to active progressive Radicalism and Labour interests'. Produced by the Cooperative Printing Society its editor was McSheedy.

The appearance of a challenge to consensus politics in the area had already galvanised other sections of the local press. The *Walthamstow Guardian*, a long-standing and respectable paper, derisively referred to as 'granny' by the *Walthamstow Whip*, became apoplectic in its coverage of local events. Headlines such as 'Disgraceful Proceedings', 'The Vicar Grossly Insulted' and 'Council Room Door Forced and Public Admitted. Councillor to be Prosecuted,' became common place. Events in which McSheedy himself, later known as 'the stormy petrel of Walthamstow', took part were fully covered.

Against a highly charged background, the *Reporter* rapidly achieved a circulation of about 2000 copies, and through its pages McSheedy continued to offer a long-running radical critique of local affairs. It was not until 1903 that a conventionally violent dispute with the shareholders led to his resignation and the paper's collapse.

If radical and progressive politics were in a sense squeezed out of the metropolitan papers by market forces, local publications could still offer an alternative line of access to a general audience. The means of production were available through a scattering of small-scale, radical printers whose output could easily accommodate local newspaper production. In Walthamstow the Buck brothers, pioneer socialists who were arrested in 1912 under the provisions of the Mutiny Act, built up an active printing business from very obscure beginnings, largely through the production of some seven local papers.[30] The commercial symbiosis between printer and newspaper could have a political dimension and only the Registration and Libel Act of 1881 presented an obstacle to radical publication at this level.

By the end of the nineteenth century the complex networks of the local press were providing very full cover across the London area. Assessments of circulation levels are as problematic as ever. Directory and other published information is hard to interpret and there were some extravagant claims based on a supposed number of readers rather than sales or print runs. Overall, circulations showed a modest upturn from the 1850s. It seems possible to suggest that, by the last decade of the century, the outer London weeklies such as the *Barnet Press* were selling up to four or five thousand copies, and that in the more densely populated inner areas the equivalent figure was up to nine or ten thousand. Individual regional papers could greatly exceed these upper limits and even in the 1860s the *Clerkenwell News* was selling about 25 000 copies a week.[31] However, in general the depth of cover was achieved more through the publication of multiple titles than through the achievement of dramatic circulations.

At the same time, the pervasive character of the locals was emphasised by the widespread use of free publication. This had always been an option for the low-key advertising sheets of the first phase and during the later decades a range of more sophisticated publications were floated on the rising tide of income from commercial and personal advertising. In the late 1880s a chain of free locals were produced at the Free Press Steam Printing Works, Bon Marché Buildings, Brixton and a guaranteed 5000 copies of each of the five titles were delivered from house to house through the streets of south London. The way in which this material could complement the paid-for output was suggested by Thomas Baines in his comments on the *South Hampstead Advertiser*. 'It has met a want of the district', he wrote in 1890, 'as a considerable proportion of the houses change their tenant every three or four years, who consequently take so little interest in local matters that they will not *purchase* the local paper.'[32] Some of the more radical political material was also distributed gratis and any assessment of the level and range of readership has to take account of this.

The only omission from the spectrum of local output which continued to strike observers was the lack of any general daily paper specifically concerned with London issues. The *Clerkenwell News*, known in the 1860s as *The Times* of the local press, seemed capable of assuming a general role. However, following Edward Lloyd's takeover, it was simply subsumed into the metropolitan daily output.[33] In the 1880s the idea of a London-wide daily was still in circulation and it was suggested that when 'the Corporation is reformed, and Greater London has a voice in municipal affairs, it is calculated there will be a splendid opportunity for a daily treating of local matters'.[34] In spite of several false starts such a paper did not materialise and the realities of local publication were clearly identified in the *Croydon Advertiser*. Referring to his paper's own short-lived attempt at daily publication, the editor pointed out that a

> small network of local papers has thus grown up in a kind of district which, being so close to London, does not offer those features of great local and independent spirit which distinguishes so many of the great provincial towns and cities. We claim to have proved, however, that largely dependent as they [the districts] are on the great Metropolis – now greater than ever – they are still capable of supplying very liberally good local organs of thought and activity.[35]

Having offered a broad view of the development of the London locals largely from the production side, it remains to be asked how these publications related to the communities they served. The physical presence of the local paper was evident enough. The thumping and grinding of the mechanised presses working through the night, usually on Thursdays or Fridays, in High Street premises had its own galvanising effect on neighbourhoods. Trouble over the noise and vibration of steam-powered printing had cropped up in the 1820s,[36] and after repeal the problem became more general. The *Kensington News* office had to be relocated twice, first after the introduction of gas and later of electricity.[37]

In other respects the London locals were, and are, less obtrusive. Alan Lee's use of the term 'parochial' reflects one strand of contemporary comment which dismissed the penny and halfpenny locals as 'miserably weak and pointless', filled with trivia, and established merely as 'a trap to catch advertisements'.[38] There is no doubt that in many cases, particularly in that of the printer-owned papers, such comments had a degree of substance. A proportion of the first-phase output began life as low-key advertising sheets with few pretensions.[39] However, any sign of success generally led the proprietor to identify the financial benefit of balancing advertising with editorial input. Whether the starting point was provided by motives of profit or public benefit, the realities of newspaper production led to a very similar end-product – one which had broadly political as well as commercial characteristics.

The campaigning role of the London locals deserves some careful analysis. Its force was variable and likely to be reduced in the medium term by heavy reliance on local government for both information and advertising. In the short term, shifts in ownership and changes in the mode of production could prove equally damaging. The reformist character of the *Kingston and Richmond Express*, for example, was completely undermined when its new proprietor began to replace the compositors with unskilled labour and embarked on a ruthless programme of wage-cutting.[40]

Within Greater London, local papers had an importance both as business enterprises and as vehicles of communication. On the other hand, they formed part of the general structure of the London press and the relationship between the local and metropolitan papers also needs closer examination. At the most pragmatic level the London locals (then as now) served as a staging post in the movement of journalists and others through the press, and any general view of the London newspapers in the nineteenth century must accommodate the local output. At a more theoretical level, the sometimes rootless debates about the development of commercialisation and the survival or decay of liberal pluralism must also take account of this alternative line of London newspaper production.

Notes

1. A.J. Lee, *The Origins of the Popular Press in England 1855–1914* (London, 1976) pp. 70–1, 280.
2. A machine-readable catalogue of the titles and holdings of the London locals is in course of preparation at the British Library Newspaper Library.
3. William Edwin Baxter, *Notes on the Practical Effects of Repealing the Newspaper Stamp Duty, the Advertising Duty and the Excise Duty on Paper* (Lewes and London, 1852) p. 8.
4. 'Centenary Souvenir Supplement 1833–1933', *Kentish Mercury* (20 October 1933) 3.
5. Baxter, *Notes*, p. 8.
6. *North London Record* (25 February 1860).
7. *Newspaper Press* (July 1868) 157.
8. *Newspaper Press* (August 1868) 182.
9. 'Centenary issue, 1869–1969', *Kensington News and West London Times* (10 January 1969) 5.

10.   E. J. Hobsbawm, 'The Nineteenth Century Labour Market', in Centre for Urban Studies (ed.), *London Aspects of Change* (London, 1964). Hobsbawm takes his information on the London locals from *May's British and Irish Press Guide* for 1880.
11.   *Newspaper Press* (October 1868) 218.
12.   London and Suburban Newspaper Company, papers in the Public Record Office, London (PRO), BT 31, 6281 Box 1721.
13.   *Newspaper Press* (April 1868) 103.
14.   *Newspaper Press* (December 1871) 20.
15.   H. R. Pratt Boorman, *Your Family Newspaper* (Maidstone, 1968) p. 21.
16.   'Hertfordshire', *Post Office Directory of the Six Home Counties* (London, 1845).
17.   See, for example, comments on the *Woolwich Gazette* and the *Mid-Surrey Gazette* in the *Newspaper Press Directory* (London, 1864) 82 and (1879) 156.
18.   Gwyneth Cowing, 'The Story of the Barnet Press', in W. H. Gelder (ed.), *Historic Barnet* (London, 1984) pp. 91–104. Also B. J. White, 'A History of the Barnet Press' (typescript, Barnet Museum, 1978).
19.   Edward Strong's advertisements offered a very wide range of printing services, including ball cards in gold, silver and bronze, as well as all kinds of stationery and bookbinding to order. For example, *Bromley Record* (February 1862).
20.   Boorman, *Your Family Newspaper*, p. 96.
21.   Lee, *Origins*, pp. 80, 82.
22.   Listed in the *Newspaper Press Directory* (London, 1865) 25. The companies' newspapers are bound together in the British Library and the fact of termination is noted in manuscript at the end of each run.
23.   *Newspaper Press* (April 1867) 95; *Newspaper Press Directory* (London, 1873) 42.
24.   White, 'History', p. 18. See also the *Tottenham and Edmonton Weekly Herald* (6 July 1861).
25.   'Jubilee Supplement', *Croydon Advertiser* (15 February 1919).
26.   Aled Jones, 'Reporting Nineteenth Century Elections: The Gibson-Rendel Correspondence', *JNPH*, III (1986–7) 17–22.
27.   What follows is based mainly on the account in Sir Edward Clarke, *The Story of My Life* (London, 1918).
28.   Deian Hopkin, 'Local Newspapers of the Independent Labour Party 1893–1906', *Bulletin of the Society for the Study of Labour History*, XXIX (1974) 28–37.
29.   The best account of the prolix local papers published in Walthamstow is contained in R.G.C. Desmond, *Our Local Press* (London, 1955).
30.   Desmond, *Local Press*, pp. 38–9.
31.   James Grant, *The History of the Newspaper Press*, vol. III (London, 1872) p. 165. By 1866 the *Clerkenwell News* was appearing five times a week.
32.   F.E. Baines, *Records of the Manor, Parish and Borough of Hampstead* (London, 1890) p. 274.

33. Under Lloyd's management the paper became the halfpenny *Daily Chronicle*.
34. *Printer's Register* (6 April 1885).
35. 'Jubilee Supplement', *Croydon Advertiser* (15 February 1919).
36. Charles Knight, *Passages of a Working Life*, vol. I (London, 1864) p. 163.
37. 'Centenary issue', *Kensington News* (10 January 1969) 5.
38. *Newspaper Press* (May 1868; April 1869).
39. Desmond, *Local Press*, p. 18.
40. *Printers Register* (6 May 1890) 9.

9

The Early Management of the *Standard*

DENNIS GRIFFITHS

The *Standard*, London's only surviving evening newspaper, was founded in 1827. For the rest of the century the paper provided keen but critical support for Conservatism, and made an important contribution to the political and literary life of the capital. This study of the origins, early growth and maturity of the *Standard* in nineteenth-century London will examine the paper's editorial management and its role as a focus for cultural and political writing.

The origins of the *Standard* lie in the journalistic activities of the Baldwin family, a press dynasty founded in Cromwellian times by Richard Baldwin. Charles Baldwin, son of Henry Baldwin, founder of the *St. James's Chronicle*, launched the *Standard* in May 1827 to provide London with an independent Tory paper. Its motto, 'Signifer, statue signum, hic optime manebimus', was intended to be a rallying call to the Old Tories who had been left in the cold by Canning's coalition government of April 1827, and throughout the nineteenth century the paper continued to maintain close relations with the Conservative Party. However, the *Standard* retained also a degree of political independence that often infuriated Conservative leaders. Its ability to provide support for the party while remaining free from its editorial control was due largely to the skill of the early editors and managers.

The man chosen by Charles Baldwin as the first editor of the *Standard* was Dr Stanley Lees Giffard, already the successful editor of the *St. James's Chronicle*. Born in Dublin in 1788, Giffard was to retain the trust of his proprietor from 1819 until his death in 1858. Educated at Trinity College, Dublin, where he took his MA and later LLD, he entered the Middle Temple and was called to the bar in 1811. Making no progress as a barrister, he turned his attention to literature and was quickly recognised as the most distinguished and powerful political writer of the day. As an editor, Giffard was in the true Baldwin tradition: violently anti-Catholic and bitterly opposed to emancipation. It was said that 'he looked upon the Roman Church as simply a political conspiracy carried on under the name of religion'.[1]

Within four years of assuming the editorship of the *Standard*, Giffard was a celebrity, and was described by Sir Denis Le Marchant as an 'honest Orangeman, and as violent and fanatical as most of his faith'. So honest, in fact, that he could reject a gift of £1200 from the Duke of Newcastle, who had been impressed by 'a masterly article which had appeared in the *Standard* of the previous evening in opposition to the Roman Catholic claims'.[2] Giffard was not without his critics, however, as is apparent in the following remark from John Gibson Lockhart, editor of the *Quarterly Review*, to J.W. Croker in 1835:

McGinnis's superior in *The Standard* is a man of a different cast and calibre and *he* is really worth thinking of. He, too, is poor – often embarrassed, and thence irritable, sulky and dangerous. He is, however, extravagantly vain and no man more seducible by the least show of courtesy from persons of high rank.[3]

No doubt this could be said, too, of Giffard's assistant editors, the well-known literary figures, Dr William Maginn and Alaric Alexander Watts.

Maginn, immortalised by Thackeray as the Captain Shandon of *Pendennis*, was born on 10 July 1794 in Cork, where his father maintained a private school for boys. In this school, Maginn's brilliance in classical studies was so remarkable that he entered Trinity College, Dublin at the age of eleven. On his return to Cork, after graduation, he taught classics at his father's school, achieved the LLB degree and in 1819 became an LLD of Trinity, and before the age of twenty-five he was fluent in seven languages. Little wonder that Maginn's biographer, Edward Kenealy, could assert that: 'His memory was prodigious, the strongest in the world. It was a rich storehouse of all learnings so that it might with propriety be called, like the sublime Longinus, the living library'.[4]

Maginn began his journalism by contributing to the *Literary Gazette* and *Blackwood's Magazine*. In 1824 he joined the *Representative* as its Paris correspondent, being taken on by a young Benjamin Disraeli. Recalled from Paris, Maginn directed his energies once more to *Blackwood's* and the *Literary Gazette* before being approached by Theodore Hook to write for *John Bull*. Now a well-known figure in Fleet Street, Maginn had many friends of influence, one of whom was Thomas Barnes, editor of *The Times*. But it was to Charles Baldwin and the *Standard* that he turned in 1827. From the very first days, Maginn's brilliant writings and acerbic wit were features of the *Standard*, and although he wrote anonymously his style was immediately recognisable and won him many admirers. One contemporary described him thus:

> A bright genius undoubtedly he was, with lovable qualities that bound friends to him amid all his dissipation, his want of principle, his discreditable dodges to escape for a time the consequences of his mode of life; and in the thick of it all, harassed by creditors and hiding from Bailiffs, he sent out to the Press papers that display acute insight, scholarship, and critical skill, and trifles of rollicking entertainment and rare humour. He would write a leader in *The Standard* one evening, answer it in *The True Sun* the following day and abuse both in *John Bull* on the ensuing Sunday.[5]

Maginn is also credited as being the first person to call *The Times* 'The Thunderer'. In an article that appeared on 15 February 1830, in the *Morning Herald*, he described *The Times* as 'The Great Earwigger of the Nation, otherwise the Leading Journal of Europe, otherwise The Awful Monosyllable, otherwise The Thunderer – but more commonly called The Blunderer'.[6]

Despite this undoubted genius as a writer, however, Maginn was intent on destroying himself with drink. In 1836, following an article in *Fraser's Magazine*, he was challenged to a duel by Grantley Berkeley, considered a crack shot. Fortunately for Maginn, Berkeley missed with his three attempts, and Maginn's second, Hugh Fraser, then insisted that the duel be broken off. The years of heavy drinking were taking their toll, and Kenealy, another loyal friend, could write of him: 'He is a ruin, but a glorious ruin, nevertheless. He takes no great care of himself. Could he be induced to do so he would be the first man of the day in literature'.[7] By 1836, however, Maginn's financial situation was desperate, and despite aid from the King of Hanover, Sir Robert Peel and Thackeray, he was thrown into Fleet Prison for debt. This did not, however, prevent his contributing to the *Standard* and to *Punch*. Compelled to obtain his discharge as an insolvent, he emerged broken-hearted and in an advanced stage of consumption. On his release from prison, Maginn, broken in health and spirit, moved to Walton-on-Thames, where he died on 21 August 1842.

Alaric Alexander Watts was a very different character who, during his years on the *Standard*, was to prove a most loyal and valuable servant for Giffard. 'I know of no man', averred Giffard, 'whose integrity is more pure; no man whose genius is of a higher order; whose conduct, in all relations of life, is more deserving of admiration; no man in whose friendship I feel more highly honoured.'[8] Watts more than repaid that trust when, as a result of Giffard's serious illness, he served as editor of the *Standard* for three months in the late summer of 1839. In a warm acknowledgement of Watts's service Giffard told him: 'You and I have known each other for fifteen or sixteen years, a very great part of the allotted life of a man, and we have never had a difference of political or private opinion'.[9]

Born in London on 16 March 1797, Watts led a varied life as tutor to the family of a dentist to the Prince Regent, and a temporary clerk in the office of controller of army accounts before working as a sub-editor on the *New Monthly Magazine*. He soon became well-known in London literary circles and commenced to write for the *Literary Gazette*. As a result he was offered and accepted the editorship of the *Leeds Intelligencer* at a salary of £300 per annum. There he remained until 1825 when he left for Manchester to edit the *Courier*, resigning twelve months later to commence part-newspaper publishing. He arranged that provincial newspapers, with their titles and leading articles set up, should be printed at No. 1, Crane Court, Fleet Street, and that the local intelligence and local politics should be added in the country by the local bookseller and printer by whom the paper was published and who was, titularly, its proprietor. As his son, Alaric Alfred Watts, was to write later in his father's biography: 'This was the origin of what, in the printing trade is, I believe, designated "partly-printed newspapers". For the credit of having originated this method of newspaper issue there have been many claimants. For whatever it may be worth, it belongs to my father'.[10]

Upon Giffard resuming the editorship of the *Standard* once more in the autumn of 1839 he was profuse in his thanks to Watts, writing on 10 October: 'I resigned my place as principal editor of the *Standard* to you, with an expectation that my friends in Bridge

Street would feel the advantage of securing your services as my permanent successor, and had it not been for your very kind offer, I should have died in harness. I firmly believe this'.[11]

With his earnings from the *Standard* and the *United Services Gazette*, Watts was receiving more than £1000 per annum. But, despite the efforts of Charles Baldwin, he now became involved in litigation with his partner over the *Gazette*, and with debts of more than £3000 Watts lost the court action and co-ownership of the *Gazette*. But his troubles were not yet over, for 'he was arrested outside his beautiful home at the suit of a paper-maker'. Unable to pay, Watts was declared a bankrupt in 1850. However, his fate was not to be the tragic ending of Maginn. In 1853 Watts accepted an appointment in the Inland Revenue Office, where his son held a high position, and after pleas on his behalf he was awarded a Civil List pension of £100 a year by the Prime Minister, Lord Aberdeen, in January 1854. His later days were thus spent in some comfort, including editing the first issue of *Men of the Time*. He died on 5 April 1864, in Notting Hill, and was buried in Highgate Cemetery.

Although as editor, Giffard's political hopes had been a disappointment – his campaigns against Catholic emancipation and parliamentary reform had both been unsuccessful and now he had lost his final battle, the repeal of the Corn Laws – events during the 1840s were to provide some consolation, for it was then that his son Hardinge Stanley joined him on the *Standard*. But journalism was to prove to be a temporary diversion in Hardinge's career. As a lawyer he sought advancement in politics, and following defeats in the General Elections of 1868 and 1874 he was successful in November 1875, being appointed Solicitor General by Disraeli and knighted. Ten years later, Lord Salisbury appointed him Lord Chancellor. Hardinge was promoted to an earldom in his third tenure as Lord Chancellor and held this position until 1905. He is best known for his work, *Halsbury's Laws of England*.[12]

As an old man, he was able to tell his grandson, the present Earl, of his experiences on the *Standard* in its formative years and of being involved, as a special constable, with Feargus O'Connor, leader of the Chartist demonstration at Kennington Common on 16 April 1848. 'I came across a big policeman, twice as big as myself, who was being sent with a message to Feargus O'Connor, the head of the movement, and I went with him. He said, I suppose with some irony, "I suppose, Sir, you are protecting *me*."'[13]

While young Hardinge Giffard was being introduced to the

mysteries of the press, the proprietor of the *Standard* had decided to call it a day. Having reached the age of seventy, Charles Baldwin retired and after 1844 left the active management of the business to his son Edward. Unlike Henry, his father, Charles Baldwin had been fortunate in his relationship with the Establishment. On his retirement he reflected with pleasure on the great strides achieved with the *Standard* as a political force and as a commercial proposition. From its early beginnings the circulation of some 700 or 800 copies each evening had risen within a matter of years to more than 3500. Now, through the efforts of the past fifty years, there was established a highly respected and successful newspaper group and he was confident that in his son, Edward, there was a worthy successor with the knowledge and ability to take the *Standard* to even greater heights.

For the new proprietor it was a time to expand the business the further, and his first act was to develop the *Morning Herald*, which he had recently purchased from the Thwaites family. In writing of the purchase, James Grant described Edward Baldwin as a thoroughly enterprising and enlightened trader in journalism, 'who, two decades after Dudley's death, bought the *Morning Herald* from the little group of fifth-rate capitalists to which it had gone'. At once he entered on a course of spirited rivalry to *The Times*, which set all its resources in motion to crush the new competitor. According to Grant, 'so excellently did his Continental intelligence service work that, very early in his proprietorship, the *Herald* won European reputation for the promptitude, the accuracy and the fulness of its despatches from beyond the seas'. Giffard, in addition to his editorship of the *Standard*, was now given supreme control of the *Morning Herald*, and, with Baldwin, he determined to engage the best editorial talent available, almost regardless of costs and to raise the honorarium paid for leading articles from three guineas to five guineas.

For the first few months, the paper, with its highly paid staff, suffered considerable losses, but then the circumstances changed dramatically. In 1845, a railway boom led to frenzied speculation usually alternating with periods of panic. There was a 'perfect mania of railway companies' and so great was the influx of long advertisements that the *Morning Herald* sometimes ran to twenty pages or 120 columns. Not only did the *Morning Herald* gain large sums from the advertisements but the sales also increased and during 1845 it achieved a daily average of 6400, its highest since

1837, although in the panic year of 1848 it dropped to 4800 and by 1854 had fallen to 3700.

On 17 November 1845 *The Times* exposed the competing railway schemes, showing that there were some 1200 projected railways seeking to raise more than £500 million.[14] The bubble burst immediately, although Baldwin, believing that the good times would return, continued to conduct his business in the most lavish manner, even increasing the pay of his parliamentary reporters from five guineas to seven guineas per week – and all the while his circulation continued to fall. For *The Times*, however, it was to be a different story; for by 1852 its sales were to exceed 52 000, ten times that of the *Morning Herald*. Edward Baldwin's recklessness was now apparent to all, and by the end of the 1840s his fortunes were very much on the wane. The *Standard* had commenced the decade with an annual circulation of 1 040 000 or 3320 copies per day; now, in 1850, its sales had fallen to 492 000 or 1220 per day. The *Morning Herald*, as noted, was similarly affected; from a peak of 2 018 025 per annum in 1845 – the railway mania – it was down to 1 139 000 or 3635 per day. By the mid-1850s the sales of the *Standard* had fallen even further and was down to barely 700 copies per day. It was a state of affairs that could not last, and in the spring of 1857 there appeared a short notice in *The Times* announcing the bankruptcy proceedings of Edward Baldwin, and with it the end of almost 200 years of his family's involvement in the London newspaper world.

James Johnstone, the new owner, bought the *Standard* and the *Morning Herald* during the summer of 1857 for £16 500. A senior partner in the firm of Johnstone, Wintle, Cope and Evans, James Johnstone had for many years held an official appointment in the Bankruptcy Court, which he now resigned. For the first few weeks, Johnstone continued to conduct the *Standard* and the *Morning Herald* in the same manner as the Baldwins, but, finding that he was producing at a loss, he decided that drastic measures were necessary. He therefore reduced the price of the *Standard* from 4d. to 2d., doubled the pagination to eight and converted it into a morning paper. The date of this changeover was Monday 29 June 1857, and in his leader Giffard announced that the paper 'quits the ranks of the Evening Journals and today takes its place besides *The Times* and its contemporaries to compete with them in every excellence, to be less only in price'.

The introduction of this new-style *Standard* now posed a direct threat to *The Times*, and its circulation dropped 2000 copies a day within a matter of days. As *The Times* was to admit in its official history:

> The ability with which the twopenny *Standard* was conducted – Robert Cecil, later Lord Salisbury, was one of its leader writers – constituted an undeniable threat to the supremacy of *The Times*. Even *The Daily Telegraph* considered the 2d. eight-page *Standard* to be a very desirable money's worth in comparison with its own four pages for 1d.[15]

But Johnstone was not yet finished, and on 4 February 1858, 'the entire town and country trade was staggered by an announcement that the *Standard* was about to reduce its price to 1d. without any reduction in size'.[16] Thus the editor noted in his leader column, 'we this day publish *The Standard* at the price of ONE PENNY, which, we venture to predict, will yet become the current charge for newspapers throughout the kingdom'.[17] At the time of introducing the eight-page *Standard* as a morning paper, Johnstone had also launched a new Conservative evening paper entitled the *Evening Herald*, in connection with the long-established *Morning Herald*. Priced at 2d., it was not a success, even though much of the material was copied from its sister paper, and it expired on 21 May 1865. As for the *St. James's Chronicle*, which had for so many years been the bedrock of the Baldwin family fortunes, there was no future for it in the Johnstone plans and he finally sold the paper to Charles Newdegate, Tory MP for North Warwickshire, and within a matter of weeks Newdegate had converted the *Chronicle* into a weekly.

Encouraged by the success of the new-style *Standard* and the increased press capacity available, Johnstone now decided that the time had come to revive the evening edition, which had ceased publication three years earlier. The title was easily agreed, the *Evening Standard*, and it was felt that with the advent of the electric telegraph there was an increasing demand for up-to-the-hour news. The first issue of the relaunched paper took place at 3.15 pm on Thursday 11 June 1859, and the man selected as editor was Charles Williams, yet another Protestant Irishman. Williams's forte, however, was as a special foreign correspondent and he was to cover the Franco-Prussian War, the Armenian Crisis in 1877 and the Second Afghanistan War in 1878–9. He was then appointed editor of the pre-Harmsworth *Evening News* before joining the *Daily Chronicle*, which he served as a special correspondent at the Battle of Omdurman in the Sudan in 1898. He died in Brixton on 9 February 1904.[18] Succeeding Williams on the *Evening Standard* was John Moore Philp, who was to remain there until 1864. Previous to this he had spent two years on the sub-editors' table on the *Standard*. Philp left the *Evening Standard* for the *Daily Telegraph*, but rejoined the *Standard* as a sub-editor in 1880, and remained there until his death in 1903.

The new editor of the *Standard* and its sister papers and the man mainly responsible for the circulation problems at *The Times* was Thomas Hamber, who was described by his contemporaries as 'a thin, spare but manly figure' and known everywhere as the 'Swiss Captain' through his services with the Swiss Legion in the Crimean War.[19]

Under the Johnstone style of management and the enthusiasm of Thomas Hamber, who succeeded Giffard as editor in 1855, the *Standard* now began to attract a much better calibre of writer. One of these was Lord Robert Cecil, a friend of Hamber from Oxford. Lord Robert Cecil, the third Marquess of Salisbury, could later recall that in his youth he had eked out a living by writing leaders for newspapers and especially the *Standard* in Shoe Lane. Other well-known writers on the paper at this time included T. H. S. Escott, who covered the political scene, and Joseph A. Scoville, who as 'Manhattan' reported the American Civil War from the Southern viewpoint. George Alfred Henty was also employed by the paper and was to report campaigns in Abyssinia, the Franco-Prussian War and from the Ashantee Expedition. The growing commercial success of the paper enabled Johnstone to settle the paper's debt to the Conservative Party, which had held the mortgage on the newspaper's premises. Nevertheless, Hamber was still very much in the pay of Disraeli and would endeavour to write to please the Conservative leader. Aiding Hamber in this task was Alfred Austin, a future Poet Laureate, who had recently been engaged as leader writer. Austin became aware that Hamber's policy 'chiefly consisted of charging a granite wall'. Austin soon realised, however, that while 'Hamber won cheers by the constant raising of impracticable war cries, he also had his own axes to grind'. Hamber was now proving too troublesome even for Johnstone and was summarily dismissed in October 1872. Johnstone's son, James Johnstone Junior, briefly took up the editorship,[20] and was followed for an equally short period by the Tory Party agent John Eldon Gast.

Deciding that the *Standard* needed an experienced newspaper-man as editor, Johnstone appointed William Heseltine Mudford, a man of courage, energy and firmness of purpose who, undoubtedly, was one of the great editors of the nineteenth century. As a journalist, Mudford took an interest in all aspects of London life and society and had a large circle of friends. But with his appointment as editor, there came a distinct change in his manner. It was the high-time of dining out, but, while other editors were seen everywhere, Mudford remained aloof. Indeed, 'he was not to be seen at a dinner party or a reception, or any other social entertainment; he refused all the invitations which were at one time freely offered.'[22] *The Times* also observed that

> He carried out the same system in his office. Amid the turmoil of conducting the business of a great newspaper, he lived like a recluse. He was a kind of Chinese Emperor, Japanese Mikado in Shoe-lane – the mysterious and awe-inspiring inhabitant of a Forbidden City, only accessible to a very few principal attendants and acolytes.[23]

Johnstone was a great admirer of Mudford's talents, but, unfortunately, their working relationship was not to last long, for on Tuesday 22 October 1878, the paper announced the death of its proprietor. In a fulsome tribute, Mudford wrote:

> Through good and evil report, with many peculiarly harassing difficulties to overcome, and with the scantiest assistance from many quarters to which he might have fairly looked for support, Mr Johnstone carried out the work which he had set himself to accomplish and, happily, he lived to see *The Standard* in the full tide of that success which it had been the aim of his life to secure for it.[24]

Within a matter of weeks, the future of the paper was revealed in Johnstone's will. The key clause stated that

> By a codicil to the will the testator directs that Mr Mudford is to remain as editor of *The Standard* for his lifetime or until such time as he shall voluntarily resign the editorship; and further directs

that the paper is to be carried on in every respect as it was at the time of his death.

To be awarded complete editorial and managerial freedom of the *Standard* for life at a salary of £5000 per year was one of the most extraordinary acts of faith in nineteenth-century journalism, and there can be few other examples in the British press of one man being granted such absolute power over a national newspaper. As editor, Mudford was very much his own man and beholden to no party, although he must have been pleased to learn of the following remark from Gladstone: 'When I read a bad leader in *The Standard*, I say to myself, Mr Mudford must be taking a holiday'.

Apart from Austin, who continued for much of the time to lead a country existence, the other leader writers often felt the sting of Mudford's caustic comments. To T. H. S. Escott, who had recently rejoined the paper, Mudford wrote: 'I think you had better rest a day or two. Your Friday's leader was hardly up to yr. mark & the one last night must fall under the same criticism'. T. E. Kebbel, a long-serving writer, was another associate reproached by the editor, although he described Mudford as 'a kind-hearted man – nay a warm-hearted man – in reality, though his manner was often cold and a trifle constrained, arising, I thought, from nervousness rather than from any want of real sympathy'.[25]

Mudford was certainly fortunate in taking over a profitable business. Much money had recently been spent on modern machinery and during that very year, 1878, the *Standard*'s new building had been completed in St Bride Street. By his own efforts the paper already possessed a first-class editorial staff. G.A. Henty, Charles Norris-Newman, John Cameron and Hector Macpherson were special correspondents of the highest order and, with such leader writers as Austin, Escott and Kebbel, plus more than half-a-dozen parliamentary staff, all backed up by the superb professionalism of his assitant editors, Byron Curtis, C. Blythe and, later, Sidney Low, the *Standard* was greatly admired for 'the port-wine flavour in the solid rhetoric of its editorial pages'.

Under Mudford's direction, the *Standard* now became a radical journal with Tory predilections and an exponent of British imperialism. On the whole it was succeeding admirably as a steadying influence on the Tory Party with its healthy and stimulating criticism. The paper prided itself on being in close touch with all aspects of contemporary British life and its being privy to

Cabinet secrets. Given all this, it is no wonder that the *Standard* in the mid-1880s was daily selling more than 250 000 copies (an official return for 23 September 1882 recorded a circulation of 255 292) and was readily acknowledged as one of the most prosperous and influential journals of the day.

However, in little more than a decade, the *Standard* lost its direction, saw its influence wane, and its sales surpassed by other daily papers. The basic cause of the *Standard*'s decline is not difficult to discern: the journal simply could not adapt to the changing patterns of the 'New Journalism'. Mudford was a man far too entrenched in his ways, a man who was not prepared to move with the times. In his arrogant confidence in the ability of his newspaper he failed to recognise the inroads being made by brasher rivals such as W. T. Stead's *Pall Mall Gazette*, T. P. O'Connor's the *Star* and Alfred Harmsworth's *Daily Mail*. This was not a journalism with which Mudford wished to be associated, and on 31 December 1899 he retired, leaving the new century to the new editor, Byron Curtis. Unfortunately, Curtis was not the man to stop the rapid decline in the paper's fortunes, and four years later the *Standard* was sold to Arthur Pearson, abetted by Lord Farringdon and the Tariff Reform League. In the twentieth century the management of the *Standard* was set to follow a very different course.

Notes

1. Unpublished memoir of Dr Stanley Lees Giffard (Halsbury MS), p. 16, Halsbury private papers, in the possession of the third Earl of Halsbury.
2. Halsbury MS, p. 16.
3. Halsbury MS, p. 16.
4. Harold Herd, *Seven Editors* (London, 1955) p. 71.
5. Undated memo., *Standard* Library files.
6. *Morning Herald* (15 February 1830). The paragraph is signed 'P.P.P.', initials that William Jerdan assigns to Maginn, quoted in Herd, p. 75.
7. Undated notes, *Standard* Library files.
8. Halsbury MS, p. 20.
9. Halsbury MS, p. 20.
10. Alaric Alfred Watts, *Alaric Watts: A Narrative of his Life* (London, 1884) p. 140.
11. Halsbury MS, p. 18.
12. Halsbury MS, p. 18.

13. Halsbury MS, p. 18.
14. *The Times* (17 November 1845).
15. Morison, S., *The History of 'The Times'*, vol. II, (London, 1939) pp. 297–9.
16. *Standard* (4 February 1858).
17. *Standard* (4 February 1858).
18. *Sell's Dictionary of the World's Press* (London, 1904) p. 86.
19. T. H. S. Escott, *Masters of English Journalism* (London, 1911) pp. 197–202.
20. Burton Blyth to Montague Corry, 30 December 1876, Bodleian Library, Oxford, Hughenden Papers, B/XX/A/193.
21. Alfred Austin, *Autobiography* (London, 1911) p. 106.
22. *The Times* (20 October 1916).
23. *The Times* (20 October 1916).
24. *Standard* (22 October 1878).
25. Stephen J. Koss, *The Rise and Fall of the Political Press in Britain*, vol. I (London and Chapel Hill, NC, 1981) p. 237.

10

The Growth of a National Press

LUCY BROWN

There can be no doubt, on any definition, that by the 1890s the British press operated on a national scale. First of all it was true in respect of the numbers of titles in existence and their circulation: in 1892 there were seventy-four daily morning and eighty-five daily evening papers in the United Kingdom. Every town of any size had probably two (one for each party) and possibly four dailies, morning and evening, providing national and international news, as well as the advertisements and news of its own circulation area. Though the circulations of these might be very small by modern standards, their combined effect would have been massive, and a good proportion of the population would have seen a paper (not necessarily bought one), or at any rate spoken to someone who had read that day's news.

Secondly, and equally importantly, there was the network of telegraphs and cables, and the use made of them by the news agencies. News arrived, as contemporary magazine writers were never tired of telling their readers, almost instantaneously from the four corners of the world, and could be reported almost simultaneously in London and the remotest provincial town. Thirdly, there was the fact that the largest London papers, and Reuters and the Press Association, operated with sufficiently large resources to be able to compile their own reports and make their own analyses, not being necessarily dependent (though in practice many of them were so) on guidance from governments. The influence of the press is suggested by some of the events of the period: the political effects of sensational court cases and the growth of the cult of monarchy point in that direction. By 1885 it could be factually accurate to say that 'the nation held its breath' as it waited for news of Gordon in Khartoum.

We can go back fifty years, to the 1830s, and see how things

compare. The technical conditions were obviously different. There
was no telegraph, the first newspaper use of which came in the
following decade. *The Times* could afford a network of foreign
correspondents, but foreign news was far more limited in its range
of places of origin, and in the delay between an event and the
arrival of a report on it. Provincial newspapers received parliamentary and foreign news when the London papers arrived, and were
thus, willy-nilly, restricted to a role as recounters of local affairs
and secondhand reporters of what the London papers had already
said. Where opinion was concerned, however, they often had an
important role in representing and leading local groups. Newspapers, as is well known, were highly taxed: in the early 1830s the
rates were 4d. a sheet for the Stamp Tax, a tax on pamphlets of 3s.
an edition, an advertisement tax of 3s. 6d. per advertisement, and
the paper duty at 3d. per pound weight. It can be hardly surprising
that papers were few in numbers and small in circulation. Outside
London there were no dailies, and those in London, other than *The
Times*, achieved tiny circulations.

There is, however, a limited sense in which one can talk of a
national press, based on the character of its reporting. The content
of the early nineteenth-century press has not been the subject of
systematic study, but certain features are clear. London papers
were primarily concerned with national politics, and provincial
papers took their news, and general news-values, from them.
London papers, as far as can be judged from a small number of test
cases, took account of the provincial news, collected and digested
it, and on special occasions sent reporters by stagecoach down into
the provinces.[1] The various explosions of popular discontent in the
provinces – Luddism, Peterloo and the response to it, the Reform
Bill riots – which are a distinctive feature of the period between
about 1800 and 1848, were adequately reported in the London
papers, and thus brought to the attention of Parliament. It is
important to remember that, however struggling and however
heavily taxed the British press was, it never became merely a
vehicle for social gossip and fashion, and that the stamped as well
as the unstamped press was heavily involved in the political issues
of the time.

The unstamped press is a distinctive feature of the 1830s, and
has been studied more fully than its legitimate counterpart, particularly by Hollis and Wiener.[2] In it, political information could be
extended to a much broader class of people: without the burden of

taxation the great majority of unstamped papers could be sold for a penny, compared with the 7d. charged for *The Times*. They were produced by a very different class of publisher or editor, and would seem at first sight to be introducing a dramatic enlargement of the role of the press. Nevertheless, on closer examination they appear as an eccentric and short-lived episode. In the nature of things their circulation figures cannot be known and, with the exceptions of the *Poor Man's Guardian* and *Chambers' Edinburgh Journal* (which was hardly a newspaper), the unstamped papers listed by Hollis did not last more than two years, and in most cases were considerably shorter-lived. A great many of them appeared and disappeared during the near-revolutionary months between September 1831 and June 1832, when the conflict over the Reform Bill was at its height.[3] Similarly, the stamped *Northern Star* reached a circulation of 36 000 for a few months in 1839 in the first flush of Chartist agitation, but was unable to maintain it.[4] The popular radical press does not fit neatly into the history of the evolution of British newspapers. They did not acquire steady readerships, they carried a greater proportion of comment and exhortation relative to news, and they did not give the regular supply of information over a period (of whatever kind) that is the distinctive feature of a newspaper. They occupy a place somewhere between the pamphlet and the newspaper.

The 'legitimate' newspaper press reacted in a surprising way to the situation of the 1830s and to the campaign for the abolition or reduction of the 'Taxes on Knowledge'. On the face of it any reduction in these should have been a clear benefit, since it would widen the range of people who could afford to buy taxed newspapers, and narrow the gap in price between the stamped and unstamped press. (With a newspaper, most of the costs of production are constant whatever the circulation, the only significant items to increase necessarily with circulation being the costs of newsprint and of distribution.) Yet the campaign cannot be said to have received enthusiastic support from newspaper proprietors. Newspaper taxation was, admittedly, a minor matter in comparison with the Reform Bill agitation, and debates proceeded in a slow and uncertain way through the sessions of 1832–5. H. L. Bulwer, the radical, opened a debate on the question in June 1832; failed to do so in July 1833; and introduced debates in May 1834 and August 1835. Hollis, recounting these episodes, adds 'it is hard to judge the attitude of Parliament to these three motions, as only the leading radicals, the Chancellor, and the Attorney-General ever spoke in the debates. The number of those voting was always low'.[5] The advertisement duty was halved in 1834, and the stamp duty reduced to 1d. in 1835, in years when budgetary surpluses made tax reductions easy. Pressure for change came from philosophic radicals inside and outside Parliament, rather than from campaigns by newspaper proprietors and editors. They might be concerned about the competition they suffered from the unstamped press, but they did not like the alternative of repeal either. It has been argued that a major reason for their resistance was that the stamp carried with it the right to free postage and re-forwarding – an argument against repeal but not against reduction of duty. There was also a pervasive but ill-defined fear of cut-throat competition if the taxes were removed. It has been stated that disapproval went to the length of not reporting abolitionists' meetings which, if true, indicates that the status of the national press had not advanced very far if opposition to the removal of crippling duties went to such extremes.[6]

Over the following twenty years two lines of development are noticeable. In technical matters development was slow, and there is a gap of more than thirty years between the introduction of steam-printing in 1814 and the first rotary press made by Applegath in 1848. That rate of progress may be contrasted with the calico-printing industry, where roller-printing had appeared in the 1820s, and the slow progress in newspaper-printing technology may be accounted for by the small resources available for research and development outside the offices of *The Times*. Development was equally slow in another direction. Attempts to organise the systematic distribution of news through agencies were not made until the 1860s. The first general agency is considered to have been William Saunders's Central Press of 1863, though in foreign news Reuters agency had been established in London since 1851.[7] While the agencies could, once a telegraph network existed, forestall the arrival in the provinces of the London papers with their news, it might still have been advantageous, in the days of the stagecoaches, for an agency to assemble and distribute news.

Nevertheless, though the history of the newspaper press does not show the drive and innovation, for example, of contemporary railways or textile manufacture, there was substantial growth between the mid-1830s and the mid-1850s. By the end of that period the world of the newspaper was beginning to have a recognisably modern shape. The reductions in taxation were followed by increases in circulation or in frequency of publication. A number of major provincial papers, for example the *Manchester Guardian* or the *Leeds Mercury*, appeared thrice weekly. *The Times*, with a circulation of around 60 000, was at the height of its reputation by the 1850s. But the most substantial development had been the immediate success of the popular Sunday papers, *Lloyd's Weekly* (1842), *News of the World* (1843) and *Reynolds's Newspaper* (1850). From the beginning they were made up according to a recipe in which police-court reporting was the predominant ingredient, which they had inherited from the stamped and unstamped police-court reporters of the 1830s.

There were also substantial developments in organisation and practice. The cable and telegraph network, though still skeletal and not reaching beyond western Europe in 1850, was, nevertheless, in existence, and the fact was marked by P. J. Reuter's arrival in London in 1851. The establishment of the Provincial Newspaper Society was equally important.[8] It had been set up in April 1836 after (significantly it was not before) the reduction of the stamp duty, so that provincial owners and editors could discuss and act together. Before that time communication between them had been rare, and the initiative in bringing them together had come from an advertising agency, not from the papers themselves. The leadership of this organisation, which survived and was later to sponsor the establishment of the Press Association, was in the hands of the major provincial papers, such as the *Manchester Guardian* or *Liverpool Albion*.

The attack on the remaining newspaper taxes was revived in April 1851, at a time when radicals in the House of Commons enjoyed some political leverage, and a select committee, chaired by Milner Gibson, was appointed. In connection with this the Provincial Newspaper Society canvassed its members on their attitudes to the idea of repeal, and the replies give a rare survey of opinion. They were asked three questions: whether they approved of the repeal of the paper duty, of the stamp duty and of the advertisement duty (or, in the last case, whether the duty should be repealed on small advertisements only). The majority rejected the first and second proposals, and on the third a bare majority only, twelve out of twenty-three, supported the total repeal of the advertisement duty. At a meeting in the autumn of 1852 a larger, but unstated, number voted for the repeal of the paper and advertisement duties, but still voted for the retention of the penny stamp duty. There were still twenty votes for the retention of the paper duty.[9] These are striking figures to come from a newspaper press which was predominantly Liberal in its sympathies.

The evidence given to the select committee was similar.[10] Alexander Russel, editor of the *Scotsman*, and Mowbray Morris, manager of *The Times*, both opposed repeal of the stamp duty, fearing that the end of free postage would enable provincial newspapers to undercut them in their territories. As the *Scotsman* had ambitions to have a national circulation north of the Border, this complaint is understandable. (The *Manchester Guardian*, which did not give evidence, took a similar line.[11]) but the argument was somewhat undermined by Abel Heywood and W. H. Smith. Speaking as wholesale distributors, one in Manchester and the other in London, they both said that most of what they handled travelled by rail and not by post – a point overlooked by some writers on the subject. The advocates of repeal came, as twenty years before, from radicals and the people who sought moral improvement from a cheaper press – from C. D. Collet, and the Society for the Abolition of the Taxes on Knowledge, from a clergyman of the Church of England, from spokesmen for mechanics' institutes, and from minor papers such as the unstamped *Norwich Reformer*. None of these discussed the effects of taxation in restricting the market, or in thus limiting newspaper resources for carrying out their main function, the collection and transmission of news. These questions were raised, not very fully, by Horace Greeley of the *New York Times*, M. J. Whitty of the *Liverpool Journal*, and Frederick Knight Hunt of the *Daily News*. The last of these was the only one to mention what became a major grievance of the London papers a generation later: that they had no copyright in news which they had gone to great trouble and expense to collect.[12] This, more than the postal concession, left them vulnerable to provincial competition.

Taken as a whole the evidence showed little insight or interest in the probable future of the newspaper press over the next decade or two. It was defensive, almost defeatist, in tone. It was perfectly true that *The Times* would face stiffer competition in Manchester if the duties were repealed, but there were a great many other places where a reader with a serious interest in foreign affairs, parliamentary business, religious disputes or any of the matters on which *The Times* pronounced magisterially, would not conceivably be satisfied with a local paper. The reactions of newspapers in the Provincial Newspaper Society's survey were even stranger: they feared competition, yet if repeal made a difference it would be to their advantage. How, it might be asked, could newspapers be endangered by cheaper paper or untaxed advertising? Above all, none of the contributors to the debate seem to have delved very far into the economics of an expanding market. They had had experience, in some sectors of the business at least, of expanding circulations after 1836; surely a further reduction in price, in an increasingly prosperous country, would continue the process.

It may be useful to look at the subject from a different perspective – that of fiscal history. In the Napoleonic period indirect taxes on a great many commodities were very high, and in the forty years or so after the peace one after another of these taxes became the subject of systematic campaigns for reduction. These campaigns developed common features, one group of lobbyists learning from its predecessors. Merchant or manufacturing interests formed associations and acted together – the Manchester Chamber of Commerce, the West India Committee, the council of the Anti-Corn Law League and the Provincial Newspaper Society should be seen in relation to them. They developed a line of argument which reappeared again and again: reductions in price would stimulate demand, benefiting both themselves and the community.[13] Cheaper goods conveyed a social benefit – cheaper timber, better housing, cheaper coffee, less drunkenness. Newspaper editors and proprietors, who reported these arguments, should, of all people, have been familiar with them. Yet, in the arguments about the Taxes on Knowledge, it was argued that the cheaper article would be worse.

The reasons for such an attitude can only be speculated upon. It may be that the leading figures in the newspaper world, having grown up twenty or thirty years before, remained haunted by their memories of the unstamped press, and fearful of the threat of the sort of government persecution that had followed Hetherington and Cleave, though by the time of the Great Exhibition such a fear would seem unreasonable.[14] They may have believed that cheapening of newspapers would favour Lloyd and Reynolds disproportionately. They may have felt a general Arnold-like fear that the only market outside the existing circle of newspaper readers was among a brutalised populace. Alan Lee noticed that the general attitude that more meant worse persisted in places until the end of the century.[15] It is certainly true that these proprietors and editors did not conform to the familiar notion of 'Victorian values' – of independence, shrewd understanding of the market, and thrifty determination to make money. An alternative suspicion must be that these men were not primarily businessmen, but minor local politicians treating their publications as economical self-supporting props for party interests, and so were anxious to avoid change. Whatever the reason – to return to the subject of this essay – one cannot say that a national press had really arrived so long as such views remained dominant: over the following twenty or thirty years they began to fade away.

Notes

1. I have explored this further in 'London's Knowledge of the Provinces in the Early Nineteenth Century', *JNPH*, III (1986–7) 10–16.
2. Patricia Hollis, *The Pauper Press: A Study in Working-Class Radicalism of the 1830s* (London, 1970); Joel H. Wiener, *The War of the Unstamped: The Movement to Repeal the British Newspaper Tax, 1830–1836* (Ithaca, 1969).
3. See the bibliographies in Hollis, *The Pauper Press*, pp. 318–28, and Wiener, *War of the Unstamped*, pp. 281–5.
4. Ivon Asquith, 'The Structure, Ownership and Control of the Press, 1780–1855', in G. Boyce, J. Curran and P. Wingate (eds), *Newspaper History from the Seventeenth Century to the Present Day* (London, 1978) p. 100.
5. Hollis, *The Pauper Press*, p. 62.
6. William Thomas, *The Philosophic Radicals: Nine Studies in Theory and Practice, 1817–1841* (Oxford, 1979) p. 317 ff.
7. On Reuters see Michael Palmer, 'The British Press and International News, 1851–99', in Boyce *et al.*, *Newspaper History*, pp. 205–19.
8. H. Whorlow, *The Provincial Newspaper Society, 1836–86: A Jubilee Retrospect*, (London, 1886) p. 14 ff.
9. Whorlow, *Provincial Newspaper Society*, p. 53.
10. Select Committee on Newspaper Stamps, Minutes of Evidence, *Parliamentary Papers* 1851 (558) XVII.
11. David Ayerst, *'Guardian': Biography of a Newspaper*, (London, 1971) pp. 115–16.
12. Newspaper Stamps, qn 2315 ff.
13. See, for example G.R. Porter, *The Progress of the Nation*, 3 vols, (London, 1836–43) *passim*.
14. Both Hollis, *The Pauper Press*, and Wiener, *War of the Unstamped*, discuss this fully.
15. A.J. Lee, *The Origins of the Popular Press in England, 1855–1914* (London, 1976) pp. 53–4.

Part III
Directions in Journalism Studies

11

Victorian Periodicals and Academic Discourse

B.E. MAIDMENT

I

Among contemporary scholarly periodicals the *Victorian Periodicals Review* and the *Journal of Newspaper and Periodical History* are the specialist focus of research and they bring together empirical information in a cumulative way as well as permitting some investigation of the complexities of editorial policy, readership analysis or ideological position. The common purpose and will of these periodicals is readily apparent, but so are the disparate purposes and methodologies of the contributors, and it is useful to try to think why so little of this specialist, formalistic, approach to periodicals has been taken up elsewhere in scholarly publishing.

My overwhelming sense of that range of contemporary scholarly periodicals which I read across the fields of English literature, social and economic history, cultural theory and art history is that there is almost no attention paid to Victorian periodicals in themselves, though many articles and essays depend on evidence drawn from periodicals to substantiate, illustrate or reinforce arguments constructed out of other kinds of scholarly evidence. These vague impressions keep returning me to a central difficulty which has become the focus for this paper. While Victorian periodicals are widely present in contemporary scholarly monographs, biographies and essays as a source of illustrative or confirmatory evidence, there is at the same time a startling absence of any well-developed corpus of work studying the generic issues specific to periodicals – the complex mediations of, say, editorial policy, wood engraving technique, readership definition, sales figures, distribution patterns and finance which underlie, or perhaps even construct, the statements of opinions, beliefs or

143

values which scholars read off from the diligently researched page
or microfilm.

The overwhelming empirical presence of Victorian periodicals,
the sense that they had something to say on everything, makes
them a crucial and obvious resource. Yet it is just this bagginess,
this variety, this hugeness, which makes precise attention to
periodicals as a genre, or hierarchy of genres, with their own logic,
rules and determinants, so difficult to sustain. Most scholars come
at periodicals obliquely from a particular interest in a particular
individual who wrote for periodicals, or from an issue or event
which was described in periodicals, or from research on books,
pictures or performances which were reviewed in periodicals.
Often, after the complexities of archive research, or the identification of obscure original sources or the synthesis of bafflingly
divergent secondary interpretation, the apparently unequivocal
statements of opinion made by a review in the *Quarterly* or the *Art
Journal*, even with a qualifying caveat about particular points of
view, offer a welcome haven of certitude in a shifting methodological and theoretical world.

Yet, as even a quick glance at contemporary periodicals will
suggest, the dangers of reading social values from magazines
without consideration of their highly mediated nature are acute.
Consider the serious-minded contemporary commuter, addicted to
serial publications not just as a passing pleasure but as part of a
ritualised passage between work and leisure. Confronted with
cornucopian bookstalls, what generalisations about ideology could
he or she make, given his or her tremendous advantage over the
historical scholar of having the whole pattern of periodical publications available at a glance? Some major recent tendencies might be
grasped easily enough – the growth of a new breed of essentially
practical women's weeklies, for example, apparently still rooted in
Victorian concepts of gender; the extraordinarily detailed and
celebratory glossy monthly depictions of English cottage style and
an associated lifestyle; the recurrent, but unsuccessful, attempts to
produce a 'general interest' magazine for men, apparently doomed
by the male addiction to specialist publications stuffed with small
ads and technical data; the careful gradations in assumed readership between the various women's weeklies and monthlies; and
so on. Yet it is, of course, precisely this ability to generalise, to see
interconnection and similarity, to find pattern that keeps so many
scholars of the Victorian period from mounting any attempts at

empirical description, let alone classification, of Victorian serials. The range, interconnectedness, and consciousness of each other among periodicals, which is visible to us on any railway station, is precisely what can never be recovered from ranks of bound volumes in a library stack. One obvious task for periodicals research, then, is to re-think modes of empirical description of Victorian periodicals so that, however modest we may feel confronted by the size and complexity of the subject, we might at least have a chart or a map of major tendencies. I shall return to these needs later.

Partly these difficulties stem from the inevitability of selective survival, that combination of accident, prejudice and available resources which ensures, say, the survival of many complete runs of a low circulation but influential journal like the *Edinburgh Review*, but which also ensures that a mass circulation popular fiction journal like the *London Journal*, so widespread that its presence was taken for granted by most Victorians, so unselfconsciously ephemeral that its survival was never an issue, so far down the cultural scale that librarians or scholars never put in a plea for its preservation, can now scarcely be found in anything like a complete run. The task of comparative evaluation is clearly a necessary one, so that quantity can be read against influence, the essay against the gothic romance, as genres which structure meaning in Victorian Britain. Alongside these empirical tasks, then, is a need for modes of reading which are not so overwhelmingly self-conscious that they turn attention away from the periodicals themselves. This can be supplied, it seems to me, through the use of contemporary discourse theory.

These issues may appear of course banal to anyone seriously engaged in research into Victorian periodicals. But our reading of contemporary periodicals may suggest another set of problems which cannot be overlooked, the complex relationship between periodicals and ideology. To continue the contemporary analogy, one genre of periodicals which could be confidently linked to the late 1980s is that of magazines, relatively expensive, well-produced in colour, either monthly or weekly, which describe, or imagine, 'traditional' country life and interests. The genre is exemplified both by the continuing success in an urban industrial society of established journals like the *Field* or *Country Life*, and by the emergence of new monthlies like *Country Living* or even, unbelievably, a specialist publication on *Traditional Kitchens*. How might this genre be characterised ideologically? That Britain in the late 1980s permitted the growth in numbers, wealth, self-confidence and self-awareness of social groups who lived in the style of the country gentry described by these magazines? The inference here is that some close correlation between subject matter, readership and economic reality does exist. Or might we assume that Britain in the late 1980s was full of suburban dreamers who confronted a pessimistic analysis of contemporary society by fantasising a world of almost feudal pastoral serenity (which, of course, had never existed historically) as a consolatory ideology of Britishness and moral value? If so, in whose political and social interests would such a vision be, and how can such interest groups be identified within the editorial policy? Or are these magazines much more closely related to the economics of consumerism, read not for confirmation or escape, but for pragmatic details of specialist joinery firms, house prices, decorating tips and saleroom information? In short, consumerism re-packaged and disguised as lifestyle. This is an issue crucially related to readership – periodicals like these might well be read only occasionally on railway journeys, sickbeds, or when needing specialist information about available tradespeople or products. Many left-wing young art historians, who may oppose hunting, shooting and waxed jackets, use *Country Life* as a necessary source of architectural information. So the problems of ideological readings are even further complicated by the apparently inexplicable mismatches between implied reader and actual reader, mismatches commonly available to the sociological commuter – the post-punk rebel engrossed in *Elle*, the tidy accountant ignoring the stock market for the *Stock Car*, the elderly man carrying *Q*.

These are simply ways of reminding ourselves of the commonplace difficulties of periodicals research; that the overwhelming empirical presence of Victorian periodicals must be recognised, but must in no sense be mistaken for completeness – abundance must not be confused with wholeness; that the relationships between magazines and ideology are complex and problematical, not to be overcome by simple exposition of expressed point of view; that the readership of periodicals cannot be glibly inferred from their content and address.

Given these recurrent difficulties, the need now is to look at the gains made both by an increasing empirical knowledge of periodicals, exemplified most spectacularly by *The Wellesley Index*, and also to look to theoretical developments, especially those made in discourse theory, which may fundamentally alter how we read periodicals as historical evidence. Inevitably such purposes require the examination of the relationship between discourse and ideology, and therefore some sense of the specific place occupied by the discourses of periodicals within that hierarchy of discourses by which social meaning is constructed. Only at this point can we be sure of moving beyond a use of periodical literature which is essentially illustrative. If we regard periodicals not like fossil hunters, in search of specimens to fill a cabinet, but like theoretical geologists or theologians, as expositions of processes by which change occurs and is made legible, then I think a quite major shift in thinking will have occurred. As a way of trying to explain these perhaps pretentious, certainly portentous, generalisations, I want to examine in detail a recent article in the *Oxford Art Journal*, Andrew Hemingway's 'Cultural Philanthropy and the Invention of the Norwich School'.[1]

II

I am not suggesting that Dr Hemingway's article is entirely a 'representative' one, nor that it is, in spite of evident virtues, a major contribution to scholarly debate. It does, however, seem to me to illustrate a number of important tendencies. The *Oxford Art Journal* is an established, but relatively new, journal aimed both at extending the range of current places available for publication beyond the London art market-, dealer, and museum-based art history magazines and at making available recent methodological debates in a subject (art history) which is very conscious of the need to reform long traditions of connoisseurship and antiquarianism into a more self-conscious academic discipline. It is thus a professional journal, in which scholarly publication is largely aimed at fellow teachers and students and where changing research interests are implicitly linked to syllabus revision and changing pedagogic method. Dr Hemingway represents this newly professionalised subject by holding a post in Art History at the University of London. His specialist field – English landscape painting in the late eighteenth and early nineteenth century – is precisely one of those sites where long-established traditions of nationalistic, iconographical readings of celebratory pastoral have

been challenged by more sophisticated, more politically disillu-
sioned Marxist scholars, whose interest has been in the complex
inter-relationship between traditions of pictorial representation,
patronage, genre and ideology. Accordingly Hemingway's subject
– the Norwich school of painters – is an obvious candidate for a
re-reading by using the conceptual framework already applied to
Richard Wilson by David Solkin, or to Constable by Michael
Rosenthal, John Barrell or Ann Bermingham.[2] To write on this
subject at all necessarily requires the reader's awareness of a
scholarly discourse already noted and discussed elsewhere in the
periodical literature.[3] One important assumption in Hemingway's
use of the *Oxford Art Journal* is that of his reader's ability to position
this journal within contemporary discourse – an obvious enough
point, but one which advertises how hard it would be to reconstruct that specific context in a hundred years' time, when a
scholar would need access not only to the *Burlington Magazine* or
Art History, but also to *Block* and other smaller specialist journals.

Hemingway's article raises further issues of this kind because, in
a rather touching personal note, he describes the new article as
being to a large extent a revision of his own earlier substantial
book on the Norwich school. Put another way, his article represents a personal engagement with new and relatively untried
modes of analysis, an individual attempt to use more ambitious
theoretical concepts as they become available to a committed
practising teacher. (Perhaps I ought to say that I have never met Dr
Hemingway, and know nothing of him and his career other than
what can be gathered from the published works I have cited.)
Without wanting to overstate the case, and turn all the little
psycho-dramas of academics engaging in new and possibly
threatening critical ideas into heroic fictions by, say, George Eliot,
nonetheless I think it is legitimate to read Hemingway's critical
progress as an exemplary one, in which methodological fashions
and the academic economy, as well as genuine serious-
mindedness come into play. Hemingway's new argument is not
directly concerned with the re-interpretation of Norwich School
landscapes, but rather with challenging the use of the term itself as
a descriptive category. His challenge, interestingly enough, is not
mainly that the term has been constructed for the convenience of
traditional art history, but rather that it was the product, not of any
local subject matter, style or common mode of representation
intrinsic to the pictures, but of a complex history of local cultural,

social and economic forces in whose interests it was to construct a specifically Norwich school of painting. These interest groups, Hemingway argues, expressed their power, or at least defined their terms, through a number of specific discourses, of which the local periodical press was one. Accordingly, Hemingway's argument depends not on using periodicals merely to illustrate formed opinions, but rather to show that newspapers were one of a range of discourses in which, and through which, cultural values were negotiated. In many ways this seems to me a crucially changed way of using evidence from local sources. In other ways, it concerns me that this mode of argument leads Hemingway away not just from pictures, but ultimately away from periodical discourse to resolve his argument on a reading of the widest kind of political and ideological discourses – paternalism, industrial economics, patriotism. I want to pursue a little further what seem to me the strengths and limitations of these kinds of approaches.

III

Hemingway's argument is built around his perception of a hierarchy of discourses, each of increasing significance. The first of these is the discourse of landscape painting itself, which is peripheral to Hemingway's particular purpose in this article. The second is that of the local Norfolk press, in which Hemingway identifies confusions and contradictions which subvert an overall attempt to create a coherent School or 'family' of local artists as an expression of a cultural progress in East Anglia which might be offset against an evident economic decline in the first half of the nineteenth century. The third discourse is that of the national press, which, Hemingway suggests, did not give any weight or authenticity to the concept of a specific Norwich School of painting. The fourth discourse is that of retrospective and collective exhibitions of paintings by Norwich artists sponsored by 'the late nineteenth-century bourgeoisie', especially the Colman family, and aimed not so much at encouraging contemporary art as at establishing the bourgeoisie as a progressive cultural force within a geographical area characterised by a decline in economic and cultural importance. This leads Hemingway out, by way of conclusion, to those most generalised discourses which are central to the

construction of ideology – economic and industrial systems, paternalism, municipal intervention and middle-class cultural progressivism. The conclusion is that 'In the context of the depressed rural
economy of late nineteenth-century Norfolk, and in a small city
dependent on relatively minor service industries, the bourgeoisie
needed to find some basis for municipal and regional pride – the
Norwich School was one of the "plumes" remaining in the "city's
cap"'. Then, in case we have missed the point, Hemingway
concludes:

> Two more points need to be made briefly in relation to the
> themes of cultural philanthropy. . . . Firstly, the Colman Galleries
> in Norwich Castle Museum are a monument to the discernment
> and benevolence of the Colman family. But this discernment and
> benevolence were made possible by their wealth, and that
> wealth was produced by the untold and grinding labour of
> thousands who have no monument. . . .
>
> Secondly, whatever the underside of the Colmans' largesse, it
> did rest on a kind of progressive ideal of education and enlight-
> enment, however paternalist its cast.[4]

Within this determining structure of inter-related levels of discourse, Hemingway's treatment of newspaper evidence is exemplary. He finds evidence, not just of a single point of view, but of
one local newspaper, the *Norwich Mercury*, locked into the national
'discourse of bourgeois progressivism' which Hemingway sees
exemplified in the *Westminster Review* and the Society for the
Diffusion of Useful Knowledge, while another, the *Norfolk Chronicle*, despite showing considerable pride in local artistic production,
seemed unwilling to institutionalise this pride into an ideological
construction as definite as the Norwich School. As a brief but
pointed study of the interconnections between local interest
groups, the ideological and cultural values which underpin art
criticism, and the relationship between local cultural issues and
wider ideological discourses, Hemingway's handling of his
periodical and newspaper sources seems to me as productive as it
is unostentatious.

But the central question left in my mind both by Hemingway's
polemical conclusions and by that particular hierarchy of discourses presupposed in his article, is one concerning his apparently inevitable shift of focus away from the pictures themselves (on
the grounds that paintings do not contain within themselves any

intrinsic, transcendental value) towards local discourses of power, authority and social value, which are ultimately only to be understood as representative of a wider hegemonic process by which the bourgeoisie inscribes its own cultural values on society through economic dominance. Hemingway's implicit arguments, although they are never consciously described, are that economic power enables cultural dominance, and that cultural negotiations over values are entirely subordinate to economic determinants. Such assumptions seem to me to simplify the hierarchy of discourses which underpins Hemingway's exploration of his theme.

Firstly, I think it is crucial to re-inscribe the discourse of landscape painting itself back into this hierarchy, not simply at the bottom as a construction of bourgeois art history, but as a series of culturally significant gestures through which social values are mediated through representation into artefacts. I think Hemingway abandons pictures for economics too quickly and too willingly.

Secondly, I think that Hemingway subordinates periodicals too much in his scheme of hierarchies of discourse. I am using his article as a roundabout plea for a general recognition of periodicals as discourse rather than as evidence, and of course any such recognition requires further acknowledgement of the variety and relative importances of different discourses as the means by which ideology is constructed. Yet there is a danger here that scholars might ascribe another merely evidential role to periodicals rather than looking at the complex rules of magazines themselves. I find Hemingway's hierarchy of discourses an authoritarian one, with its apparently inevitable slide from formalist into culturalist into economic discourses. The issue of where to place magazines within social discourses of meaning and power is still an open one, and whatever claims that might be made for periodicals research in the future will, I think, centre on the ability of scholars to describe periodicals as a historically important discourse using the kinds of perceptions shown by Hemingway's approach. Up to now, claims for the importance of Victorian periodicals have been largely made by our sense of their enormous physical presence in Victorian culture. The result has been a kind of appalled modesty on the part of recent research at the weight, variety and methodological difficulties of approaching the subject at all – a modesty clearly to be found in the 'Samplings and Soundings' approach of Shattock and Wolff's pioneering volume.[5] It is perhaps inevitable that something so deeply assimilated into Victorian culture as the periodical should be regarded as less formally self-conscious, less highly mediated, more directly informative than the highly constructed literary texts, paintings and artefacts central to the college syllabus. Put simply, periodicals have been far too useful as a source of information and evidence for scholars to want to apply the textual sophistication, generic formulations and structural complexity of literary criticism to them. Yet it is now possible – and I find this liberating – to read periodicals as merely some of those many complex discourses by which values are imposed or negotiated (depending where you stand in the Gramscian perspective) within society. It is yet to be established just how important and complex the discourse of periodicals may turn out to be, but I am as yet unwilling to turn, as Hemingway does, to the economic and legislative as, without challenge, the dominant area of ideological process.

IV

What does all this mean practically? One major problem for the development of research work on Victorian periodicals is the awkward way in which periodicals connect with academic disciplines, college courses (with their clear assumptions about academic disciplines), and theoretical debates. The author-based, issue- or problem-based, canon-based, or theory-based syllabus has little place for any direct focus on periodicals. Until there are, specifically, courses on ideology or on discourse, it is unlikely that periodicals, as a subject in themselves, will attract much attention from scholars. As subject disciplinarity becomes even more rigidly enforced by the economics of education cut-backs, there is little encouragement to pursue the inevitably interdisciplinary approaches required to make sense of Victorian periodicals. There are a few signs that these needs have been partially recognised, ranging from the one-time existence of the postgraduate course at Aberystwyth to the emergence, in some polytechnics at least, of undergraduate courses in discourse.[6] Thinking of my own teaching, I use periodicals in a course on popular graphic images for Design History students, and as part of interdisciplinary courses with a strong methodological and theoretical interest for English and History students. So syllabus reform, both at the level of individual courses and at wider levels of course planning is not impossible, and needs urgent consideration. Periodicals, as I hope my essay has begun to suggest, offer real educational opportunities – they allow students access to source material while at the same time requiring them to think self-consciously about the nature of the material they are using and the ways in which they are using it. It may seem over-optimistic to envision major changes in academic disciplines and institutional structure, but it is important to stress that the study of Victorian periodicals brings together descriptive and analytical skills with methodological and theoretical self-consciousness, and that these combined demands could well be used to structure progressive and interesting syllabuses.

Similar inhibitions seem to me to characterise the available places offered for publication by the scholarly press, which is almost totally orientated towards either traditional disciplinarity or towards self-consciously theoretical essays where the focus is on 'reading' as much as 'text'. Outside the specialist *Journal of Newspaper and Periodical History* and *Victorian Periodicals Review*, itself the expression of enthusiasm under constraint rather than of any wide scholarly recognition, it is hard to find any essays which focus directly on the formal characteristics, generic formulations or social significance of periodicals. There is little sign that editors of scholarly magazines encourage work on periodicals either through special issues or general editorial policy. So changes in the available places for publication of scholarly work are another priority.

A case still has to be made for the centrality of the study of periodicals as a scholarly project. Such a case will be unpopular as it involves a critique of the narrowness of academic disciplinarity, a critique of the evidential and illustrative uses to which periodicals have traditionally, and usefully, been put, and a sympathetic awareness of the theoretical debates centred on notions of ideology, hegemony and discourse. It will also require unceasing empirical attention of the kind which underpins *The Wellesley Index*. Yet, in spite of all these inhibitions, it seems to me that there is now enough accessible theoretical work and enough empirical evidence for scholars to focus precisely on periodicals as a subject in their own right. We can now explain, rather than just assert, how important Victorian periodicals were, not just in illustrating or reinforcing ideologies, but actually in constructing them.

Notes

1. A. Hemingway, 'Cultural Philanthropy and the Invention of the Norwich School', *Oxford Art Journal* II (1988) 17–39.
2. D.H. Solkin, *Richard Wilson: The Landscape of Reaction* (London, 1982); M. Rosenthal, *Constable: The Painter and His Landscape* (New Haven, 1983); J. Barrell, *The Dark Side of the Landscape: The Rural Poor in English Painting 1730–1840* (Cambridge, 1980); A. Bermingham, *Landscape and Ideology: The English Rustic Tradition 1740–1860* (Berkeley, Calif., 1987).
3. For a polemical survey see N. McWilliam and A. Potts, 'The Landscape of Reaction' originally published in *History Workshop Journal* in 1983 and reprinted in A.L. Rees and F. Borzello (eds), *The New Art History* (London, 1986) pp. 106–19.
4. Hemingway, 'Cultural Philanthropy', 31.
5. J. Shattock and M. Wolff (eds), *The Victorian Periodical Press: Samplings and Soundings* (Leicester, 1982).
6. North London Polytechnic's newly submitted English Studies Degree has a compulsory first year course called 'Discourse', for example, and similar undertakings under different names occur in several Polytechnic degrees.

12

Sources for the Study of Newspapers

JOEL H. WIENER

In this paper I have tried to give some thought to the use of sources for the study of newspapers, and the unlikely result is that I am *almost* prepared to conclude that newspapers are too speculative, too problematic, to be used as sources at all. They present enormous difficulties and have many lacunae. In short, they resemble all too closely Corker's comical definition of the news in Evelyn Waugh's *Scoop*, that it is 'what a chap who doesn't care much about anything (else) wants to read'.[1] Notwithstanding this scepticism, however, I believe that newspapers are perhaps the best general source we have for the study of many aspects of Victorian life, including both its enlightening features and its unanticipated pleasures and adventures.

The fundamental problem with newspapers as source is that they embody a basic schism in the use of evidence: between the 'authoritative' and the 'subjective' (to use the terminology of Lucy Salmon[2]), or put another way, between the private and the public. (Virginia Berridge employs the analogous terms 'history' and 'popular culture' to describe much the same division.[3]) The authoritative/private side of newspapers refers to their external documentation, what one might consider to be their objective aspect. Who is the editor? Sub-editor? Proprietor? Publisher? Who writes the newspaper's leaders and its news stories? How is the paper put together? Does it contain unacknowledged patterns of construction or meaning in its contents, or private relationships between those who put it together which we, as readers, should be aware of but almost certainly are not.

The difficulties in reconstructing the authoritative/private side of Victorian newspapers are overwhelming. Not only are we ignorant of the detailed histories of many of these papers, but we often lack information about most of the key people connected with them.

Part of the problem has to do with the transient quality of
newspapers, making them seem, in A. P. Wadsworth's witty
phrase, like butterflies and mushrooms. The editors of a large
number of Victorian newspapers are ciphers to us, at least for
substantial tracts of time, and this is truer still of the mass of
'anonymous' sub-editors, assistant editors and reporters. I understood this for the first time when I worked on the unstamped
press, and I have recently confirmed it for many of the elaborately
produced, better-known newspapers of the second half of the
century.

The quality and character of newspapers are shaped by the
'authoritative' input of journalists. This is so whether they are
collaborative efforts or, as is true of much of the unstamped press,
dependent upon the activities of individuals. Thus Henry Hetherington was the printer and publisher of the *Poor Man's Guardian*,
the leading unstamped paper of the 1830s. That may be all one
needs to know for a history of the struggle against the 'taxes on
knowledge' because Hetherington was the public symbol of that
struggle. But for a sophisticated understanding of the paper,
including its political and economic ideology, it is essential to
know something about its two anonymous editors, Thomas
Mayhew and Bronterre O'Brien, and how and under what circumstances they contributed to the paper. Here is another example
of this point. In 1833, Hetherington was almost prosecuted for
sedition for an article signed by 'Palafox, Jr.', which urged reformers to come armed to public meetings. This provocative piece
was written by the well-known freethinker Julian Hibbert,
although few people knew it at the time. My point is that this type
of objective information usually cannot be located in the text of the
newspaper itself. One must dig into other sources to uncover it.

The obstacles to writing the histories of newspapers are well
known to scholars. First and foremost, there is the general problem
of anonymity, which greatly exercised writers in the nineteenth
century and has made life unendurable for some scholars in the
twentieth. In my reading of the twopenny *Illustrated Times* (1855–
72), one of the key papers of the century in terms of a breakthrough
into popular journalism, I discovered from external sources that
the author of its most intriguing column, 'The Lounger at the
Clubs' (the first important gossip column of the century), was
Edmund Yates, who subsequently became the editor of the *World*
and other society papers.

There is also the problem of the many 'silent' contributors to newspapers, including above all the sub-editors, who played an increasingly critical role in the nineteenth century. Most 'subs' worked in obscurity, although their tasks were varied. Some, like Horace Voules (who managed *Truth* for Henry Labouchere), were editors in all but name. Others like Thomas Catling, who sub-edited *Lloyd's Weekly Newspaper* for more than fifty years, contributed few ideas of substance to their paper;[4] still others such as Ernest Parke, a great sub-editor of the *Star* and the *Morning Leader*, were eloquent crusaders for the cause of reform. This theme touches upon the related questions of newsgathering, which Lucy Brown has systematically explored,[5] and of political influence, which Joseph O. Baylen has impressively analysed.[6] On the subject of political influence, it is worth pointing out that Stephen Koss in his two-volume history of the political press (in the writing of which he consulted more than a hundred archives), states emphatically that it is 'impossible to say who read what newspapers for which particular (political) features'.[7]

There is also the often intricate question of the connection between proprietor and editor. No general work on this subject has been written, although the extent to which a proprietor or publisher intervened in the running of a newspaper is, obviously, a key to an understanding of the history of that newspaper. The proprietor may have been, for all intents and purposes, *the* editor, like Edward Lawson of the *Daily Telegraph*; or a dominating personality like Lord Northcliffe, who demanded results from his editors but otherwise allowed freedom to such as Thomas Marlowe of the *Daily Mail*; or an 'aloof constitutional monarch' like George Newnes, who scarcely intervened at all with his editors, who included E. T. Cook and J. A. Spender of the *Westminster Gazette*.

I cite two additional examples from my own work to illustrate the difficulties in recreating the 'authoritative' side of newspapers. When studying the unstamped press I discovered that 'dummy' publishers and proprietors occasionally came to life as a way of evading the tentacles of the law. More recently I learned that when William Howitt lost control of the *People's Journal* to his editor, John Saunders, in 1847 after a rousing battle, his publisher, William Lovett, ceased to have anything further to do with the paper. This meant (and the effects of it can be traced in the pages of the *People's Journal*) a diminished coverage for those causes with which Lovett was associated, particularly the activities of his National Association for Promoting the Political and Social Improvement of the People.

There is a historical pattern to the analysis of the authoritative/ private side of newspapers which may help us to consider further the problem of sources. The history of early nineteenth-century newspapers is easier to reconstruct than that of later ones because of the ease with which many of them were put together. Some were literally the products of individual effort, including the many publications of Richard Carlile. At this end of the journalistic spectrum, the person who cobbled the newspaper together – mostly for political reasons – was often the editor, publisher, proprietor, vendor, correspondent, advertiser and purchaser. Yes, even purchaser. As unlikely as it may seem, Carlile occasionally bought copies of his own newspapers cheaply from distributors and then circulated them gratis to prospective supporters.

After the mid-century expansion of the press, particularly the coming of a New Journalism in the 1880s and 1890s, newspapers became more sophisticated. Each unit of the paper was now a cog in the end product, including the many paid journalists who had no parallel on earlier newspapers. As a result of their collaborative efforts, it is harder to write a narrative history of late-Victorian journalism, in the same way, perhaps, that it is more difficult to reconstruct the history of a film than a book. To complicate matters, the 'objective' component of journalism also contracted in the late nineteenth century. Political and parliamentary news diminished in importance, as did leaders. For example, when the first issue of the *Daily Mail* appeared on 4 May 1896, *The Times* provided, as was its custom, more than 80 inches of leader material; the *Daily Mail*'s leaders, on the other hand, pithy and abbreviated, added up to only 17 inches. In substitution for leaders, increased coverage was given to subjects of cultural and social interest, a theme to which I will return.

It seems to me that the subjective/public side of the press (its cultural matrix) presents as many theoretical problems as the authoritative one. One key question is: what does the final product, the newspaper itself, tell us? Is it a unique entity? Or does it reflect the 'times', possibly in the context of class relationships or another general category? The question of readership is crucial, and it is particularly difficult. Until the 1890s, sales figures for newspapers were not audited or certified. Therefore, much of the conjecture about the readership of Victorian newspapers cannot be definitively resolved. Except for the years 1837–54, when reliable stamp returns are available for some newspapers, the historian is mostly reduced to guessing at the number and character of readers at any given time during the nineteenth century. Papers frequently made exaggerated claims about their circulation: understandably so, since the financial prizes were considerable – profitable advertising, perhaps even survival if a 'bandwagon' effect could be created. As I learned from my work on the unstamped press, the self-sustaining 'circulation' of many of these papers bore little relation to reality. Almost every party, including the government (which might then justify suppressing the newspapers) had a vested interest in exaggerating the number of sales.

There are additional difficulties in connection with readership. It has been claimed on the basis of scanty evidence that for every purchaser of a newspaper in the early nineteenth century there were as many as thirty readers.[8] Newspapers were, to be sure, circulated in reading rooms and coffee houses, read aloud by working men, and either resold or given away on the days subsequent to their publication. But it is impossible to measure with any accuracy the extent to which this was done, and unless one can be precise, generalisations about circulation are more easily made than substantiated. The obstacles are formidable even closer to the present. Kennedy Jones claimed that it was a common practice in the 1890s for newspapers to overprint an edition so as to increase 'sales'. This necessitated destroying the extra unsold copies of the paper, and involved a financial loss. But such a loss might be more than compensated for by increased advertising. Almost certainly this practice has been resorted to in the launching of newspapers in more recent times.

Even if it is possible to establish who the readers of a newspaper were – clerks, shopkeepers, housewives, artisans or the proverbial 'man on the knifeboard of the omnibus' who purportedly read the *Daily Telegraph* with avidity – an important question remains: what is the nature of the relationship between those creating the paper and the readers? In a sense, this is the time-honoured problem of how public opinion is shaped. Does the content of a newspaper predominantly reflect the views of its writers? Is it substantially shaped by its readers? Does it, in a less specific way, reflect the political and cultural ethos of the period? J. A. Spender is rightly perceived as an editor who 'created' opinion in the influential *Westminster Gazette*. Yet he tells us that when writing for the paper he felt like a politician delivering a speech from a balcony to a crowd in a fog-filled street below.[9] If Spender was so uncertain of his audience – literate and educated as it was – how can historians poring over obscure Victorian newspapers a century after the fact feel a degree of assurance about their discoveries? Another leading Victorian editor, Sir Edward Cook, concluded that there were three ways in which a newspaper editor might influence his readers: by initiating opinion, mirroring it or guiding it. He then added a confusing proviso: that in the case of *The Times* (and presumably other papers) the triple influence often occurred simultaneously, or at the very least in overlapping ways.[10]

There is another question to be resolved. Which sections of a newspaper can be used as evidence in writing about its subjective/ personal features: sports news, leaders, gossip, foreign reports, advertisements, literary criticism, crime, sex, unsolicited letters from correspondents? It is difficult to be certain. *Private Eye*, for example, is following a well-tried Victorian convention in fabricating 'letters' from its readers. This device was employed by the *Daily News* and several of its rivals in the late nineteenth century to generate sales. Content analysis, therefore, as valuable as it is, must be used with caution. A paper's political views are not always a precise barometer of its influence or, indeed, of its typicalness. The *Sun*'s coverage of the 1987 General Election at times seemed to be little more than a transcription of the sexual fantasies emanating from Conservative Central Office. Yet more likely than not, a majority of the paper's readers voted for the candidates of the Labour Party. Will this be evident to a historian writing about Margaret Thatcher's victory a century from now?

Stephen Koss makes a similar point in his history of the political press. He tells us that the *Manchester Guardian* had only a fraction of the circulation of the *Daily Mail* in 1900; yet it exercised far greater political influence because its leaders were carefully read by people in a position to shape public policy.[11] In the case of Edmund Yates's *World* it was almost certainly gossip and 'celebrity' columns that interested readers. With respect to T.P. O'Connor's *Star*, the 'Jack the Ripper' stories in the autumn of 1888 undoubtedly animated its readers, not the impassioned politics of its editor.

Once more a knowledge of the history of the nineteenth-century press is useful to an understanding of its value as a source. With the coming of a New Journalism in the later decades of the century and the emergence of a mass readership, newspapers became more 'subjective'. News accounts largely replaced the older type of political analysis, but for the most part it was 'descriptive reporting' or human interest material that attracted readers. A 'good story' became the chief desideratum, the *how* and *what* of the story becoming more important than the *why*. In the earlier years of the nineteenth century, newspapers tried to meet the needs of a specialised readership; by the 1890s, many papers had become selective in their coverage as they sought to provide a less class-specific audience with 'All the News That's Fit to Print' (the motto of the *New York Times*). Their objective was to produce the best story; or, as Northcliffe colourfully affirmed it: 'If a dog bites a man, that ain't news; if a man bites a dog, that's news'.

In addition to the authoritative and subjective aspects of the press, there is a third complicating factor: the personality of newspapers. This is at base the way in which they comport themselves. Anything that may be described as constituting the heartbeat of a paper is relevant to its personality: typography, price, the placement of articles, the use of headlines and pictures, the predominant influence of editors or proprietors. E. T. Cook focused on personality when he used adjectives such as 'grave', 'deliberate', 'weighty' and 'subdued' to describe the *Pall Mall Gazette* under John Morley; whereas under W. T. Stead it was, he believed, 'a demon for work, insatiable in curiosity and interest, and ceaseless in its interrogation of public opinion'.[12]

The personality of a newspaper may also reflect its relationship with its readers, and as in the case of *The Times*, the weight of a particular tradition. It may stand in for an institution like the cheap Sunday paper or the late-Victorian evening paper, which was generally intended to be read and discarded quickly. More profoundly, it may reflect national differences. There are, to be certain, significant distinctions between American and British newspapers, as Rupert Murdoch discovered when he transferred his base of operations to New York in the late 1970s. Some of his techniques of popular journalism adapted easily to the new mould, such as the use of garish headlines (which were originated in the United States by Joseph Pulitzer and William Randolph Hearst); others did not, including the 'tit and bum' journalism of the *Sun*, which was not successful when Murdoch tried it briefly in the *New York Post*. My point is that it is necessary to decode particular newspapers, in the same way a psychologist 'reads' the personality of his patients, and that the clues to such a decoding are likely to be found in sources other than the newspaper itself.

Having indicated the difficulties in using newspapers as sources, the harder task is yet to come. What can be done to surmount these obstacles? First of all, it is advisable to plunge into the study of newspapers without waiting for preliminary projects to be completed. However useful such projects may be, much good historical work is empirical. One fumbles along, makes foolish mistakes, ignores solid evidence, goes over the same ground repeatedly, and sometimes, against the odds, emerges with a few interesting conclusions. The preliminary work (including a bibliographical compilation) should proceed *simultaneously* with the study of newspapers, not in blissful disregard of it. Stephen Koss read newspapers and also compiled as much information about them as he could. That is why his work is so valuable.

Is there more specific advice to offer? Everything in a newspaper, however insignificant it may seem, is potentially of interest, which complicates the matter. Sources for the study of the press may include newspaper archives with marked files; publishers' records; data from advertising companies; memoirs, diaries and letters; information about the readers of newspapers; printers' archives; and, of course, the private correspondence of journalists, proprietors, politicians and occasional contributors to the press, in short, of anyone who helped newspapers to take form. In my own work on the unstamped press I have made extensive use of Home Office, secret service and Treasury Solicitor's papers to track down radical newspapers and learn more about them. I have also profitably consulted the John Johnson Collection at the Bodleian Library, the Francis Place and Barry Ono Collections at the British Museum, and provincial manuscript and local history collections. Some of this material I learned about systematically through the National Register of Archives and other valuable repositories of information; much of it – uncatalogued and difficult to come by – I stumbled upon by chance.

Can the use of sources for the study of newspapers and periodicals be facilitated? Several years ago Gordon Phillips proposed the creation of a national press archive. This excellent suggestion was intended to assist in the centralisation and exchange of information about newspapers. I am not certain if it is a feasible idea. But if such an archive could be established, it would help researchers immensely because, at present, they are dependent upon an uncoordinated miscellany of sources. Bibliographical work is also essential. One thinks of the impressive *Waterloo Directory of Victorian Periodicals, 1824–1900* (1976), the Research Society for Victorian Periodicals' unpublished Key Serials Project, and *The Newspaper Press in Britain: An Annotated Bibliography* (1987), edited by David Linton and Ray Boston, which includes many useful references to printed sources. There is a risk in placing too much emphasis on bibliography because this may increase our confusion by showing *how much work remains to be done*. Yet, no bit of information should be slighted. While accumulation is not in and of itself a virtue, the more we know about particular newspapers the better. A 'Wellesley Index' project for newspapers is also a possibility. Obviously, it would not be possible to replicate the quality of the original in dealing with newspapers because of the sheer problem of quantity. But if there is a way to centralise information about authorship, this would be an enormous boon.

Finally, there is a project which is, I believe, worthy of serious consideration. This is a Dictionary of Victorian Journalists, to include analytical biographies of editors, sub-editors, illustrators, reporters, columnists and all other persons significantly connected with the press. It is imperative that we become more knowledgeable about the human element behind journalism. Over the years I have compiled notes about numerous journalists, some of whom notwithstanding their importance do not put in even a cameo appearance in the *Dictionary of National Biography*, Boase's *Modern English Biography* or other leading biographical sources for the Victorian period. Among such journalists are Ernest Parke and Horace Voules, both of whom I have already mentioned (Voules was the business manager of *Truth*, the *Echo* and the *Pall Mall Gazette*, and a key personality in the evolution of financial journalism); William Beatty-Kingston, a famous 'special' of the *Daily Telegraph*; and T.H.S. Escott, who edited the *Fortnightly Review* from 1892 to 1896, and was both a prolific writer and an influential historian of the press. We need to know more about these journalists and others like them if we are to understand fully the Victorian press. I had thought at one time of trying to launch a multivolume Dictionary of this kind but I am now convinced that such a project must be a collaborative venture but one well worth doing.

Having focused on the difficulties in studying newspapers, I want to conclude this essay on an inspirational note. To do this I choose the words of *Life*, the American photo magazine, when it issued its prospectus in 1936. It seems to me that this eloquent text makes the case for studying newspapers, even assuming that many difficulties are likely to be encountered. *Life* affirms the function of newspapers as follows: 'To see the world; to eyewitness great events; to watch the faces of the poor and the gestures of the proud; to see strange things – machines, armies, multitudes, shadows in the jungle and on the moon; to see man's work – his paintings, towers and discoveries; to see things thousands of miles away, things hidden behind walls and within rooms, things dangerous to come to; the women that men love and many children; to see and take pleasure in seeing; to see and be amazed; to see and be instructed'.[13] Corker might disagree with this statement, and so too, for contrary reasons, might Northcliffe. But that, after all, is precisely why the study of newspapers in all their disparateness is such a fruitful activity. It will and must continue.

Notes

1. Evelyn Waugh, *Scoop* (Boston, Mass., 1977) p. 191.
2. Lucy Salmon, *The Newspaper and the Historian* (New York, 1923) p. 35.
3. Virginia Berridge, 'Content Analysis and Historical Research on Newspapers' in Michael Harris and Alan Lee (eds), *The Press in English Society from the Seventeenth to Nineteenth Centuries* (Rutherford, NJ, 1986) pp. 200–18.
4. Thomas Catling, *My Life's Pilgrimage* (London, 1911) p. 195.
5. Lucy Brown, *Victorian News and Newspapers* (Oxford, 1985).
6. J. O. Baylen, 'Politics and the New Journalism: Lord Esher's Use of the *Pall Mall Gazette*', in Joel H. Wiener (ed.), *Papers for the Millions: The New Journalism in Britain, 1850s to 1914* (New York and London, 1988) pp. 107–42.
7. Stephen Koss, *The Rise and Fall of the Political Press in Britain*, vol. I (London and Chapel Hill, NC, 1981) p. 416.
8. G. A. Cranfield, *The Press and Society: From Caxton to Northcliffe* (London, 1978) p. 119.
9. Here is another observation by Spender which makes much the same point: 'The readers of the modern popular newspaper may frequently be heard saying that they hate its politics and pay no attention to its leading article, but they cannot help being affected by its headlines, its catch phrases, its presentation of the news, the stress which it lays on some things, the veil which it draws over others'. J.A. Spender, *The Public Life*, vol. II (New York, 1925) p. 111.

10. Another great Victorian editor, E. T. Cook, once stated: 'To be interesting and to be helpful; those are the two essentials of the good Editor, and unless he interests us, he will not be able to help us'. J. W. R. Scott, *Faith and Works in Fleet Street: An Editor's Convictions after Sixty-Five Years in Journalism* (London, 1947) p. 46.
11. Koss, *Rise and Fall*, vol. I, p. 412.
12. Quoted in W. T. Stead, 'Character Sketch: February: *The Pall Mall Gazette*', *Reviews of Reviews*, VII (1893) 155.
13. 'Prospectus', *Life* (1936).

13

The Golden Stain of Time: Preserving Victorian Periodicals

SCOTT BENNETT

The essays in this book focus on the people who wrote Victorian periodicals, or produced them or read them. This focus is sustained by the conviction that there is no better way to get at the human vitality, the tangle of ideas and consciousness, the variety of communities and the quotidian reality of Victorian Britain than through its periodicals. Indeed, the study of periodicals for what they represent has all but displaced the study of what they are as things in themselves.[1]

If we continue to neglect the study of periodicals as tangible objects, especially as objects made of paper, we will gravely imperil the study of those things that Victorian periodicals represent. Paper made in the last 150 years is chemically self-destructive, and the loss of the verbal record of the nineteenth century is not inconceivable or far-fetched. That we will lose part of the record is a dead certainty. For the first time in its 2000 year history, paper in the nineteenth century was being made to satisfy the demands of an explosively growing and widely literate population. The paper that resulted, and the paper that we continue to make to this day, has virtually no chance of surviving for the long term. The title page of an 1860 paper sample book (Figure 13.1) suggests how fragile the medium of printed communication among the Victorians is becoming. Those who are attracted to modern history should relfect on what it will be like for those who come after us, when they find that the Renaissance or even the Middle Ages are better documented than the nineteenth and twentieth centuries.

Paper was, in fact, an extraordinarily significant feature of Victorian life. Paper was to the urban revolution what iron was to the industrial revolution.[2] The output of paper marked the advance

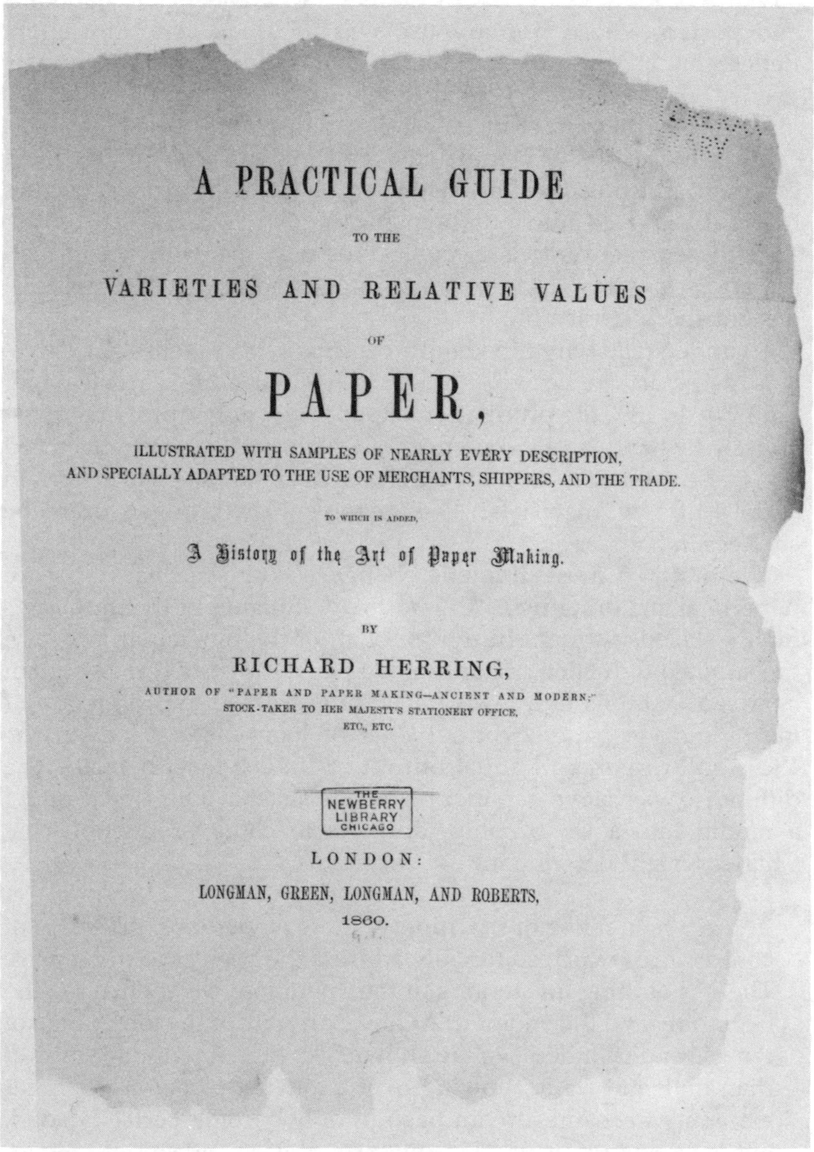

A PRACTICAL GUIDE

TO THE

VARIETIES AND RELATIVE VALUES

OF

PAPER,

ILLUSTRATED WITH SAMPLES OF NEARLY EVERY DESCRIPTION,
AND SPECIALLY ADAPTED TO THE USE OF MERCHANTS, SHIPPERS, AND THE TRADE.

TO WHICH IS ADDED,

A History of the Art of Paper Making.

BY

RICHARD HERRING,

AUTHOR OF "PAPER AND PAPER MAKING—ANCIENT AND MODERN;"
STOCK-TAKER TO HER MAJESTY'S STATIONERY OFFICE,
ETC., ETC.

THE
NEWBERRY
LIBRARY
CHICAGO

LONDON:

LONGMAN, GREEN, LONGMAN, AND ROBERTS,

1860.

FIGURE 13.1   *Deteriorating title page of a British paper sample book published in 1860.*

of urbanism just as surely as the output of iron marked the advance of industry. Think of the flood of broadsheets, handbills and posters whose primary use was in urban communication. Reflect on all the printed forms that municipal governments needed, or on the need for tickets and train schedules and city directories. Think most of all of Victorian periodicals. Paper was everywhere in the Victorian city, and paper is by far the most common and most widely-dispersed carrier of Victorian culture that has survived into our own postindustrial, suburban world. Take these paper records away, leaving only the country's industrial artefacts, its land uses, its buildings, and how well would we understand Victorian life?

To understand why nineteenth-century paper is self-destructive, it is necessary to describe briefly the nineteenth-century paper industry. In 1800 the production of paper was accomplished almost entirely by hand, and the owners of Britain's 450 paper mills faced two key economic issues: the high cost of labour and the uncertain supply of raw materials. The new century brought dramatic changes in both areas.

The first and most dramatic change was the mechanisation of paper-making, bringing to an end the dominance of the industry's highly skilled vat men. In the first half of the nineteenth century, the annual production of hand-made paper dropped from a high of nearly 20 000 tons to a low of 4000 tons, while the production of machine-made paper overtook that of hand-made paper in the 1820s and rose to an annual output of 100 000 tons in 1860.[3] The difference was between paper made one sheet at a time by dipping a mould into a vat of pulp, and the machine production that Charles Knight described:

> In the whole range of machinery, there is, perhaps, no series of contrivances which so forcibly address themselves to the senses. There is nothing mysterious in the operation; we at once see the beginning and the end of it. At one extremity of the long range of wheels and cylinders we are shown a stream of pulp, not thicker than milk and water, flowing over a moving plane; at the other extremity the same stream has not only become perfectly solid, but is wound upon a reel in the form of hard and smooth paper. This is, at first sight, as miraculous as any of the fancies of an Arabian tale. Aladdin's wonderful lamp, by which a palace was built in a night, did not in truth produce more extraordinary effects than science has done with the paper-machine.[4]

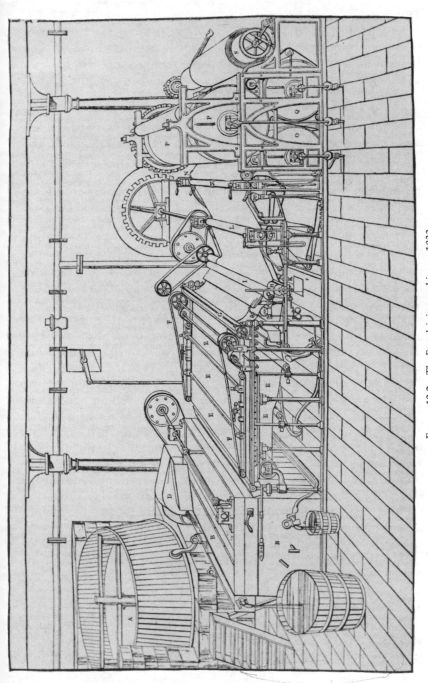

FIGURE 13.2 *The Fourdrinier machine, c. 1833*

Source: Charles Knight, 'The Commercial History of a Penny Magazine', *Penny Magazine*, II (1833) 381.

This marvel was the Fourdrinier machine (Figure 13.2), a French invention developed in England with the financial backing of London's most substantial stationers, the Fourdrinier brothers. The new machine was first licensed to paper manufacturers in 1807. By 1837 there were 279 machines reported at work in the United Kingdom.[5]

At the beginning of the century, vat men in the southeast of England were organised in the Original Society of Papermakers and could expect to earn 4s. a day, with steady employment and beer money extra. They were among the best-paid artisans and maintained this position throughout the century. But as the Fourdrinier machine came to dominate production, the workforce grew rapidly and changed dramatically, bringing much lower-paid children into the industry in unprecedented numbers. As late as 1841, men over twenty accounted for sixty-two per cent of the persons employed. But only twenty years later, in 1861, while the paper-making workforce in Great Britain had grown by a factor of 2.4, men over twenty accounted for only thirty-three per cent of the workforce. The employment of women over twenty rose only slightly, from nineteen per cent in 1841 to twenty-three per cent in 1861. The dramatic change came in the employment of children. They were nineteen per cent of the workforce in 1841, but forty-four per cent twenty years later.[6] The consequent reduction in the labour cost of paper and the heavy capitalisation of the industry required by the Fourdrinier machine were key factors in the dramatic increase in paper production. Knight wrote in 1833 of how material published to be 'read by thousands instead of tens and hundreds, has already caused a large addition to the demand for printing-paper'. Knight's *Penny Magazine* alone consumed the annual output of two Fourdrinier machines working ten hours a day and producing about three miles of paper each day.[7]

With paper production growing so rapidly, some uncertainty about the supply of raw materials for it was felt. The centuries-old dependence on linen rags could not be maintained, and it was not until after the invention of the cotton gin in 1793 that the supply of cotton rags was abundant enough to quiet concerns about raw materials. Those concerns were evident in the publication of Matthias Koops's 1800 book on paper, printed – by way of demonstration – on paper made of straw and recycled waste paper, with a few pages made from wood pulp.[8] But with cotton rags in good supply, several decades passed before British manufacturers were forced to turn to other materials. One indicator that rags could not meet the growing demand for paper, especially in the amounts needed for periodical publications, was the production of paper made from esparto grass. Edward Lloyd established his own esparto estate in Algeria and began production at his own paper mill in 1861, to maintain supplies for *Lloyd's Weekly Newspaper*.[9] For the next twenty years, esparto was the principal alternative to rags for the manufacture of paper in Britain.

It was not until the 1880s that wood pulp became a significant raw material for British paper, though it had been developed almost forty years earlier, first in Germany and then in Canada and the United States.[10] Once wood pulp began to be used, it quickly established its dominance. By 1901 Britain imported only 16 000 tons of rags, compared to 194 000 tons of esparto and 448 000 tons of wood pulp.[11] With a copious supply of raw material assured by the seemingly endless forests of Scandinavia and North America, large-scale paper-making machines were constructed, dwarfing the Fourdrinier machines of the beginning of the century. In 1893, the largest paper machine in the world was put into production at Star Mill, Feniscowles, near Blackburn. It produced paper nearly 12 feet wide, making between 75 and 80 tons of paper weekly.[12] This was a more than twenty-fivefold increase over the productive capacity of the machines built in the 1830s.

It was not just writing and printing paper that was produced in great abundance. Paper was a highly versatile manufacturing material. By 1868, when the song 'The Paper Age' was popular in London music halls, paper was being used to make barrels and table tops, vests and raincoats, slippers, machine belts and carpets. The following year an American manufactured a railroad car wheel using strawboard between the hub and tyre (Figure 13.3). This wheel was widely used on Pullman cars for the next thirty years. Paper was also used to build a 50-foot high chimney in Breslau in 1877, and for the construction of observatory domes and rowing shells. Compressed paper was commonly used in Britain to make railway car interiors, drain pipes, and even military field-hospital buildings. By the end of the nineteenth century, paper was a common part of everyone's life. If you wore cuffs or collars, or corsets and petticoats, they might well be made from paper. Many things were now manufactured for national and international markets and so had to be labelled with paper. Whatever was not labelled was wrapped in paper, whether it was meat from the

FIGURE 13.3 *The Allen paper car wheel.*

Source: John H. White, Jr., *The American Railroad Passenger Car* (Baltimore, 1978) p. 535.

butcher or gunpowder charges for the navy.[13]

Paper had thus become the most ubiquitous industrial product of the nineteenth century, but it had also become one of its least durable products. Paper, like every other organic matter, is inherently subject to deterioration. But well-made paper kept in reasonable conditions is wonderfully durable. Most of the paper made through the eighteenth century is physically sound and promises to remain so. The paper lost from the last two millennia of production has been lost primarily to fire, to the ravages of war, to floods and leaking roofs, to insects, and to dealers in scrap paper. Nineteenth- and twentieth-century papers are subject to the same enemies, but they are also uniquely self-destructive.

Paper is a strong interlocking mat of cellulose fibres (Figure 13.4). The strength of that mat was significantly weakened by numerous industrial innovations introduced to boost production and lower costs. Among the four most significant of these was, first, the Hollander beater. Whatever the raw material, whether it was linen rags, grass or straw, Egyptian mummy wrappings, tobacco plants or wood, it had to be macerated into a pulp. Until the end of the seventeenth century this was done by water-driven stampers. The Dutch, wishing to speed production without increasing the energy used, turned their windmills to operating a rotary device that increased production eightfold. Unfortunately the new beating machine considerably shortened the length of the cellulose fibres. As larger vats, more power, and higher rotary speeds were used in the nineteenth and twentieth centuries, paper strength was correspondingly weakened.

As the demand for paper grew, the need to use dyed and badly stained rags increased. A process to use chlorine as a bleach was patented in 1792 and quickly came into general use in making paper, creating the second major factor in paper deterioration. Cellulose is a polymer of glucose. As a polymer, the cellulose molecules consist of many repeating units of glucose forming a chain anywhere from a few hundred to several thousand glucose units in length. The longer the chain, the stronger the paper. These cellulose chains are broken by a number of chemical processes. One of them is oxidation, and chlorine is a strong oxidising agent. Early in the nineteenth century, before paper-makers had much experience with chlorine bleach, their use of it led to the rapid oxidisation of paper. A chemist named John Murray complained, in 1824, of a Bible published by the British and Foreign Bible

FIGURE 13.4   *Paper pulp made from cotton linters, magnified 115 times.*
Source: Paulette Long and Robert Levering (eds), *Paper-Art & Technology*
(San Francisco, 1979) p. 40.

Society in 1816, just eight years before, that was already '*crumbling, literally, into dust*' and of writing paper so unstable that a letter sent from England to Naples would be unlikely to survive long enough to reach its destination. The principal nineteenth-century historian of paper recollected that in his father's time poor bleaching practices sometimes had the result 'that an entire ream [of paper] . . . might be as readily snapped asunder as a piece of rotten wood, merely by giving it a sharp blow against the back of a chair'.[14]

Alum-rosin size was a third factor contributing to paper deterioration. Paper must be sized so that ink does not feather out through the capillary action of cellulose. Since the mid-seventeenth century, it had been customary to use a somewhat acidic alum (potassium aluminium sulphate) in combination with animal gelatine or glue for sizing, after the paper had been made into sheets. Time and labour would be saved if the size could be added to the pulp itself, and in 1807 Moritz Illig invented such a process by combining the alum with rosin. The process produced sulphuric acid as a by-product of the reaction between the two ingredients. This acid, working through hydrolysis, breaks the cellulose chain and is probably the most significant cause of paper deterioration. This problem was compounded later in the century when, to lower cost, aluminium sulphate was substituted for potassium alum. The new material was likely itself to contain residual sulphuric acid from the process of its manufacture.

The fourth most significant factor in paper deterioration was wood pulp. Wood is a bountiful source of high-grade cellulose, but it contains other materials as well, the most important being lignin. Cellulose chains bind together in wood to form hollow structures, or fibres. Lignin occurs both in the cellulose cells and between the fibres to give wood its structural strength. Lignin remains in the paper when pulp is prepared simply by grinding the wood (as is done for newsprint); and on exposure to light the lignin rapidly breaks down into acidic compounds. The result is brown and easily broken paper, the chemical change in paper with which almost everyone is familiar. Lignin can be separated from wood cellulose, and often is, but the processes for doing so are chemically harsh; they also shorten fibres and accordingly weaken the paper.[15]

These four technical innovations in nineteenth-century paper-making are evidence that the causes of paper deterioration are numerous and relate to both the structural nature of paper and the chemical processes of paper-making. What these destructive innovations have in common is the nineteenth-century drive to increase the production of paper greatly and to lower its price. Technical innovation made the century the paper age. But it is paper that is incapable of carrying the permanent record of its own time, as is evident in the landmark studies of William J. Barrow. Barrow studied book papers manufactured between 1507 and 1949. His findings indicate a dramatic decline in paper strength and an equally dramatic lowering of the pH value (that is to say, an increase in acidity).[16] Barrow gave nineteenth-century papers specially close attention. Table 13.1 clearly documents the growth in the use of rosin–alum sizing, the move from rag to wood-based paper, and the loss of good fibre length. The bad consequences of these changes are evident every time we go to the library to use a Victorian periodical.

The study of Victorian periodicals and of the age they so fully represent has no future if the paper on which these periodicals were published has no future. What can be done to preserve these papers and thereby secure the future of the Victorian past?

There are, broadly speaking, four things that must be done. The first is to ensure that library materials are kept in environmentally favourable and stable conditions. For paper, this means a temperature of 64°F and relative humidity of fifty per cent. It also means the filtration of dust and air-borne chemical pollutants, and the shielding of paper from the ultraviolet spectrum of light. All of these environmental conditions, but especially those of temperature and humidity, control the rate at which acid hydrolysis and oxidation occur. Frequent, extreme fluctuations in these conditions are especially damaging to paper.

Environmental controls are vitally important because most research material spends most of its time on library shelves. But it is used from time to time, and after unfavourable conditions of temperature and humidity, nothing is more damaging to Victorian periodicals than the people who use them. Little changes in user behaviour will make a difference. For instance, we have to stop dropping books into book drops. But more than anything else, we must learn patience and tolerance for partially out-of-focus results at the copying machine. Copiers are designed for single-sheet operation, and there is little hope that libraries can use them without substantial damage to library materials. Photocopying has become a way of life in academe; it promises to be the way of death

TABLE 13.1 *Loss of Strength in Nineteenth-Century Paper*

Decade	No. folds Unlinked area CP	No. folds Unlinked area WP	Tear resistance CP	Tear resistance WP	pH Unlinked area (cold extraction)	% Papers with rosin	Fibre % rag	Fibre % mixture	Fibre % chemical wood	Fibre % good length	Fibre % medium length	Fibre % poor length
1800–09	18	14	28.70	29.60	4.6	0	100	–	–	96	4	–
1810–19	22	15	23.60	25.40	4.7	0	100	–	–	94	6	–
1820–29	27	20	30.20	29.50	5.2	0	100	–	–	82	16	2
1830–39	35	21	30.00	30.00	5.8	2	100	–	–	84	16	–
1840–49	35	23	36.00	36.30	5.4	10	100	–	–	84	16	–
1850–59	15	10	33.40	34.10	5.1	32	92	8	–	84	14	2
1860–69	8	5	22.20	21.80	4.9	42	84	14	2	64	30	6
1870–79	3	2	18.60	16.60	4.5	94	20	70	10	36	30	34
1880–89	2	2	19.50	19.30	4.6	98	0	60	40	30	40	30
1890–99	2	1	20.90	20.80	4.6	98	0	80	20	22	50	38

CP = Tested in the direction of cross printing
WP = Tested in the direction with printing

SOURCE: Table 3, *Permanence/Durability of the Book—V* (Richmond, Va., 1967) n.p.

for much of the nineteenth- and twentieth-century library material we copy.

Any library able to support significant nineteenth-century research will have vast quantities of acidic paper. At most large, long-established research libraries in North America, eighty per cent or more of the collections are on such paper.[17] Virtually all of our collections are therefore at risk, but the hazard is of two kinds. One relates to paper that has already become so brittle there is no known way to extend its life, while the other relates to paper not yet in that condition but which will certainly become brittle if nothing is done.

To illustrate this difference and its consequences, two simple paper tests were done on a copy of the *Illustrated London News*, testing one volume for each five years between 1844 and 1914. The first test was the 'double-fold' test. It is generally thought that paper which does not break when folded against itself four times is durable enough for continued library use. Paper that fails this test is regarded as brittle. Table 13.2 indicates that the paper used in the *Illustrated London News* in the 1860s and 1890s, and in 1914, passed this fold endurance test; all the remaining sample volumes failed. The second test was a measure of the paper's pH (that is, its acidity) using 'colorpHast'® strips, which give reasonably useful measures but require the paper to be wetted for the test. To avoid unnecessary damage, only those fragments of the *Illustrated London News* that had come loose during the double-fold test were tested for pH. The paper tested a consistent 4 on the pH scale, which means that the paper is 1000 times more acidic than paper which is chemically neutral (7 on the pH scale). This reading is consistent with Barrow's findings about nineteenth-century paper. These tests indicate that sixty per cent of this run of the *Illustrated London News* is now so brittle it will not survive further use; it also has a characteristic pH level that indicates further rapid embrittlement is likely.

What can be done? For that part of the run which is already so brittle it will not sustain further use, there is at present no alternative to reformatting – the third response to paper deterioration. Reformatting involves preserving the intellectual content of a title in another format, but the paper – the periodical itself – is irretrievably lost. By far the most common new formats are microfilm and microfiche, and libraries can expect to spend at least $60 a volume preserving brittle paper through reformatting. The

TABLE 13.2 *Embrittlement Tests Conducted on the* Illustrated London News, *1844–1914*

Year	1844	1849	1854	1859	1864	1869	1874	1879	1884	1889	1893	1898	1904	1909	1914
4-fold test	2	2	4	4+	4+	4+	2	1	2	2	4+	4+	4	2	4+
pH*	4	4	4				4	4	4	4			4	4	

* Measured with colorpHast® indicator strips.

estimated cost of reformatting only the brittle part of the *Illustrated London News* is $2556.

The question of what to do about acidic but not yet brittle paper – the other forty per cent of the *Illustrated London News* – is more complicated. One option is to do nothing until it becomes too brittle to use, and then reformat it. Alternatively, further deterioration of the paper might be halted by deacidifying it. Conceivably the paper might be chemically strengthened at the same time, so that the documents of the Victorian age will remain useful over a much longer time. We might in this way avoid reformatting a great deal of the paper the Victorians used to tell themselves (and us) about their world.

A number of people are developing processes for the large-scale deacidification of paper, which is the fourth means of responding to paper deterioration. Pilot deacidification plants are now serving the National Library and the Public Archives of Canada, the Bibliothèque Nationale and the Library of Congress. The British Library has been experimenting with a process that will both deacidify and strengthen paper. These initiatives have demonstrated that library material can be deacidified on a mass scale at $5 a volume – one-twelfth of the cost of reformatting. That being so, it appears the non-brittle part of the *Illustrated London News* could be deacidified for approximately $142. The cost difference between reformatting and mass deacidification is dramatic and provides a compelling rationale for moving quickly to develop mass deacidification capabilities.

In preserving Victorian periodicals we preserve not only the printed record of an age, but also our own ability to remember. Or more accurately, we exercise our ability to make things memorable. On this subject there is no one better to heed than John Ruskin, who surely among the Victorians had the most acute sense of the value of memory and of the process of making things memorable. Writing of memory as one of the *Seven Lamps of Architecture*, Ruskin was concerned with buildings rather than with paper. Indeed, he attributed a higher importance to architecture than to the written word as a record of human experience. Nonetheless, what he wrote applies with as much force to paper documents as to buildings:

The greatest glory of a building is not in its stones, nor in its gold. Its glory is in its Age, and in that deep sense of voicefulness, of stern watching, of mysterious sympathy, nay, even of approval or condemnation, which we feel in walls that have long been washed by the passing waves of humanity.... [I]t is in that golden stain of time, that we are to look for the real light, and colour, and preciousness of architecture; and it is not until a building has assumed this character, till it has been entrusted with the fame, and hallowed by the deeds of men, till its walls have been witnesses of suffering, and its pillars rise out of the shadows of death, that its existence, more lasting as it is than that of the natural objects of the world around it, can be gifted with even so much as these possess, of language and of life.[18]

We study Victorian periodicals and all the other verbal record of the nineteenth century because that record has taken on the golden stain of time, because it has been gifted with language and life. Ruskin was clear about the obligation we bear to objects so gifted:

Watch an old building with an anxious care; guard it as best you may, and at *any* cost, from every influence of dilapidation. Count its stones as you would jewels of a crown; set watches about it as if at the gates of a besieged city; bind it together with iron where it loosens; ... and do this tenderly, and reverently, and continually, and many a generation will still be born and pass away beneath its shadow.[19]

There is today no voice speaking so powerfully as this about preserving the most abundant artefact of the Victorian age, its paper. But if we read Ruskin with any imagination, if only we will look at the floor after a day's work with nineteenth-century paper, if we will just notice the odour of disintegration that pervades library stacks, we will know enough to get on with the urgent preservation job before us. If, however, we fail to act, even as nineteenth-century paper crumbles in our hands, we will have added to those failures that Ruskin called, with great sadness, the mysteries of life.

Notes

1. For instance, there is no descriptive bibliography of Victorian periodicals, even though they were by far the most characteristic product of the nineteenth-century printing press; see Scott Bennett, 'Prolegomenon to Serials Bibliography: A Report to the [Research] Society [for Victorian Periodicals]', *VPN*, XII (1979) 3–15. John S. North (ed.) *Waterloo Directory of Irish Newspapers and Periodicals, 1800–1900, Phase II* (Waterloo, Ontario, 1988) is the best published model now available for the bibliographic representation of Victorian periodicals.

2. See Michael Wolff, *Urbanity and Journalism: The Victorian Connection* (Leicester, 1980). The omnipresence of paper in the nineteenth century is well represented in *The John Johnson Collection [of printed ephemera]: Catalogue of an Exhibition* (Oxford, 1971).

3. See Figure 9 in D. C. Coleman, *The British Paper Industry, 1495–1860: A Study in Industrial Growth* (Oxford, 1958) p. 206.

4. Charles Knight, 'The Commercial History of a Penny Magazine', *Penny Magazine*, II (1833) 382.

5. Coleman, *British Paper Industry*, p. 198.

6. See Coleman, *British Paper Industry*, pp. 299 and 292.

7. Knight, 'Commercial history', 379 and 384.

8. Matthias Koops, *Historical Account of the Substances Which have been Used to Describe Events and to Convey Ideas from the Earliest Date to the Invention of Paper* (London, 1800).

9. Edward Lloyd's *A Glimpse into Paper-Making and Journalism* (London, 1895) is cited by Lucy Brown, *Victorian News and Newspapers* (Oxford, 1985) p. 12.

10. Marjorie Plant, *The English Book Trade* (London, 1939) p. 337; James Strachan, 'The Invention of Wood-Pulp Processes in Britain During the Nineteenth Century', *The Paper-Maker and British Paper Trade Journal*, Annual Number (1949) 6.

11. Coleman, *British Paper Industry*, p. 344.

12. See the 'Chronology of Paper and Allied Subjects' in Dard Hunter, *Papermaking: The History and Technique of an Ancient Craft* (New York, 1943) p. 370.

13. See Hunter's 'Chronology', pp. 357 ff.; and John H. White, Jr., *The American Railroad Passenger Car* (Baltimore, 1978) pp. 534–8.

14. John Murray, *Observations and Experiments on the Bad Composition of Modern Paper* (London, 1824) pp. 7, 11; Richard Herring, *Paper & Paper Making, Ancient and Modern* (London, 1858) p. 93.

15. For a fuller account of the industrial changes that made paper less durable, see Verner W. Clapp, 'The Story of Permanent Durable Book-Paper, 1115–1970', *Restaurator*, Supplement No. III (1972) 8–35.

16. See *Permanence/Durability of the Book*, a series of seven research reports published by the W. J. Barrow Research Laboratory, Inc. (Richmond, Va., 1963–74).

17. See, for instance, Gay Walker *et al.*, 'The Yale Survey: A Large-Scale Study of Book Deterioration in the Yale University Library', *College & Research Libraries*, XLVI (1985) 122.

18. E. T. Cook and Alexander Wedderburn (eds), *The Works of John Ruskin*, vol. VIII (London, 1903) pp. 233–4.
19. Cook and Wedderburn (eds), *Works*, vol. VIII, pp. 244–5.

14

Technology and the Periodical Press

DEIAN HOPKIN

I

The debate over the condition and prospects of the periodical press has been with us in one shape or form throughout the present century and for much of the latter half of the last. With each new technical and organisational development, fresh doubts have been cast over the future of the established press. The style and vigour of the New Journalism, for example, admirable enough in its way, was nevertheless seen to transform journalists and newspapers into '"complete machines" ... lacking creativity and initiative'.[1] And yet few observers of the press would doubt that, whatever else, in the longer term, the New Journalism placed the periodical press on a surer footing than hitherto.

An essay on our contemporary concerns with technology might seem peripheral to a volume dealing, in the main, with nineteenth-century developments and yet it may be argued that examining the current debate over the impact of rapid and wide-ranging technological change on the press and other media enables us to reflect on the kind of issues which confronted those commentators in the past who have sought to balance the notion of technological progress with the defence of values. The debate is perennial but the outcome of new developments and their impact is rarely as damaging as the pessimists claim.

The late Victorians and the Edwardians, in particular, took this debate very seriously, as they did most things. Take the *Contemporary Review*, for example, a profoundly serious and eclectic journal. Sandwiched in between articles on the exorcism of hydrophobia, the preservation of the African elephant, a delicate piece on bachelor women, a robust attack on teaching history backwards and familiar sounding articles entitled 'The Bitter Cry of London

Ratepayers' (*plus ça change*), one can find discussions by eminent commentators on the Hooligan Journalism, the demeaning effect on literary standards of the gambling ingredient and the appropriateness of journalism as a career for either graduates or, more controversially, women. 'Whither wholesome reading?', asked a mortified Albert Cave.[2] This new media, which explicitly and unashamedly addressed itself to a mass readership, and was epitomised by the dreadful *Titbits* and the potentially more dreadful *Daily Mail*, was to transform the very idea of publishing, removing for ever the redeeming qualities of scarcity and inaccessibility. Instead of literature being concerned with the high-minded and the highly placed, this literature sought a lowest mass common denominator, in the process forcing all periodical literature ever downwards in the scales of taste and propriety. Yet, despite it all, Edwardian commentators were generally optimistic – if the public were degenerate, the nation's opinion leaders would eventually prevail and standards would be restored. Quite how was not clear, but spring water would inevitably arrive into this sewer. Evidently, the Edwardians never anticipated some late twentieth-century tabloids.

From time to time, fresh debates have begun; prompted in the 1920s by the emergence of radio, in the 1950s by the arrival of television, and in the 1980s by the development of the 'Third Media'.[3] Once again, questions have been raised about the ability of print media to compete with what, at this moment, appears to be a promised land of inexpensive electronics. But once again, it may be that reports of a death are premature. As always, the central question is technological but linked with it are questions of economics, the relationship with consumers and finally politics.

At this point it can be argued that there is no need to define too closely which part of the periodical press is being discussed; indeed, many of the remarks in this essay apply equally to the whole of the printed word, in whatever physical form it appears, whether it appears in the form of a book, periodical or personal letter. Technological and economic issues, not to mention politics and institutional factors, affect all forms of printing.

II

The rapidly evolving technology, mechanical and electronic, is affecting periodicals in two particular ways: first by its impact on the production and distribution of the printed word, and secondly by the prospect it offers of an alternative to the printed word. The first of these is well-established and familiar to all of us. At the macro-level, we are talking about the great strides made in the printing press, direct key operations, remote printing, colour printing and so on. What this involves, however, is the enhancement of old practices or their replacement by new versions – so the direct key operation simply enables the journalist to undertake tasks which other people did, just as remote printing enables copy to be produced in several places, something which was done in the past. In this context, one need only be reminded of the emergence of syndication at the end of the last century to conclude that the principle of multiple production is by no means novel. Another remarkable recent development, the laser printer, effectively dispenses with the pie and with linotype but the end-product is identical – it is the same task as before, now carried out more quickly, cheaply and effectively.

At what might be termed the micro-level, the change appears to be more far-reaching. Through word processing and desktop publishing, it is possible for an individual to undertake tasks which were hitherto only possible on a much larger scale or, in some cases, through professional activity.[4] It is at this level of what might be called micro-printing and even micro-publishing that we observe the greatest impact, because it alters the locus and organisation of printing and publishing and brings to an end traditional divisions of labour. The distinction between author, producer and consumer becomes blurred. At the very minimum the author is the producer.

There are other implications, not least in the size of the necessary audience, with micro-printing capable of being economically sustained through far smaller output than could ever have been the case in the earlier technology. It might be argued that this was also the case with offset litho, but a counter argument would be that in such technology there were high minimum levels of actual output to incorporate the not inconsiderable costs of composition, proofing, plate-making and final production. In the new technology, major cost reductions can be seen in every stage up to the actual printing process. Nevertheless, even at the micro level, the change is of scale and quality but not of function. Desktop publication is publication by any other name. The author remains the author, and the product is permanent even if it can be easily altered.

The more far-reaching but difficult technological area to discuss, simply because it is so very new, is electronic publishing, an area of production which has only become possible at all through the advent of electronic processing, mass storage and distributive systems. Two technologies have come together here – computing and telegraphy. The outcome is networked distribution and this is certainly revolutionary in two obvious ways. First, the distinction between production and distribution becomes meaningless, and secondly the notion of the product itself changes.

In the past publishing was a permanent process, even if the material was regarded as ephemeral. So a newspaper might be relevant for a day, but its form was durable. An individual copy of an Edwardian socialist newspaper or a Victorian literary journal can be consulted for so long as they are physically preserved. Once printed they exist, in theory, for ever. Above all, the words of the Edwardian editor as written in 1901 are precisely the words that the historian in the year 2001 reads. The meaning or common usage of such words may well change, and their context will certainly appear different – but their physical form is inalienable. Indeed, that was locked the moment the compositor put the plate to bed.

The next stage, creating a bridge between production and consumption, between text and reader, necessitated the construction of a distribution machinery – sometimes homespun, in that papers were delivered door to door or handed out on street corners, or through the more complex route of the specially created commercial channels. Either way, someone had to mediate. Without physical distribution, the periodical remained an incomplete product, a meaningless entity lying on a warehouse shelf. Moreover, the distribution had a specific time scale attached. Once that time scale was exceeded, the product itself had changed – yesterday's newspaper is no longer a newspaper; it is a source of past news.

Electronic publishing differs from conventional print-publishing in a number of respects. It is, for example, an eternally malleable process. This is not to say that the content is not durable, but it is not necessarily permanent. At no point is the act of communication embodied in a physical form; it exists, as the spoken word, in the ether, but it has characteristics which go far beyond the spoken

word and, indeed, the printed word. In electronics, the word
becomes a reference point and a component, capable of being
transformed, altered, re-referenced and concatenated. The word
ceases to be an individual entity. Its context can be altered, its
function can be changed.

Beyond this, the distribution is determined by accessibility to the
electronic medium itself, the medium of production. Theoretically,
it can reach everyone simultaneously. But more important, with
access to the medium anyone can obtain everything which is
generated within it. In practice, all kinds of constraint can exist –
there may be limits to the access but they are imposed limits. At the
same time, the audience can either be targeted in highly systematic
ways or can itself demand highly specific aspects of the medium.

In this sense, the electronic periodical differs qualitatively from
the printed periodical.[5] The aim of the newspaper in the past was
to create the impression that all information was the true business
of all its readers. At the same time, the readers were defined by
their willingness to physically subscribe to the medium – they had
to buy the specific newspaper or periodical in question. In the
electronic media, the reader elects to receive that portion which he
wishes to see.

The main current limitation of such electronic reading material is
physical – the speed of access and the flexibility of the browsing
capability. However systematic and speedy the computer, it does
not match the human eye and the power of experienced reading.
Besides it is a physically more taxing activity, and it does involve
certain keyboard skills of a limited kind. So long as one is unable to
stuff a terminal in a coat pocket, or lounge over the breakfast table
with it, it will never supersede the book or the magazine.

All this may soon change – improvements in screen technology
and input devices, or the arrival of parallel processing, may all
make the activity of reading from a terminal, or whatever output
devices are offered, much easier in future. Moreover, it is already a
great deal easier to retrieve archived newspapers through online
systems. To that extent we have already moved some way beyond
Gutenberg's world; if printing facilitated the expansion of information, the technical and physical restraints remained considerable.
Generating the printed word entails processes of prior selection
and editing which then impose limitations on the extent to which
information is being disseminated. The electronic word imposes no
such *a priori* restrictions on selection or dissemination.

Modern technology is advancing at a speed more rapid than the most zealous predictions of the past, so that the user-hostility of today's mechanical environments may well dissolve into the user-indulgence of tomorrow. The technology is in a state of constant improvement, bringing it ever nearer to what might appear to be the perfect man–machine interface – the replication of the human mind. Advances in voice-activated systems, in super-mouse activity, in totally integrated software, parallel processing, so-called intelligent systems and cybernetics, mean that the technology is directed toward a neo- and proto-human goal. At the present time, the advance shows no sign of letting up. It is questionable, however, whether any piece of hardware will match the power or dexterity of the hand and eye coordination which conventional browsing and reading entail, hence the considerable interest currently being shown in new departures such as neuro-computing.

More importantly, even where a new technology exists there is no guarantee that it is implemented. We have seen historically that all manner of constraints exist to slow down, even prevent, the introduction of new technology – existing institutions, bureau-cracy, compatibility between technologies, investment write-offs, the problems of labour. Indeed, the idea of the paperless society, a common prediction only a few years ago, seems to be as far off as ever, if the amount of hard print generated by every computer is any indication. Above all, there may be substantial cultural barriers inhibiting the spread and use of new technology and which even divert such technology into unforeseen and unprofitable direc-tions. Indeed, one often wonders whatever happened to all those hundreds of thousands of micros bought in the first flurry of the Sinclair revolution; now that domestic arcade games have lost their novelty, they are probably lying in some dusty corner or remote drawer. A classic instance of new technology being used for very old pastimes.

III

The second major area to be considered is economic and here there are three aspects – the economics of production, receiving and development. Implicit in this discussion are the issues of control, both of the media and of the resource-base, the division of labour, and the relationships between producer and consumer. In terms of production, we can see major changes in the scale and cost of operations, while at the same time world economic conditions dictate the degree to which groups or individuals can actually receive or respond to new technology.

Clearly the economics of producing periodicals have changed – the levels of required activity, the facilities needed, the reduction in the marginal costs and so on have all contributed to reducing the costs of periodicals to the level that it is possible to publish very small runs directed at a highly specialised audience. The bottom line at which profitability begins should, by now, be very low. In practice, we know that this is not always so, and this is where the mystery of cost accounting intervenes. Nevertheless, the economics of print suggest that, largely because of new technology, old-fashioned publishing still has a very bright future.

However, different considerations apply to electronic media. At all levels of electronic activity, there is an inherent discrimination, based on access to technology. One could argue, of course, that access to the printed word is limited by resource, and indeed one has often encountered letters to the press railing against the high and increasing price of books and the consequent limitation of knowledge to social patricians. But there is a difference between the resources required to buy a book, which is one-off investment, and the resources required to gain and maintain access to electronic media. For one thing, it involves both capital outlay of a considerable order together with substantial maintenance and replacement costs. Electronic information depends on the electronic media itself, in a way that the printed word does not. One can still read a book printed on the Gutenberg press after 500 years, whereas most ten-year-old computers are totally incapable of coping with current packages and programs. Indeed, a serious obverse problem is that modern computers cannot easily read early paper tapes (a major problem at this moment for archivists in the United States and Britain, for example, who are in possession of prodigious quantities of early machine-readable census material that no machine can be found to read). There is an inherent economic process in modern technology which requires even recent products to be declared obsolete.

It is this reliance on extraneous media which makes the problem so acute, and in consequence so highly discriminatory. The only thing that can be said in its favour is that the unit cost of the medium itself is reducing so that it is becoming more widely available. Even so, at the bottom line, one can envisage a world in which large numbers of people are permanently denied access to certain forms of knowledge. One way of resolving the problem of access and of wide-area usage was found by the French network system MINITEL which has out-performed its British equivalent simply by giving the hardware free to its customers. This has boosted access and usage enormously even if, as it seems, it has not done very much for the morality of the subscribers, considering some of the more exotic services which have been offered in the system.

All of this, however, is conducted in a developed economy. The problem is quite different in Third World countries who cannot even offer the telephone service which France has, let alone Minitel terminals.[6] Even in the developed world itself there is another problem. Technology constantly offers economic savings. It has been estimated that information processing and storage has fallen in cost by a factor of three every two years over the past twenty years, while the size of each unit of capacity has dropped a thousandfold in the same period. It is tempting to try to take advantage of this – better to spend a million on a new computer than to spend three millions on a new building. Yet, one wonders if these are real economies – the life-cycle of electronic technology is notoriously short.

On the other hand, there is a compelling argument which says that the new media are less extravagant with natural resources than the old, certainly less than newspapers. It seems quite logical to argue that creating one central body of information in a very tiny physical space which is used only when it is specifically accessed is less profligate with resources than the vast output of our newspaper industry which involves the felling and pulping of trees, the fuel for transport and for processing, the chemicals and other materials for printing, the electricity for printing and the fuel for distribution, not to mention the initial costs of vast machines and means of transport, or the costs of storage – and all of this for a medium which at best is only partly accessed. How many of us can claim to have read and used every word in every newspaper we have examined in a typical week?

The electronic media have an appeal for all sorts of people, not least the bibliographical accountants. New worlds of information or knowledge may be available, but should they be universally accessible? Why should access to knowledge not be controlled by market forces just as the contents of a supermarket? The problem, of course, is the checkout at this particular retail outlet, and this is why economic considerations cannot be viewed as natural. There are, as always, political implications.

IV

Before turning to some of these political aspects, it may be worth pausing at a third area of consequence, the broadly intellectual and cultural dimensions. Under the impact of new print technology, there have been important changes in the culture of journalism and in the social organisation of the industry. The changes are much more startling when one considers electronic technology, where the changes affect the social function of regularly distributed information (in other words changes in the notion of the periodical altogether and in the concept of information).

Periodicals are defined by their periodicity; regularity and, to some extent, consistency of appearance ensures that they are periodicals as opposed to books, while the precise chronology of appearance determines what sort of periodical they are and what function they perform. Hence, the monthly has a different character from the weekly and both are very different from the daily. The longer the gap between appearances, in broad terms, the more profound and considered the product because they are capable of being studied over a longer time scale – the content of a daily is geared to the fact that it is intended to be relevant within one day. In electronic publishing, in a sense, this distinction disappears because new material can appear at any time and in any form.[7] The reader accesses on the basis of availability and relevance. It is the content of the article which becomes relevant, not the form of the journal in which it appears. Within the same electronic environment, the news item, the comment, the longer piece of analysis and the part-published serial coexist. They are summoned according to need and interest. Of course, the presentation has changed, and in a sense the idea of the periodical has changed. Reading a periodical involves absorbing the totality – the structure of the whole is as important as the content of the individual item. So far, electronic technology has not been able to replicate that structure or, indeed, compete with the aesthetics. Besides, the structure of the periodical is determined by editor and publisher, not by the reader directly, whereas the structure of the online electronic journal is user-defined – a different meaning to the idea of structure.

Information itself changes in an electronic context because it ceases to be a one-way process. The whole point about interactive media is that anyone can change the content – and so information can be provided on the basis that it will evolve as it is used, a sort of publishing round-robin where the material is constantly changing; or those bedtime stories at boarding school (for those so privileged!) where someone started the story and everyone added a bit. The ultimate story was a collective act. Electronic media facilitate such acts in a way that the printed media inhibited them. The consequence of this is that literature itself may change; there are changes to authorship, editorship and to the audience.

At the simplest level, I would suggest that the act of creation in electronic media is different from the act of creation in the older forms. Anyone who has worked with word processors knows what difference it makes. At one side of the equation there is a new ease and convenience; this paper was written on a word processor over several days. Changing text, pulling in bits already written, altering words, deleting, adding, are all simple tasks. It is also easy to undertake the physical act – no more retyping, no more having to use scissors and paste. But precisely because of this new ease, there is a tendency towards a new laxity. It is so easy to change and to alter that one is more casual about it all, even more reckless. We have all heard editors complain that authors who use word processors often return proofs which are twice as long as the original, and usually only half as good.

Of course, all this is highly subjective – it doesn't have to be like that but it does, I believe, raise all sorts of questions about the psychology of writing. When the act of producing words was more cumbersome, there was an inclination to make every word count. The obverse tends to happen with word processing. And it would be interesting to hear what literary critics have to say about the style changes of the new milieu.

At a more profound level, there is a change of sovereignty away from the author to the receiver. In electronic media, moreover, there are new questions regarding the role and status of editorship and mediator. The very idea of editorship changes if the product itself has changed. Given that the printed word eventually has a final form, the idea of editorship is clear – 'the editor has the last word' literally means something concrete; he is the last to approve every word. But in a medium where there is no final form, what does editorship actually mean? Who exercises editorial control in such circumstances? Who owns the copyright to electronic words? Who decides the parameters by which access is determined?

Finally, there is the question of the audience. Leonard Courtney, writing at the turn of the century, attempted to define a newspaper as something which 'supplies something for all and pays special devotion to none. . . . It fulfils its purpose if the ordinary reader can find something on his own subject and as much as he can digest on every other'. A major problem of the late twentieth century is the problem of absorbing information which is growing exponentially. We are, moreover, a world of increasing specialisation which fuels this growth of information. And this has implications for mass communications. Technology has already created two additional rival media to the printed word. Electronic media, however, do not add – indeed, they offer the prospect of reducing the flow of information by enabling the consumer to select far more efficiently. Instead of a combination of habitual reading and serendipity, there is the possibility of menu-driven communication. The result, however, is narrowcasting and a limit on communication. If Gutenberg inaugurated an era of expanding information, it is possible that electronic media have begun to constrain it.

Technology is rarely introduced in order to transform a process. Almost without exception, technology is introduced to enhance or improve existing processes. Electronic media, for example, were introduced to speed up processes rather than to change them. The end-result may be change but there is a gap between innovation and change, and the direction which the processes themselves take may bear no resemblance to the intention of the innovators. One obvious example of this is the emergence of the database. The advent of computerisation was intended to improve the speed and reliability of certain simple tasks, later more complex ones. What was not envisaged at the outset was the creation of large, amorphous, infinitely malleable bodies of data which grew as a result of the process of carrying out the original tasks.

In the printing world this has revolutionary implications which belie the very conventional appearance of the product itself. The current issues of *The Economist* or *The Times*, or even many specialised journals, are qualitatively different from their predecessors in the way they can be used. Since all these periodicals now exist both as conventional hardcopy and as electronic databases, they can be recreated in different forms, used as a reference point, merged with one another. In theory it is not necessary to publish any of these journals in order to disseminate them. They can remain in the database until they are called up. And this transforms the idea of publishing.

V

The political implications are evident but not clear. At the heart of any debate about the significance of electronic media must be the issues of freedom and equality, and the degree to which new technology enhances or vitiates these. Unless technology broadens access to knowledge, makes mass communication easier, widens the scope for mutual understanding and enables us to live fuller and richer lives, then it will have failed. The great danger is that a technology which seems to offer a world, ends up providing only islands. For that reason I believe there should be resistance to the implementation of new technology which is not compatible with our desire for greater access, wider freedoms and greater equality. Indeed one may also ask if a technology which is essentially so discriminatory, is a particularly moral technology.

One political aspect is particularly intriguing. What does censorship mean in an electronic world? How does one actually prevent the dissemination of electronic information? On the face of it this appears fairly straightforward – if someone has control over the switch, then he has control over the current. But censorship presumably depends on there being an object to censor, something which exists. What do we mean by saying that the electronic word exists? At one level it clearly does not. It has no form. It is a series of electronic instructions with no meaning. How, in the final analysis, can that be controlled? It is interesting, and not in the least ironic, that governments have become increasingly obsessed with freedom of information at the very time when access is becoming easier.

The danger of new technology is that it is introduced irresponsibly. Innovators and entrepreneurs rarely cast a backward look at the wider implications – in each case, their objective is narrow and highly personal. The experience of the inauguration of the nuclear age should contain many lessons. Technology cannot, in my view, be divorced from ideology although it is not clear to me how, in practice, the two are reconciled.

VI

The fact is that electronic media are in their infancy. It is barely fifty years since the advent of television, and only ten years since the arrival of the microcomputer. The exponential evolution of technology is astonishing and it would be foolish to offer prognostications. Nor is it at all clear where the balance of the future will lie, especially in view of the dramatic changes in the world of broadcasting.[8] In a world where intellectualism has been displaced by accountancy, it is easy to envisage the future library being a set of coin-operated terminals just like the old American automats, offering segments of Moby Dick or Plato on a keyword search. Indeed, if television is heading towards a world of choice through subscription, why not the library? Avoiding it, if that is what we want to avoid, entails taking political decisions.

For the moment, it appears that far from displacing the older print technology, the new technology has strengthened it. It is a familiar tale. A century ago, the advent of the popular newspaper may have reduced the number of periodicals but did not restrict either their range or nature. The advent of radio and television widened the choice for the consumer, but did not bring about the end of print. And the new electronic technology has so far enhanced the older print technology by making it more efficient, cheaper and capable of wider dissemination. Indeed, one consequence of the wider use of computers has been a dramatic increase in the number of computer journals and books. In such circumstances it appears that the periodical as we have understood and cherished it will continue among us for a very long time to come as, one hopes, will the Research Society for Victorian Periodicals.

Notes

1.   'The Lament of a Leader Writer' quoted in 'How New was the New Journalism?' in Joel H. Wiener (ed.), *Papers for the Millions: The New Journalism in Britain, 1850s to 1914* (New York, 1988) p. 58. See also Laurel Brake, 'The Old Journalism and the New: Forms of Cultural

Production in London in the 1880s', in Wiener (ed.) *Papers for the Millions*, pp. 1–24.

2. Albert Cave, 'The Newest Journalism', *Contemporary Review*, XCI (1907) 18–32. See also L. Courtney, 'The Making and Reading of Newspapers', *Contemporary Review*, LXXIX (1901) 365–76.

3. There is a prodigious literature, most obviously in journals and periodicals, dealing with the current and likely impact of electronic technology on the press. A useful starting point is Anthony Smith, *Goodbye Gutenberg: The Newspaper Revolution of the 1980s* (Oxford, 1980). But see also Alvin Toffler, *The Third Wave* (New York, 1980); Gary Gumpert, *Talking Tombstones and Other Tales of the Media Age* (Oxford, 1987); Thomas L. McPhail, *Electronic Colonialism*, 2nd edn (Bury St Edmunds, 1987); D. Patten, *Newspapers and New Media* (New York, 1986). Even before the enormous technical advances of the 1980s, commentators were beginning to prophesy a dramatic change in communications; see, for example, F.W. Lancaster, *Towards Paperless Information Systems* (New York, 1978).

4. One of the most far-reaching developments in software packages in recent years has been the development of comprehensive 'desktop publishing' packages such as Ventura and Pagemaker 3.0 which, to all intents and purposes, concentrate all stages of publishing, apart from the actual printing, in the hands of the author.

5. One of the most interesting experiments in electronic publishing was conducted by Professor Brian Shackel and his colleagues at Loughborough University. B. Shackel and D.J. Pullinger, *BLEND 1: Background and Developments* (London, 1984). H.-J. Bullinger *et al.* (eds), *Human–Computer Interaction: INTERACT 87: Proceedings of the Second IFIP Conference on Computer–Human Interaction* (Amsterdam, 1987).

6. This point was well made over twenty years ago, long before the advent of the present revolution, in Leo Bogart, 'Mass Media in the Year 2000', *International Journal of Mass Communication Studies* (1967) 221–35.

7. See, for example, B. Shackel *et al.*, *BLEND-5: The Computer Human Factors Journal* (London, 1986). For some general observations about the impact of these processes on specialist academic publishing see Deian Hopkin, 'Historical Journals and New technology', in *Proceedings of the 16th International Congress of the Historical Sciences, Stuttgart, 1985* (Paris, 1987).

8. *Broadcasting in the Nineties; Competition, Choice and Quality: The Government's Plans for Broadcasting Legislation* (HMSO, 1988).

Suggestions for Further Reading

REFERENCE WORKS

Fulton, Richard D. and C.M. Volee (eds), *Union List of Victorian Serials* (New York and London, 1985).

This lists locations of selected nineteenth-century British serials in some American and Canadian libraries.

Houghton, Walter E. (ed., vols I–III); Walter E. and Esther R. Houghton and Jean H. Slingerland (eds, vol. IV); Walter E. Houghton and Jean H. Slingerland (eds, vol. V), *The Wellesley Index to Victorian Periodicals 1824–1900* (Toronto, 1966–89).

An index which lists the contents and author (where known) of each issue between 1824 and 1900 of forty-three periodicals. Informative introductory essays are provided for each journal, and an index by author ends each volume. Volume V is a cumulative author index. An important feature of this project has been attribution of authorship; this and other editorial procedures have been aired in *VPN/VPR* over the years.

Linton, David and Ray Boston, *The Newspaper Press in Britain: An Annotated Bibliography* (London and New York, 1987).

2909 entries including some unpublished dissertations; main orientation of selection is the twentieth-century newspaper (as distinct from periodical) press, but includes entries on Victorian journalism.

Madden, Lionel and Diana Dixon, *The Nineteenth-Century Periodical Press in Britain: A Bibliography of Modern Studies, 1901–1971* (New York and London, 1976).

Books, articles and unpublished dissertations on the periodical and newspaper press.

Sullivan, Alvin (ed.), *British Literary Magazines*, 4 vols: *The Augustan Age and the Age of Johnson, 1698–1788; The Romantic Age, 1789–1836; The Victorian and Edwardian Age, 1837–1913; The Modern Age, 1914–1984* (Westport, Conn., 1983–85).

Each entry, by periodical title, consists of a short article followed by brief outlines of information sources and publication history. Entries for titles appear in the volume for the period in which the title began; thus the entry for the *Quarterly Review* appears only in *The Romantic Age*. *British Literary Magazines* covers more titles for the Victorian period than *Wellesley*'s format permits, and for titles not in *Wellesley*, its entries, while uneven, can be useful at an early stage of research.

198

Vann, J. Don and Rosemary T. Van Arsdel (eds), *Victorian Periodicals: A Guide to Research* (New York, 1978).
   An invaluable series of introductory bibliographical articles on aspects of the Victorian periodical press. A second volume appeared in 1989.
Wiener, Joel H., *A Descriptive Finding List of Unstamped British Periodicals, 1830–1836* (London, 1970).
   A comprehensive annotated bibliography with locations.
Wolff, Michael, John S. North and Dorothy Deering (eds), *The Waterloo Directory of Victorian Periodicals, 1824–1900: Phase I* (Waterloo, Ontario, [1976]).
   [Includes nearly 29 000 entries of titles from appropriate items in the *Times Tercentenary Handlist*, the *British Union Catalogue of Periodicals*, Mitchell's *Newspaper Press Directory*, the *British Museum Catalogue of Newspapers, 1801–1900*, and the *Union List of Serials in the United States and Canada*. Although entries overlap, and details are incomplete and unverified, the *Waterloo Directory* is the most inclusive single listing of Victorian periodicals.
North, John S. (ed.), *The Waterloo Directory of Irish Newspapers and Periodicals, 1800–1900: Phase II* (Waterloo, Ontario, 1986).
   This second phase of the Waterloo project lists nearly 4000 Irish newspaper and periodical titles, and includes indexes by subject and personal name. Entries are more detailed than in Phase I, and benefit from a shelf check of one issue from each title.

PERIODICALS

Journal of Newspaper and Periodical History, ed. by Michael Harris (London, 1985–). Quarterly. Includes articles on the press of all periods, reviews of recent books and dissertations, and updates on recent research. Mainly historical and bibliographical approaches.
Prose Studies, ed. by Ron Corthell (London, 1978–). Three issues a year. Started as *Prose Studies 1800–1900* but now publishes articles on prose of all periods. Recently special numbers have abounded, and articles often engage with current theory.
Publishing History, ed. by Michael Turner (Oxford, 1977–). Appears irregularly, but biannual. Contains long and scholarly articles. Mainly historical and descriptive.
Victorian Periodicals Review, ed. by Barbara Quinn Schmidt (Edwardsville, Ill., 1967–). Quarterly. Began as *Victorian Periodicals Newsletter* and purveyed projects and reports of the Research Society for Victorian Periodicals. Now the main publisher of research in the field, it includes articles, reviews, notes and announcements. A variety of approaches, but mainly descriptive, historical and bibliographical. Includes an annual bibliography of articles published in English on the Victorian press, and has published a number of important bibliographical supplements.
Victorian Studies, ed. by Patrick Brantlinger. (Bloomington, Ind., 1965–) Quarterly. An interdisciplinary, scholarly journal which only occasionally publishes articles on Victorian journalism, but does regularly

review books in the field. Includes a full and inclusive annual bibliography of Victorian studies in its summer number.

Year's Work in English Studies, ed. by Laurel Brake (Oxford, 1919–). Annual narrative and evaluative bibliography which includes a review of the year's work in Victorian periodical and publishing studies.

BOOKS

Aspinall, Arthur, *Politics and the Press, 1780–1850* (London, 1949).

Boyce, George, James Curran and Pauline Wingate (eds), *Newspaper History from the Seventeenth Century to the Present Day* (London and Beverly Hills, Calif., 1978).

Brown, Lucy, *Victorian News and Newspapers* (Oxford, 1985). Concentrates on 1860–1890, and examines the provincial and London press to 'establish the processes behind the finished result'. Copious documentation of sources.

Curran, James and Jean Seaton, *Power Without Responsibility: The Press and Broadcasting in Britain*, 3rd edn (London and New York, 1988). Although nineteenth-century journalism figures only in two early chapters, the framework of the entire analysis is pertinent to the Victorian press. Contains an excellent bibliography.

Harrison, Stanley, *Poor Men's Guardians: A Record of the Struggles for a Democratic Newspaper Press, 1763–1973* (London, 1974).

Hollis, Patricia, *The Pauper Press* (London, 1970).

James, Louis (ed.), *Print and the People, 1819–1851* (London, 1976).

Klancher, Jon P., *The Making of English Reading Audiences, 1790–1832* (Madison, Wis., 1987). Cultural criticism which draws on semiotics and theories of discourse. It is one of the few works on readership of the nineteenth-century press.

Koss, Stephen, *The Rise and Fall of the Political Press in Britain*, 2 vols (London, and Chapel Hill, NC, 1981 and 1984).

Lee, A.J., *The Origins of the Popular Press in England 1855–1914* (London, 1976).

Read, Donald, *Press and People 1790–1850* (London, 1961).

Shattock, Joanne, *Politics and Reviewers: The 'Edinburgh' and the 'Quarterly' in the Early Victorian Age* (Leicester, 1989).

Shattock, Joanne and Michael Wolff (eds), *The Victorian Periodical Press: Samplings and Soundings* (Leicester and Toronto, 1982).

Walters, Huw, *Y Wasg Gyfnodol Gymreig: The Welsh Periodical Press, 1735–1900* (Aberystwyth, 1987).

Webb, R.K., *The British Working Class Reader, 1790–1848* (London, 1955).

Williams, Raymond, *The Long Revolution* (London, 1961).

Wiener, Joel H., *The War of the Unstamped: A History of the Movement to Repeal the British Newspaper Tax, 1830–1846* (Ithaca, 1969).

Wiener, Joel H. (ed.), *Innovators and Preachers: The Role of the Editor in Victorian England* (Westport, Conn., 1985).

Wiener, Joel H. (ed.), *Papers for the Millions: The New Journalism in Britain, 1850s to 1914* (New York and London, 1988).

Index